Profiling Serial Killers

Profiling Serial Killers

and other crimes in South Africa

MICKI PISTORIUS

PENGUIN BOOKS

PENGUIN BOOKS

Published by the Penguin Group
Penguin Books Ltd, 80 Strand, London WC2R 0RL, England
Penguin Group (USA) Inc, 375 Hudson Street, New York, New York 10014, USA
Penguin Group (Canada), 90 Eglinton Avenue East, Suite 700, Toronto, Ontario, Canada M4P 2Y3 (a division of Pearson Penguin Canada Inc)
Penguin Ireland, 25 St Stephen's Green, Dublin 2, Ireland (a division of Penguin Books Ltd)
Penguin Group (Australia), 250 Camberwell Road, Camberwell, Victoria 3124, Australia (a division of Pearson Australia Group Pty Ltd)
Penguin Books India Pvt Ltd, 11 Community Centre, Panchsheel Park,
New Delhi – 110 017, India
Penguin Group (NZ), Cnr Rosedale and Airborne Roads, Albany, Auckland 1310, New Zealand (a division of Pearson New Zealand Ltd)
Penguin Books (South Africa) (Pty) Ltd, 24 Sturdee Avenue, Rosebank, Johannesburg 2196, South Africa

Penguin Books (South Africa) (Pty) Ltd, Registered Offices:
24 Sturdee Avenue, Rosebank, Johannesburg 2196, South Africa

www.penguinbooks.co.za

First published by Penguin Books (South Africa) (Pty) Ltd 2005

Copyright © Micki Pistorius 2005

ISBN 0 143 02482 5

Typeset by CJH Design in 10/13pt Bookman
Printed and bound by Interpak Books, Pietermaritzburg
Cover design: Mouse Design

*This book is dedicated to the memory
of my father
Calie Pistorius*

Contents

Acknowledgements

My thanks to the following for their input and assistance:

Associated Intelligence Network, Anne Davies (Metropolitan Police, London), Gavin de Becker (Gavin de Becker Inc, Los Angeles), Advocate Beverly Edwards (State Prosecutor, Johannesburg), Dr Charmaine Elliot (Graphologist), Nate Gordon (Academy for Investigative Training, USA), Roy Hazelwood (ex-FBI profiler), Dr Eric Hickey (California State University), Dr Gerard Labuschagne (Investigative Psychology Unit, South African Police Service), Robert Ressler (ex-FBI profiler), Avinoam Sapir (Laboratory for Scientific Interrogation, USA), and the following South African Police Service detectives: A J Oliver, Philip Veldhuizen, Allan Alford, Bushie Rambardhursing, Vivian Bieldt, Mike van Aardt and Frans Visagie.

The author and publisher gratefully acknowledge the following persons and instances for permission to quote copyright material:

Nathan J Gordon for permission to quote from *Effective Interviewing and Interrogation Techniques* (N J Gordon & W L Fleisher, Academic Press, 2002).

Material in the chapter 'Stalkers' (pp325-386) was extracted with permission from the *Journal of Forensic Sciences*, No 1 (1981) and March 1991, copyright

Introduction to Profiling

Imagine a crime scene in a patch of veld the size of two rugby fields. It is strewn with twelve female corpses in different stages of decomposition, all virtually naked, all strangled with underwear. The identities of the victims are unknown and some of them have been reduced to skeletal remains. Physical evidence has been destroyed by the weather. No fingerprints, no footprints, since the rain has washed these away; no hair or fibres, since the wind has blown them away. No semen, since the perpetrator used condoms. The murder weapons were the women's own clothing and could thus not be traced to a suspect. The women's handbags and any other form of identification has been removed. No witnesses, since the area is remote. The bodies were found by a man walking his dog in the veld; the dog picked up the scent of the decomposing bodies.

If you were the investigating officer in charge of this crime scene, what would you do? How would you go about catching the killer?

Most people would answer that they would begin by trying to identify the victims in order to ascertain whether they had all had contact with the same man. Examining missing persons reports (provided the victims had officially been reported missing), reconstructing skulls, drawing up identikits of the women's faces, pub-

lishing photographs of their clothing in the press and on television, etc – all these are processes that could take weeks or even months.

It would not help much even if all the victims were identified, since the killer did not necessarily know who they were when he selected them. Their names and identities meant nothing to him. The only thing the victims had in common was that they had been randomly picked by the same man. During the weeks and months it will take to identify the victims it is more than likely that the killer will strike several more times.

The pressure to solve the case – to find the killer – will mount. The press will have a field day and the public will be hyped up into hysteria. The killer will realise that the hunt for him is intensifying and may move his graveyard somewhere else. A major investigation costing millions of rands and requiring the time and work of hundreds of policemen and specialists could last a year or more.

If, however, the investigating officer immediately called in the help of an experienced profiler, the profiler will be able to start describing the type of man responsible for the carnage right then and there at the crime scene. Enlisting the help of a profiler will put the investigating officer in touch with the elusive killer, almost from the start.

If I had been the profiler called to this crime scene I would have advised the investigating officer to keep the discovery of the crime scene confidential, to postpone any crime scene processing, to post detectives at the crime scene round the clock, and to wait. The killer would almost certainly return to the scene in less than a week and be caught red-handed, so to speak. A detective once followed my advice in similar circumstances, and the killer was arrested the same night.

THE CONCEPTION OF MODERN PROFILING

The science of modern criminal profiling can be attributed to a psychiatrist named James A Brussel.

During 1941 New York was shaken by an explosion at a Consolidated Edison building. The year before a fake bomb had been found there. This time it was clearly a real bomb, but no one could figure out the motive for the explosion. Thirteen more bombs followed, accompanied by anonymous letters to the police. When America entered the Second World War the police received a letter from the 'Mad Bomber', as he had been dubbed, saying that he would put a moratorium on further bombings for the duration of the war. The bombings duly ceased, but the letters to the authorities did not. When the war ended in 1945, the bombings resumed. Between 1945 and 1956 another seventeen bombs exploded. Theatres, libraries, stations and subways were targeted. The police were baffled.

Someone who knew the investigating officer of the Mad Bomber case also knew James Brussel, who was the assistant commissioner of the Mental Hygiene Department of New York State. The police were under heavy pressure to make an arrest – after all, the bomber had been terrorising the city for sixteen years – and it was suggested that Brussel be asked to draw up a profile of the bomber.

Brussel studied the crime scenes and the bomber's letters and came up with the following profile: *The motive for the crime was not political, but rather the action of a disgruntled ex-employee of Consolidated Edison. The suspect would be in his fifties, a Roman Catholic of East European descent, he suffered from a paranoid disorder and a chronic physical illness, lived with older female relatives and was unmarried. He wanted to be caught.*

'When you find him,' Brussel predicted, *'chances are he'll be wearing a double-breasted suit. Buttoned.'*

Brussel advised that the profile be published as it would make the man feel important.

The newspapers began addressing open letters to the suspect, and he responded anonymously.

In one of his letters the suspect mentioned the date of an accident in which he had been injured. Consolidated Edison had merged with a number of smaller companies years before. Eventually a clerk found the file reporting the accident in the records of one of the smaller companies. The suspect was identified as George Metesky of Connecticut. Metesky lived with his two elderly aunts and a bachelor brother. He was in his fifties, a Catholic of East European descent, and he suffered from tuberculosis which had resulted from a work-related illness. When the police went to arrest him on 20 January 1957, he did not resist. He asked to be given time to change his clothing and emerged in a double-breasted suit, buttoned up. He was smiling. Neighbours commented that they had never seen George smile before.

How had Brussel come up with such an accurate profile? By matching a careful analysis of the known facts of the case with his training in the study of human behaviour, his experience in the field, and by using simple logic.

Brussel knew from his training as a psychiatrist that paranoia peaks at age thirty-five. To this he added the sixteen years that the bomber had been active to come up with his prediction that the suspect would be in his fifties. His research revealed that many convicted bombers were male, of East European descent, and that most East Europeans are Catholic. In his analysis of the suspect's letters, Brussel noted that he used expressions like 'dastardly deeds'. The man was uncomfortable with the English language, but probably read Victorian crime novels. This would point to someone of foreign origin. The bombs were meticulously constructed, wrapped in newspaper and a paper bag and

4

neatly tied with cord. The letters also showed careful attention to detail, which is an element of paranoia. The man would be very neat. The latest fashions would be too casual for his liking, and he would prefer a more old-fashioned style of dress – hence the double-breasted suit. Because he paid meticulous attention to detail, he would button the jacket. Metesky smiled for the first time in years because he was glad that he had finally been caught.

The way in which Brussel devised the profile is completely logical and not at all mysterious.

After Metesky's arrest the police played down the role the profile had played in his apprehension and focused on the discovery of the employment file as the key factor. In a sense they were justified in doing this. The profile does not carry out the arrest; the detectives do. Without the accompanying thorough investigation by the detectives, a profile is just a piece of paper.

Metesky was committed to a hospital for the criminally insane. He was released in 1973 and lived out the rest of his life quietly in Connecticut. He died inconspicuously in 1994, aged ninety. He was not, however, forgotten by serial killer David Berkowitz. Berkowitz, alias 'Son of Sam', who terrorised New York decades later, said that George Metesky was one of his heroes.

In his book *Casebook of a Crime Psychiatrist* Brussel explains that

a psychiatrist usually studies a person and makes some reasonable predictions about what he or she may do in the future. What is done in profiling, is to reverse the process. Instead, by studying an individual's deeds one deduces what kind of person the individual might be.
(NCAVC FBI, 1990)

I compare the process of profiling to analysing a work of

art. One can draw conclusions about an artist by studying his or her paintings. A crime scene is a far cry from being a work of art, but one can draw conclusions about the perpetrator when studying his work – the crime scene. As Brussel commented, it is mostly a process of reversal.

EVOLUTION OF PROFILING IN THE WESTERN WORLD

It took the FBI about twenty years after the arrest of Metesky to develop criminal profiling into a recognised investigative tool in combating crime. The pioneers of profiling in the West were originally FBI field agents with some training in the human sciences, who were eventually settled at the FBI Academy in Quantico where they established the Behavioral Science Unit in the 1980s.

The FBI defines the profiling process as

An investigative technique by which to identify the major personality and behavioural characteristics of the offender, based upon an analysis of the crime(s) he/she has committed. (NCAVC FBI 1990)

The profile cannot establish the identity of the offender, but it can narrow the scope of the investigation. In his book *Profiling Violent Crimes* (1989), Ronald M Holmes states that a profile is yet another forensic tool to complement a thorough investigation by competent and educated law enforcement officers.

In *Criminal Profiling: a viable investigative tool against violent crime* (1986), pioneer FBI profiler John Douglas states:

Unlike other disciplines concerned with human violence, law enforcement does not, as a primary objective, seek to

6

explain the actions of a violent offender. Instead its task is to ascertain the identity of the offender, based on what is known of his actions.

Douglas makes a crucial mistake in ignoring the necessity of explaining the actions of the offender. In his view, the question of *why* a crime was committed is not an important element in the final identification of the suspect. He does not acknowledge that part of what an understanding of the offender's actions reveals is the motivation – the *why* – that led to those actions. The *why* will always point to motive.

Initially, FBI profilers clearly underestimated the role of motivation and gratification of needs in the profiling process. Human beings will do nothing (that is, they will remain passive) unless they are motivated into action. A simple example is that of hunger. When a person experiences hunger – a need that is ungratified – it will motivate him into action to seek food. Motivation and gratification of needs always underlie action. The *why* is therefore a very important element in the profile. Murder is also an action that is propelled by an underlying motive. The first thing detectives will do at a murder scene is try to establish the motive behind the murder. Was it emotional anger, an issue related to money or blackmail? Anyone who will benefit from the death of the victim will immediately be identified as a suspect. Evidence collected by detectives at the crime scene will substantiate (or not substantiate) their hypotheses about the suspects they have identified. Eventually *means*, *motive* and *opportunity* form the basis of their case against a suspect which will be presented in court, substantiated by the evidence.

Serial killer investigations, however, are notorious for their lack of physical evidence, and because the motivations for these crimes are of psychological origin they are hidden. The conviction of a serial killer thus often relies heavily on the suspect's confession. The confession leads to a pointing-out of the crime scenes and the revelation of facts that could only have been known to the perpetrator. When there is no physical evidence, many serial killer cases are taken to court on the basis of the confession and the pointing-out of crime scenes, and augmented by a psychological explanation of the killer's motivation. The better the interrogator understands the suspect, the more likely he is to confess.

Although FBI profilers were pioneers in the field in the 1980s, the science of profiling has continued to evolve during the last twenty years. In *Practical homicide investigation, tactics, procedures and forensic techniques*, Gerbeth (1996) defines profiling as

> ... an educated attempt to provide investigative agencies with specific information as to the type of individual who could have committed a certain crime. It involves the preparation of a biographical sketch based upon information taken from the crime scene and victimology which is then integrated with known psychological theory ... [profiling] can be a valuable tool in identifying and pinpointing suspects; however it must be noted that the profile has its limitations. It should be utilized with sound investigative techniques.

My contribution to the field was to endeavour to add to the profile an analysis of the psychological motivation underlying the crime in order to assist the interrogator in 'pushing the right buttons' when interviewing the suspect. Violent criminals, like all the rest of us, will respond to those who understand them. But *understanding* the motive behind their behaviour should not be confused with *condoning* their behaviour.

8

ART OR SCIENCE?

Investigators sometimes complain that the profiles presented to them are vague and contain no information that they could not have come up with themselves. Profiling has been described as an 'educated guess'. Education is a vital ingredient, but guessing does not come into the equation at all. Analytical thinking, evaluation of evidence, interpreting statistics, allocating precedence to facts, formulating hypotheses, playing devil's advocate and, finally, coming to the most probable conclusion(s) is a more intricate and scientific process than mere guesswork.

According to the FBI: *The profiler's skill is in recognizing the crime scene dynamics that link various criminal personality types who commit similar crimes.* This statement predisposes, firstly, that the profiler should be able to recognise crime scene dynamics, and should therefore have training and experience in analysing crime scenes; and, secondly, that the profiler should be trained in psychology in order to be able to identify and describe personality types.

Clearly, the FBI recognises training as important in a profiler. However, formal training and academic qualifications in psychology and criminology are not enough. For instance, any qualified psychologist knows that there are more than twelve personality disorders (as defined by the DSM classification manual). Yet providing the investigating officer with a list of 'various personality types' that could perhaps be linked to a series of crimes would cover such a wide variety of suspects that it would be worthless. The profiler needs the knowledge and experience to be able to narrow down the probable characteristics of the suspect.

It is generally accepted that a profiler should at least be educated in the human sciences, preferably in psychology, and be trained and have experience in crime scene analysis. These requirements point to profiling being a science. So far, there is no 'art' to it.

Where does 'art' come into it? Profiling has been criticised as a hocus-pocus process that is based on the 'feelings' of the profiler. If the profiler has an 'instinct' for the work it is a bonus, but there are no crystal balls involved. *A profiler brings to the investigation the ability to make hypothetical formulations based on his or her previous experience* (NCAVC FBI 1990). The art of profiling involves a combination of experience and instinct. Just as detectives develop an instinct for investigation, so do profilers develop an instinct for profiling. Their 'feelings' are not based on guesswork.

To me, an instinct may also be a 'sixth sense'. For example, a person entering the home of friends will immediately be able to 'pick up the vibe' if the friends have had an argument shortly before his or her arrival. Sometimes we dislike or distrust people immediately upon meeting them. If asked why, we answer that it is just a 'feeling' or a 'vibe'.

A 'vibe' is a vibration of energy. Quantum physics teaches us that all matter vibrates, even thoughts vibrate, creating an energy field. Some people feel extremely uncomfortable in hospitals, others feel strange walking through graveyards, yet others feel elated when entering ancient cathedrals. These people are all responding to the energy fields of the environment, like a radio picking up frequencies. This is not a special gift. Everyone has the ability to respond to energy fields in this way, but some people have a greater sensitivity than others.

Crime scenes are laden with the residual energy fields of the killers and the victims and the acts that were committed there. Over time a profiler can develop a sixth sense to tune into this vibration of energy. Just as someone may be able to pick up the 'vibes' of other people, the profiler's ability to tune into the 'vibes' of a crime scene develops over time. It comes with experience.

Delta brainwaves are responsible for our instincts, so-called sixth sense, etc. There is a general misconception that we experience delta waves only when we are asleep and in a state of unconsciousness. This is not true. We can experience delta waves in a state of wakefulness. My delta brainwaves were highly activated when I was working on a crime scene and this enabled me to tune into the 'vibes' of the killer. Alpha brainwaves provide the link between the subconscious and the conscious. So my alpha brainwaves enabled me to translate this 'vibe' and my beta brainwaves enabled me to verbalise it. We all have these brainwaves, but my delta brainwaves are apparently more active than average. Through neurofeedback one can actually train one's brainwaves to become more active when one is in need of a specific function. So my ability to 'pick up the vibes of the killer' is not mumbo-jumbo (which is something I have been accused of); there is a scientific explanation for it.

My ability to tune into the 'vibes' of killers developed so intensely that I even had the same nightmares that they had. I could 'feel' when they were killing and describe the crime scene to the detectives as if I was looking through the killer's eyes, even though I might have been hundreds of kilometres away at the time of the killing. Crime scenes found later by detectives corresponded with the descriptions I had given them earlier. The more one is exposed to this sort of work, the better one becomes at 'tuning in' – but of course it comes at enormous mental and emotional cost. I developed severe post-traumatic stress syndrome. A profiler worth his or her salt will recognise that this mental damage is part of the job and be prepared for it, and also be prepared to accept therapy.

While I believe that a profiler should always trust his or her gut instinct, care must be taken that evidence is not twisted to support that feeling. Every statement in a profile must be substantiated, and all hypotheses should be explored, and accepted or discarded objectively.

The best candidate for the job of profiler is a qualified psychologist (education and training), employed by a police agency and therefore with access to police records and crime scenes (experience), who has an instinct for the work. It should be a person who is strong enough mentally to manage the post-traumatic stress.

One of the reasons why profiling has been criticised as being too generalised can be found in the differentiation between *inductive* and *deductive* profiling. In *Criminal Profiling: an introduction to behavioral science*, Turvey (1996) explains that inductive profiling relies strongly on statistical findings of research conducted on similar offenders. For example, a profiler may predict that an offender would be in his late twenties because 95 per cent of offenders who committed similar crimes were in their late twenties.

Holmes (1989) states that when he began profiling the process was surrounded by an 'atmosphere of mystery and mysticism', and he decided to interview convicted offenders to learn more about their crimes. In the 1980s FBI profilers did the same thing by conducting research on thirty-six convicted serial killers. This sort of research provides us with statistics which can be used to predict the future behaviour or characteristics of other offenders.

There is, however, a danger in relying solely on statistics of this sort. A convicted perpetrator relating his story years after the fact is actually telling a second-hand story. He may have had first-hand knowledge of what happened, but many factors may influence the retelling of the facts. Psychological defence systems come into play, and convicted offenders lie, distort, and justify their actions. Trained psychologists interviewing them are alert to such defence mechanisms, while laymen may easily be manipulated by them. Convicts' motives for participating in this sort of research may vary from being bored with prison life, to seeking attention, to a need to associate with law enforcement, to an opportunity for repeating their fantasies about their crimes, to a genuine attempt at restitution. Or they may participate because they have nothing to lose by doing so. Relying solely on their answers would be unwise. But, bearing this in mind, the research conducted in this area has been valuable and should be continued.

Inductive profiling, based solely on earlier research, is therefore a quick and easy way to come up with a profile. It would however probably be so general that it would be of not much value to the investigating officer.

What other source of information is available to the profiler? The pristine crime scene is the best source of first-hand information and the best starting point. As opposed to inductive profiling, deductive profiling is a laborious process of analysing the crime scene, the evidence, the photographs, victim profiles, post-mortem reports, and so on, to finally come up with a more comprehensive and more accurate profile. Deductive analysis, for example, would enable the profiler to predict that the suspect would be in his late teens to early twenties based on the fact that evidence of sexual acts indicated inquisitiveness as opposed to sexual experience. Inductive profiling, on the other hand, would lead to the profiler arriving at an age group based on statistical research.

A deductive profile will analyse the specific 'signature' of the offender to the extent that the possibility of confusing the offender with another is drastically reduced. The ideal profile will fit the offender like a glove. It is hard work, but it is not impossible.

I would recommend that a profiler should follow the more tedious, and sometimes emotionally draining, deduct-ive process to determine the demographics, personal characteristics and motive of the offender. Only when all other resources have been depleted should one fall back on statistics obtained from research into similar crimes. Offenders may be classified as robbers, murderers, rapists, etc, but in my experience individuals who commit psychologically motivated crimes are unique; if one relies too heavily on group statistics one could overlook intrinsic characteristics and the profile would be too generalised. The profiler should strive to compile a profile that is 95 to 100 per cent accurate.

Profiling is thus both an art and a science, performed by trained, experienced profilers who are proficient in deductive thinking and who have an instinct for the work.

FIELDS OF PROFILING

Profiling as an investigative tool is best suited to psychologically motivated crimes, such as serial homicide and serial rape. It can also be applied successfully to stalking and in the analysis of threatening letters, and has been used in cases relating to kidnapping, occult-related crimes, white collar crimes, muti murders (murders committed for the purpose of obtaining human body parts) and in the competitive intelligence arena.

DIFFERENT TYPES OF PROFILING

Criminal profiling should not be confused with other types of profiling tools also used in law enforcement. A brief discussion of these will explain how they are different.

Intelligence profiling

This involves collating information about an identified person. It will include such information as identity number, address, criminal record, weapons owned, vehicles owned, employment records, verification of academic qualifications, cellphone records, bank statements, and so on. It is used mostly to trace illegal activities in white-collar crime investigations. Vetting personnel or pre-employment screening would also fall under intelligence profiling.

Compiling a psychological profile of an identified subject is a different matter and will be discussed later (page 414). It will have application in the field of competitive intelligence, where one agency or organisation needs information about a competitor. The profile will provide predictions on the subject's future behaviour, strong and weak points, thought processes, etc and recommendations on personal interaction with the subject.

Geographical profiling

With the aid of computer mapping, by entering the location(s) of crime scenes, the most likely area of residence or place of work of the offender can be determined. The MTN Centre for Crime Prevention Studies, founded by my colleague Dr Mark Welman of the Department of Psychology at Rhodes University, has done extensive work on geographical profiling in South Africa.

DNA profiling

The DNA collected from body materials – semen, hair, bones, etc – can assist in providing the definitive identification of an individual.

Victim profiling

The victim profile is usually included in the profile of the offender and contains as much information as possible about the victim. In addition to this, it is important to include hypotheses as to why a particular victim might have attracted the offender.

PSYCHOLOGICAL PROFILING IN SOUTH AFRICA

Prior to 1994 the South African Police Service (SAPS) did not officially make use of profilers. In February 1994 I was appointed by the Behavioural Sciences Unit of SAPS to oversee a project on profiling. My appointment came about because I was the first person in the country to conduct academic research on the subject of serial killers (*A psychoanalytical approach to serial killers*, DPhil Psychology, University of Pretoria, 1996). On my first day at work I was flown to Cape Town and asked to compile a profile of the serial killer whom the press had dubbed the 'Station Strangler'. For the first time a psychologist employed by SAPS participated directly in an investigation and worked hand-in-hand with the detectives assigned to the case.

The success of that profile attracted the attention of the then national head of Murder and Robbery Units, Brigadier Suiker Britz. Later that year, on his recommendation, I was transferred to what later became known as the Serious and Violent Crimes division of the detective service where I established the Investigative Psychology Unit (IPU), with the sole aim of providing psychological profiles and psychological crime scene analyses to the detectives. A short while later I attended a course on profiling and crime scene analysis in Dundee, Scotland, conducted by Robert Ressler and Roy Hazelwood, two pioneering FBI profilers.

If my first profile of the Station Strangler had not been as accurate as it was, it is doubtful whether an independent unit specialising in profiling would ever have been established under the detective services, which is a line function of the SAPS, as opposed to remaining a project within the

Behavioural Sciences Unit, which offers a support service to the SAPS. The element that distinguished my profile of the Station Strangler from all others throughout the world was that my psychological analysis of the motive of the offender was based mainly on Freudian theories, the subject of my doctorate. Robert Ressler proclaimed this technique a world first.

My work in the IPU soon expanded to include training detectives in serial homicide and related investigations, and research and consultation on other psychologically motivated crimes, such as stalking, serial rape, threatening letters, kidnapping, muti murders, and so on. In 1997 the unit expanded with the appointment of Inspector Elmarie Myburgh, a qualified psychometrist and criminologist, and a few years later we were joined by Captain Lynn Evans, a detective who specialised in serial rape. I identified certain murder and robbery detectives in each province to act as coordinators of such investigations. I compiled a two-week course in Basic Investigative Psychology as well as a two-week Advanced course, which I presented annually to selected murder and robbery and serious violent crimes detectives and crime scene photographers. Between 1994 and my resignation in 2000, we participated in the investigation of thirty-five serial killer cases.

I resigned in 2000 with the rank of deputy director, equivalent to the old rank of colonel. The pioneering phase of psychological profiling in South Africa had come to an end. Senior Superintendent Dr Gerard Labuschagne was appointed as the new commander of the IPU about a year after my resignation. He had also achieved his master's degree in psychology on the subject of serial killers (*Serial Murder – An Interactional Analysis*, University of Pretoria, 1997). The training courses have been integrated into three weeks and renamed 'Psychologically Motivated Crimes'. During the last twelve years there have been in the region of fifty known serial killer cases in South Africa. The majority of these killers have been apprehended. Although in 2004 there were still only three staff members in the IPU, I believe my legacy is in capable hands.

Dr Labuschagne defines profiling as:

> Any activity specifically undertaken with the intent of assisting an investigator to determine the most likely type of individual to have committed a specific crime. The process would usually involve an assessment of the crime scene, attending the autopsy, examining all available docket material such as statements, photographs, forensic reports and investigative decisions. This information is then compared to any available research. Finally hypotheses are formulated regarding the type of suspect who committed the crime. These hypotheses might be verbally communicated to the investigator but would normally also be structured in a written report. The aim is to assist the investigator to focus his investigation on the most likely type of suspect.
> (Labuschagne, 2003)

THE PROCESS OF COMPILING A PROFILE

The FBI profiling pioneers provided us with what I call the 'recipe' for compiling a profile (see Table 1, page 20). I find this recipe very useful and like to use the analogy of baking a cake to describe it. Step 1: When one bakes a cake, one needs certain basic ingredients – flour, sugar, butter, eggs, milk – or else the cake will flop. Additional ingredients determine whether one bakes a chocolate cake, or a fruit cake or some other kind of cake. Usually, the more ingredients there are the fancier the cake will be. Compiling a profile follows the same principle. Certain basic ingredients are essential – or the profile will not be at all helpful – and the more ingredients one adds, the 'fancier' the profile will be. Steps 2 and 3 can be compared with the mixing of the ingredients and the baking of the cake, step 4 is the finished cake. Feedback is like adding icing; the investigation (step 5) is the eating of the cake, and the apprehension of the suspect (step 6) could be thought of as 'the proof of the pudding' ...

And just as chefs usually work with a team, so does the profiler. In this instance, the profiler and the investigating officer are the team. While the investigating officer may be the client of the profiler, the profiler relies on the investigating officer to assist in collecting the 'ingredients' for the profile. We don't always understand how chefs combine ingredients to create a remarkable dish, and in the same way the profiler's requests may sometimes sound quite alien to the investigating officer. It is important to remember that the profiler is attempting to arrive at a final product by making deductions from patterns of human behaviour. Each individual human being has a unique personality and style and habits which will be constant factors in any form of his or her behaviour. What may seem unimportant to the investigating officer because it has little value as physical evidence may be very important to the profiler because it has great psychological value. For example, the fact that an offender pulled down the skirt of a victim after he had raped her may mean so little to the investigating officer that he would not notice or report it. But to the profiler this act indicates a sense of remorse on the part of the offender, which can influence the direction of the profile.

Table 1: The FBI recipe

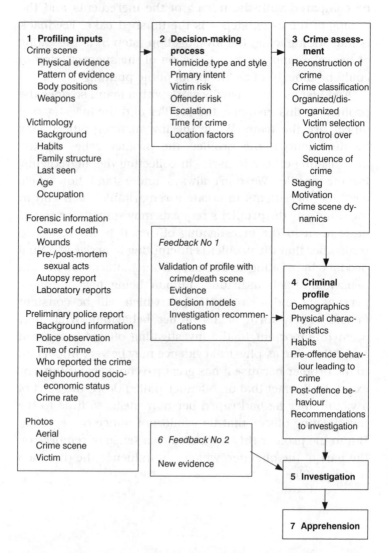

Source: Douglas, J 1986. Criminal profiling from Crime Scene Analysis. *Behavioural Sciences and the Law* 4(4).

Step 1: Profiling inputs

The crime scene

It is always best if the profiler is able to visit the pristine crime scene before the body or anything else has been touched or removed. The investigating officer is in charge of the crime scene and will immediately mark a route to the body. All those attending the crime scene must follow this route in order not to trample on or disturb evidence. I always found it best to stay behind the investigating officer and never to touch anything. I did once touch something, when I was still a rookie, and received a well-deserved tongue-lashing for it. Even so, the profiler should wear gloves and other protective gear, if available. I always kept a pair of gloves in my handbag. I would take notes while the investigating officer, crime scene photographer and pathologist carried out their work. The profiler should not be reticent about asking questions, or about pointing out objects or evidence of behaviour that might have psychological value.

If the profiler is unable to attend the crime scene, he or she will have to rely on photographs, a video and crime scene descriptions. However, the profiler should still visit the crime scene with the photographs, even after the body has been removed.

If no photographs are available, the profiler will have to rely on descriptions of the crime scene. An inaccurate description of even the smallest detail may result in a skewed profile and throw an investigation off track, so it is best to return to the crime scene with the officer who wrote the crime scene description and to mark out exactly where everything was found. This might reactivate his memory.

The crime scene is the only first-hand source of information available to the profiler, who should therefore take note of the following elements:

Physical evidence

The detectives and crime scene processors will collect evidence with forensic value. The profiler's job is to note and report on any evidence found or missing at the crime scene which might have psychological value. Examples of evidence with psychological value are:

- Cigarettes. The profiler should count how many were smoked and what brand they were. Finding many cigarette butts at a crime scene indicates that the offender felt secure enough to spend time there. He was familiar with the crime scene and had probably been there before. The profiler needs to determine what type of person would feel secure in the particular environment of the crime scene. The cigarette brand may provide a clue to identity as certain brands are associated with certain images. Cheap cigarettes might indicate a vagrant. Lipstick might indicate that the victim had also smoked at the scene. This could mean that the offender had a charming personality and succeeded in gaining the victim's trust. Are there spent matches as well as cigarette butts?

- Cans or bottles. At one of the crime scenes of the Station Strangler we found an almost empty bottle of sparkling wine right next to the decomposed body of a victim. The Station Strangler's victims were killed in a remote dune area. Since there was still liquid in the bottle and the label had not faded in the sun, yet the body had already decomposed, it was clear that the killer had returned to the crime scene long after the murder. The bottle's proximity to the body ruled out the possibility that it had been left there by any other person. When I was studying the crime scene photographs of the Cleveland Strangler I noticed that in two instances there were cold drink cans lying between the victims' legs. When I asked whether the cans had been collected for fingerprinting, I was told that the crime scenes were littered with rubbish and the detective had surmised that the cans were simply part of the environment. This may be true once, but it seemed too much of a coincidence that two of the victims should have fallen with their legs spreadeagled over a cold drink can. Potential evidence could have been lost on these occasions.

- Condoms and condom wrappers. Condoms may, of course, contain semen. Condom wrappers may indicate a brand and may be traced to a retailer. In a serial killer investigation the profiler will check whether the same brand was used on all the victims. If the victim was a prostitute, she might have provided the condom. The use of condoms indicates that the killer is sophisticated enough to know about DNA evidence and sexually transmitted diseases. I was called in during the Cleveland Strangler investigation only after many bodies had been discovered in the mine dumps to the south of Johannesburg. The detectives had been reluctant to use my services and only did so when Brigadier Britz insisted. I asked to return to the crime scenes, even though it was weeks since they had been processed. I was informed that all the evidence had been collected and the investigating officer made it clear that he felt we were wasting our time. At one of the scenes I noticed a sanitary towel and a condom wrapper on the ground and asked that it be collected. It later yielded valuable DNA evidence which would otherwise have been lost.

- Clothing. It is important to check what items of the victim's clothing are missing and what items may have been added. Serial killers often take 'souvenirs' from their victims so that they can relive their fantasies. Clothing and jewellery are the items most likely to be taken. Phoenix killer Sipho Twala connected himself to his different crime scenes by using the underwear of a previous victim to strangle his next victim. He tore the underwear into strips which he plaited into the cord with which he strangled his victims. He also tore squares of material from petticoats and rolled them into balls which he placed in his victims' mouths. All of this indicated that a lot of time was spent at the crime scene and that he was fascinated by feminine mystique, as shown by his preoccupation with the underwear. It was clear that he had knocked his victims unconscious before he stripped them. Since they were already incapacitated, why would he want to tie them up with intricately plaited cords and why would he want to gag them? Bondage and gagging were the main elements of his fantasy.

Moses Sithole, the Atteridgeville Strangler, transferred underwear from one victim to another. One of his victims was strangled with a bra which was clearly not the right size to have belonged to the victim. He also covered their heads and faces with their panties. This is an indication of *depersonalising*: the killer hates his victims.

The Station Strangler placed his victims' shoes neatly beside them, which is indicative of habitual neatness, and he re-dressed his victims very neatly after sodomising them. Their soiled underwear was discarded near their bodies. Re-dressing a victim in this way points to undoing. *Undoing* is a term used to describe the psychological process of trying to undo the action and is motivated by remorse. The covering of body parts often indicates undoing. Killers have been known to wash and even dress the wounds of their victims. Stewart Wilken covered the body of his daughter with a tarpaulin, a clear act of undoing and remorse. Apart from remorse, undoing may also indicate that the killer knew his victim. The fact that Moses Sithole covered his victims' heads was not, however, an act of undoing. His victims were found with their legs spreadeagled and their genitals exposed.

The profiler will check whether clothing is worn correctly. Have the buttons been correctly fastened, are there buttons missing, is the clothing inside out, cut or torn? If a belt is found, does it fit the victim or could it have belonged to the killer?

The victim of Willem Grobler of Louis Trichardt was wearing a jersey that had a name tag stitched to it. One cannot assume that the name would immediately identify the victim; people often wear second-hand clothing. In this case the victim had borrowed the jersey from a friend who, fortunately, was identified and who, in turn, was able to identify the victim.

The quality of the clothing may provide clues to the social standing or occupation of the victim. Shoes are particularly important because if they indicate that the victim walked to the crime scene, one can deduce that the murder had been committed there. If it appears that the victim was dragged or carried, the likelihood is that the murder, or initial assault, took place elsewhere. The Wemmer Pan serial killer, Cedric Maake, always stole the shoes of his male victims because looking smart was important to him.

- If the victim is still wearing her jewellery, the motive for the murder was not robbery. In the Cleveland case, one victim was found naked, with her jewellery displayed on her stomach. The killer's message was that robbery was not his motive. Fingers should be checked for indentations that might point to missing rings. Fingers may be amputated to remove rings. Earlobes should be checked for signs of earrings having been torn off. Moses Sithole used jewellery he had taken from earlier victims to entice his next victims. Serial killers also seem to enjoy presenting the jewellery of their victims to wives and girlfriends. When Phoenix killer Sipho Twala was arrested the police found that his shack was stacked with female clothing and the watches of two of his victims were displayed as trophies alongside his bed.

- Excreta. Excreta has no forensic value, but it could have psychological value, as will be explained in the chapter on serial killers.

- Foreign objects. Foreign objects such as umbrellas, sticks, etc are often inserted into the vaginas or anuses of victims. These objects are usually phallic and are indicative of castration anxiety or possible impotence of the killer. Other foreign objects, like stones, may be found in the mouths or throats of victims. Stewart Wilken inserted newspaper into the anuses of the boys he killed so that he would not be troubled with maggots when he later returned to the corpses to commit necrophilia.

- Handbags. Removal of the handbag of the victim to prevent identification indicates criminal sophistication to the profiler. If the contents of the handbag have been scattered the killer was looking for money or other valuables or the victim's identity document. It should be established whether the strap of the handbag has been removed. It might later come to light as a murder weapon on a different crime scene.

- Paper. Any paper, including toilet paper, tissue or newspaper, may contain forensic evidence. We returned to one of Moses Sithole's crime scenes months after it had been processed and all evidence removed. In the mean time the veld on the scene had been burned. Yet we found a fresh tissue in the place where the body had been lying. It would appear that the killer had returned to relive his fantasy.

- Body fluids. Semen, of course, has great forensic value, but it also has psychological value. Some serial killers masturbate on the bodies of their victims. The investigating officer should check on top of and underneath clothing for signs of semen. All body orifices, including the mouth, anus, navel and wounds should also be checked for semen. The profiler should request the pathologist to do this.
- Weapons. The profiler will note whether the killer brought the weapon to the crime scene or whether a weapon of opportunity was used. To whom does the weapon belong? Weapons can have a symbolic significance. A firearm may be fired from a distance; a knife may have a phallic symbolism and the killer may derive sexual pleasure from slashing and drawing blood (the term for this is *piquerism*); strangulation is a hands-on act. When a garrotte is used for strangling the victim, the killer can tighten and loosen the pressure on the victim's throat, sadistically prolonging the process of death.

  Moses Sithole placed one of his victims on her stomach, bent her legs back and tied a ligature from her ankles to her neck. When the victim became tired and tried to relax her legs she slowly strangled herself involuntarily. Sithole masturbated while watching her slow, agonising death.
- Knots. Knots may indicate whether an offender is right or left-handed and they should never be undone. The cord or other ligature should be cut and the knot preserved.

All other physical objects should be noted, including footprints and tyre tracks.

Unlike the detective, the profiler also notes non-physical elements of the crime scene such as accessibility, weather patterns at the time of the crime, and so on. The profiler needs to find reasons why a victim would accompany a stranger to a remote area. Serial killers have been known to lure their victims with the promise of employment, an indication that the killer would be confident and charming. The bodies of Sithole's victims were often found in close proximity to one another, which would tell the profiler that he showed their bodies to his latest victim in order to terrorise her.

Pattern of evidence

The pattern of evidence refers to the modus operandi, rituals and habits of the offender. Neither the investigating officer nor the profiler should make the mistake of considering only a particular modus operandi and similarities in the victims as a means of determining whether different crimes are the work of one offender. The key is the killer's 'signature' which differentiates one perpetrator from another. Although it is rare, the modus operandi and victim selection can differ in one series, but a serial offender will none the less leave his signature on the crime scene and someone who has been trained to look for it will be able to pick it up through analysis.

Different crimes can be linked to one offender through an analysis of the victims, the crime scenes, the forensic and pathology reports, interviews with surviving victims and verbal and non-verbal behaviour patterns. It is essential that the profiler analyses the pattern of evidence at the crime scene in order to determine what the signature of the killer is.

What is the difference between a modus operandi and a signature? A *modus operandi* is a learned behaviour. An offender uses a particular modus operandi because he has learned that it is effective, although it may progress as he gains experience. The modus operandi of an offender who has already served a prison sentence will be more sophisticated because he has learned from his own mistakes and those of other offenders.

The victim's reaction may also influence the modus operandi. A rapist may learn that it is better to have a knife with him because his victim will offer less resistance. So the modus operandi will be adapted to suit the demands of the crime.

A *signature*, on the other hand, is the personal stamp that a killer will leave on a crime scene. It is also called *repetitive personation*. It evolves from the killer's psychological needs which led to his developing his own particular fantasy which is then acted out in reality in the committing of the murder. Any form of ritual, whether symbolic or compulsive, is a signature.

A signature need not necessarily be a physical manifestation – like a bow around the victim's neck or writing on the victim's body. It can also manifest in verbal behaviour. Verbal and non-verbal behaviour are, of course impossible to establish in murder cases, but can be established in cases of serial rape or other sex crimes where the victim survived. It may be helpful in a serial killer investigation to interview ex-partners and wives of suspects to determine whether similar sexual acts (non-verbal behaviour) to those performed on the victims were also practised on them. A serial rapist's signature can be expressed through verbal behaviour – vulgar language, 'scripts' for the victims, apologies – as well as non-verbal behaviour, such as specific acts of violence or preferred sexual acts.

The core of the offender's ritual or fantasy will never change but the signature can become more elaborate; for example, become more violent. Elements of the ritual can also develop progressively with each crime. A signature may be absent because of the victim's response, or something disturbing the offender. Crimes committed out of doors and the level of decomposition can complicate the detection of a signature.

Body positions

This element is often overlooked by investigating officers. Descriptions of the crime scene should state whether the body was found lying on the back, stomach, side, etc. Are the legs spreadeagled or closed? What is the position of the hands, head, etc? Hands placed in a praying position on the chest may indicate undoing and remorse. Has the body been transported, dumped or displayed? Bodies displayed in a certain way usually indicate that the killer is trying to communicate something to the detectives who will find his 'work'. It may be to communicate how he feels about his victims, or it may merely be to communicate arrogance towards the police.

Stewart Wilken displayed the mutilated naked bodies of the female prostitutes he killed in public places such as parks and school grounds. He despised prostitutes and wanted them found and humiliated in death. By contrast, he hid the bodies of his street boy victims in dense bush. He covered them with palm leaves, which had an intrinsic religious meaning for him. He covered his own daughter's body with a tarpaulin and slept next to her body for months.

A displayed body may tell the profiler that the killer had enough confidence to know that he had time to display the body without being found at the scene. Killers who spend time at the scenes have been there before.

The condition of the victim's nails should not be overlooked. Manicured nails may point to the status of the victim. Broken nails may indicate victim resistance, and nail scrapings may have forensic evidential value.

The position of the body may indicate whether it was dragged. Scars on the heels and post-mortem lividity on the wrists will often reveal dragging. Tracing the drag marks may lead to tyre tracks and the conclusion that the victim was not killed at the scene.

Victimology

The profiler will compile the victim profile. As mentioned earlier, the primary factor here is not necessarily to identify the victim but rather to try to establish specifically what it was about the victim that made the killer choose her. Of course the main focus of the profile is the killer, not the victim, but there will be an idiosyncratic reason for his selection of the victim which will reveal more about the psychological make-up of the killer. It will also provide a clue as to motive. In serial homicide the victim represents a subconscious primal hurt which occurred during the killer's childhood. The profiler has to decipher the psychodynamics underlying this.

With that in mind as the first priority, the profiler's secondary focus is to take into consideration such factors as the victim's background, habits, family structure, age and occupation, when last seen, and appearance and personality. Any of these factors may be the conscious reason why the killer chose her. This is why it is important to the profiler that victims be identified as soon as possible.

Moses Sithole's victims did not have much in common as far as physical attributes were concerned. He selected women who belittled him. In his case it was important to interview the families of the victims to find out what sort of people they were.

How does one set about identifying the bodies? We have already discussed the importance of examining the clothing, and Inspector Vivian Bieldt, crime scene analyst with the South African Police Service, taught me the following which may lead to the successful identification of victims:

- Tattoos. These may place the victim in a particular category. For instance, was the tattoo professionally done (in which case it might be traceable to the tattoo artist), or self-inflicted? Gangs have tattoos by which they may be identified.

- Body markings. These include scars from surgery, old wounds, amputations, traditional markings and sports injuries. Calluses may identify occupations and perhaps even religion (time spent on the knees). Blind people may have calluses on their fingertips, as would guitar players. A cast should be made of any bite marks on the body, as this can identify the killer. A bite mark may resemble a bruise, but once the skin is removed and turned over the bite mark is revealed. The notorious American serial killer Ted Bundy was convicted on the evidence of a bite mark.

- Jewellery. Engravings on jewellery can be used to identify victims. The police sometimes publish photographs of jewellery in the press.

- Hair. The roots of the hair indicate whether it is the natural colour or has been dyed. Hairstyles may reveal whether the victim was fashion conscious and/or had the financial means to afford expensive haircuts, etc. The roots of the hair contain DNA.

- Teeth. A victim may be identified from dental records. However, many people can't afford dentistry. Smooth molars may indicate that the victim came from a rural area where hard seeds were part of her diet. People from rural areas have higher fluoride levels than the urban population. Rotten teeth can indicate age, or lack of means to afford dental care. They could also point to a mentally disturbed person who had deteriorated to the extent that personal hygiene was neglected. Stained teeth could be indicative of a smoker. Teeth that are exposed to heat will splinter and crack. Pink discolouration of the teeth may indicate strangulation, or that the body had been in water or lying face down.

- Skeletons. The age of the victim may be determined by

the condition of the teeth and examination of joints such as the wrists. The ends of the ribs in older people tend to be more concave on their inner surfaces. Abrasions on the head of the femur may indicate that the person walked with a limp. There will be excess calcium in the area of a bone that has been broken. The length of the femur gives an indication of height. The victim's gender may be identified from the pelvis and gender can also be determined from the frontal bones of the skull (just above the eyes) which are flatter in women than in men. The skull can also indicate race and can be reconstructed so that facial features are revealed.

- Stomach contents. Analysis of stomach contents provides information on what the victim ate or drank before death.
- Missing person reports. Detectives will obviously peruse missing person reports to try to find a match with an unidentified victim. There are however many illegal immigrants in South Africa who might not be reported missing. Also, many people from rural areas come to the cities to seek employment and their families probably do not expect to hear from them regularly. They, too, might not be reported missing.

In my view, the investigating officer should allocate the task of victim investigation to specific members of the team and not focus the whole investigation on this aspect. It can waste valuable time. The profiler should continue to work on the profile regardless of whether the victims have been identified. Accurate profiles have been drawn up without this information.

Forensic information
Cause of death

The pathologist will establish the cause of death. It is

unwise for the investigating officer to decide on the cause of death and note it as a fait accompli in the docket. In one case a victim was found apparently strangled, but the pathologist established that she had actually died before strangulation from a blow to the head with a blunt object. The fact that the killer continued to strangle her, although she was already dead, indicates a need to act out a fantasy.

In another case, a young girl was discovered in the well in the backyard of her home in Bellville, Cape Town. When the detectives reconstructed the crime, it was found that she had been assaulted with a blunt object and had collapsed. The killer assumed she was dead and threw her body into the well. But the pathologist found that she had actually died from drowning.

It is also often found that killers burn their victims to disguise gunshot or knife wounds.

Wounds

It is sometimes difficult to distinguish between knife and gunshot wounds, especially if the body is decomposed or covered in blood. An experienced investigating officer may make an educated guess. If it seems that the wound was caused by a blunt instrument, he will obviously look for an 'instrument' (which might be a rock) with traces of blood on it. If a gunshot wound is suspected, then he will look for the round or the shell. In one of the serial killer cases I worked on the pathologist authorised burial of the victims with bullets still inside the bodies.

Defensive wounds should be noted. These are usually found on the arms and hands of the victim, indicating that she was conscious during the attack.

Wrists and ankles must be checked for signs of bondage or handcuffing. An experienced pathologist will be able to identify these marks. The heels and the back of the victim should be checked for drag marks.

The pathologist should be able to say whether wounds were inflicted pre- or post-mortem. Post-mortem wounds do not bleed. The pathologist can also determine the depth and size of wounds and determine whether more than one weapon was used.

Pre- or post-mortem sexual acts

It is difficult to establish from a fresh body whether sex took place pre- or post-mortem. In the case of Mhlengwa Zikode, the Donnybrook serial killer, blood traces on the ground indicated the location where the victim was shot, but drag marks led to the victim's body a few metres away. The gunshot wound on her head indicated that she must have died immediately at the place where the blood was found. She had been raped, and clearly this had happened post-mortem at the place where her body was found. When asked why he had raped the dead woman, Zikode answered that her body was still warm so it did not bother him.

Sometimes it is obvious that necrophilia has taken place, as in the case of Stewart Wilken, who sodomised street boys weeks after killing them.

Serial killers often return to the scene of their crimes to masturbate. There is often fresh excreta, a strong indication that the killer had returned.

In one case a killer returned to the body of a young girl several hours after he had killed her and cut off her breast. This may be regarded as a post-mortem sexual act since he was sexually aroused by cutting off her breast. Serial killers who masturbate with 'souvenirs' in the privacy of their own homes are also committing post-mortem sexual acts. A sexual act need not be regarded only as sexual penetration.

Autopsy reports

Since it may take a long time before post-mortem reports are released to the investigating officer, it is important that the profiler or one of the members of the investigation team attends the post-mortem and takes notes. The profiler needs this information urgently and cannot wait three to four weeks for it.

Pathologists often use terminology that needs clarification for the layman and the profiler should not be reticent about asking for this.

When I was working on the profile of the Saloon Killer, Velaphi Nglandlamandla, I noticed in the post-mortem reports that most of the victims had been shot two centimetres above the left eye. Considering that they had been shot from a distance and in the dark, I surmised that the killer must have had training in the use of firearms which, indeed, proved to be the case.

The profiler may ask the pathologist to check for bite marks, semen in unusual orifices, needle marks or any other unusual 'damage' that the profiler suspects the killer might have inflicted on the victim. Serial killers often bite their victims, especially on the arms, breasts, shoulders, vagina, buttocks and thighs. Apart from checking the nails of victims for scrapings, the profiler can ask the pathologist to check the victim's teeth for traces of skin. It is perfectly possible for a victim to have bitten her assailant.

In the Atteridgeville Strangler case several bodies were discovered at one crime scene. Captain Petra Hennop, a DNA expert, found foreign blood on the clothing of one of the victims. But when she checked the crime scene photographs she could see that there was no blood on the victim's clothing. Captain Hennop followed up on the circumstances of the transportation of the body and found that the victims had been transported in the same mortuary van and that the blood of one victim had contaminated the clothing of another. Had she not been so vigilant the foreign blood might have been thought to be that of the killer. Contamination is inexcusable carelessness.

All clothing as well as all ligatures removed from victims at the mortuary should be photographed and kept.

The pathologist should inform the investigating officer and the profiler of the stomach contents and blood alcohol level. The victim's family may assert that the victim did not drink alcohol, in which case a high content could indicate that the killer forced the victim to drink it.

If a foreign objected was inserted into the body of the victim the investigating officer should take possession of it and prevent anyone from touching it. In the Cape Town prostitute case a pathologist kept the bottle that had been inserted into the vagina of one of the victims, contaminating possible fingerprint evidence.

The pathologist is able to determine if body parts are missing as a result of insect or animal activity, or if they were removed by the killer as a 'souvenir'.

In many of the serial killer cases I worked on pathologists were requested to come direct to the crime scenes. This is always advantageous from the pathologist's perspective, and it is also helpful if the same pathologist can deal with all cases relating to one specific series. Pathologists can estimate the time of death of decomposed bodies, but a forensic entomologist can determine the *exact* time of death by examining insect activity on the crime scene.

Laboratory reports

The profiler should be informed of the results of forensic laboratory findings and not have to wait for official reports before compiling the profile. Laboratory reports comprise not only those from the Forensic Science Laboratory in Pretoria, but also those from the forensic entomologist, statistics relating to similar crimes, missing person reports, and so on.

Preliminary police report

This is mainly the information contained in the police docket.

Background information

This refers to the circumstances in which the crime took place. It includes initial statements taken at the crime scene, especially the statement of the person who discovered the body, statements of the policemen who attended the crime scene as well as those of bystanders and the families of victims if any have been identified at this stage.

Police observation

This refers to a situation where the police may post an observation team at the crime scene, as well as what measures have been taken to identify the killer. It may also include investigation into cellphones, vehicles, etc.

Time of crime

This refers to the time at which the victim was killed. We have already mentioned that an entomologist can provide an accurate time of death. Inspector Bieldt, who was trained as a forensic entomologist by expert Dr Victor Mansel, describes the science of forensic entomology as follows:

> Flies lay thousands of eggs in the body. These eggs develop into maggots approximately eight hours after being laid. The maggots feed on the body, which accelerates the decomposition process. Maggots become pupae, which later hatch into flies.

During the process of decomposition the body becomes bloated and exudes a putrid odour which attracts flies. Ants will also begin to feed on the body, opening new wounds which also attract flies. Flies enter the body through the orifices or where there is blood from wounds. At this stage hairy maggots, big blue flies and green-blue flies should be collected from the scene.

Once the maggots begin feeding on the body they will create orifices attracting other insects such as the small flies called Cheese Jumpers and also the Coffin Fly, so named because it can infest a body that has been buried.

In the last stages of decomposition the body will be dehydrated. Only the skeleton, hair and sinews remain. These attract Hide, Veld and Hair Beetles.

If it is not possible for an entomologist to attend a crime scene, the investigating officer should collect the insects and take note of weather conditions, sunspots and shade, moisture, etc.

Both live and dead insects should be collected in bottles and the investigating officer should note from which part of the body they were removed. Live pupae should also be collected in order to determine later which particular fly it is.

This may seem a particularly gruesome task, but it is imperative for the profiler to know the exact date of death of the victim. The knowledge may help the profiler to determine a pattern. For example, the killer may be active only when there is a full moon, or on rainy evenings. The date of death may also correspond with a date that has significance for the killer, for example his mother's birthday. Dates are also important in investigating alibis of suspects.

The Nasrec serial killer Lazarus Mazingane abducted a young girl who was reported missing on the day she disappeared. When her body was found it was established that she had been kept captive for some days, since the body was fresh.

Another reason why establishing the date of death is important is that it may enable the profiler to identify a pattern, which could mean that he or she will be in a position to predict when the next murder is likely to take place and crime scenes may be kept under surveillance. Establishing the time the crime took place may indicate when the killer has free time. If he kills during the day it is unlikely that he has regular employment from 9 to 5 each weekday.

The Cape Town Prostitute Killer preferred to commit his crimes on rainy nights when no one would bother to check what might be going on in a car parked alongside the road with steamed-up windows. In addition, the rain washed away his tyre tracks on the farm roads where he dumped his victims' bodies. The Station Strangler's preference was to entice children to follow him at dusk. At this time of day parents were likely to be in their homes preparing supper or watching television while children were still playing outside, making the most of the fading light.

Who reported the crime?

It is important to take all the particulars of the person who reports a crime; serial killers have been known to report their own crimes. In addition, those observing the crime scene should be videoed and as many details as possible taken as they may prove to be valuable witnesses.

The Donnybrook serial killer Mhlengwa Zikode was a bystander at the scene of his last murder and even helped mortuary attendants to load the body into the van. Phoenix serial killer Sipho Twala watched the processing of his crime scenes from a short distance away. Stewart Wilken was far more bold. As an 'innocent bystander' he asked detectives questions about the collection of evidence. He later used this information in an attempt to cover his tracks. None of these activities was reported by the detectives who initially processed the crime scenes. I obtained the information when I interviewed the killers after their arrest.

It is not desirable to allow members of the public to approach a crime scene. They may disturb evidence, discuss what they saw with members of the media and prejudice the police investigation.

Neighbourhood socio-economic status

Another reason why it is important for the profiler to visit the crime scene is that it enables him or her to analyse the environment. The killer might, for instance, prefer suburbs, industrial areas, dunes, mine dumps or railway lines. The profiler must familiarise him- or herself with the killer's preferences in order to get to know his habits. Serial killers usually commit their murders or dump the bodies in places where they feel safe, and these are usually places that they know well. The profiler's task is to find out why the killer felt safe in a particular area or place. It could be that he lived there, or worked there, or had grown up there. A suspect in the Cape Town Prostitute Killer case was known to sit and read in his parked car close to a number of areas where bodies were later found.

By analysing the neighbourhood the profiler can also determine whether the community would be likely to contribute willingly to the investigation, or whether special measures would be necessary to obtain their cooperation. In the Cape Town Prostitute Killer case local prostitutes were asked to have their fingerprints and photographs taken at the Murder and Robbery Unit. They complied in their hundreds. They also wrote down the vehicle registration numbers of their clients and gave these to the police.

Analysing the environment will also indicate the likely success of surveillance. For example, in the Phoenix case it was decided that surveillance of the cane fields would be difficult because of the height of the sugar cane and the denseness of the fields. Instead, it was decided to deploy police dogs and they found a number of bodies.

Crime rate

The profiler needs to have some idea of the crime rate in the area. Captain Mike van Aardt, the investigating officer in the Jeppe Pyromaniac case, knew he would be unlikely to secure the cooperation of the residents since many of them were involved in petty crime and wary of the police.

A serial killer operative in an area like KwaZulu-Natal at a time when faction fighting was rife might be difficult to trace, since murders with a different motive will confuse the issue. A community desensitised to murder will not be likely to assist in a police investigation. An attempt should always be made to elicit the support of community leaders in such cases. In the instance of the Donnybrook serial killer the community took matters into their own hands, and two innocent men were lynched. Provision should be made to ensure that such vigilante activities do not occur.

Photographs

Photographs and videos are essential to the profiler's work. They are also displayed in the operations room and will be presented during the trial. They may also later be used for research and training purposes. The profiler needs all the crime scene and autopsy photographs, not only those selected for presentation in court. The set of photographs provided for the profiler must not be mounted.

Aerial photographs

Aerial photographs can be obtained from the Defence Force, but if these are too old new photographs should be taken. This can be arranged through the SAPS Air Wing, who have always been willing to help. In the Saloon Killer case the local forestry department volunteered the services of their aeroplane and Inspector Danie Reyneke took the photographs. Aerial photographs are mounted on one wall of the operations room. They can be of much greater value than a map of the area.

In the Station Strangler investigation aerial photographs of the dunes in Mitchell's Plain provided views of footpaths that are not discernible on a map. On the other hand, maps are important in providing street names and identifying landmarks.

Aerial photographs and maps help to establish whether the killer used a vehicle or whether he walked to his crime scenes. For instance, the dunes in Mitchell's Plain were only accessible by foot, as were the cane fields in Phoenix. But the prostitutes in Cape Town were picked up in Voortrekker Street and their bodies were dumped kilometres away on farm roads; a vehicle was definitely involved.

The profiler needs to be able to look at the crime scene in relation to suburbs, railway lines, taxi stops, bus terminals, shopping centres, schools, and so on. The employment or habits of the victims will identify important landmarks. These places can be kept under surveillance in an attempt to identify the killer approaching his next victim.

Crime scene photos

It is the responsibility of the investigating officer to instruct the photographer in what he wants photographed. There should be a number of full-length photos of the victim, taken from toes to head and from different angles. The victim's feet should never be excluded since it is important for the profiler to be able to determine whether the victim willingly accompanied the killer, or whether he dragged or carried her to the scene. There should be a close-up of the victim's face and profiles from both sides, as well as close-ups of hands and feet. Ears are particularly important as they are as unique to an individual as fingerprints.

Close-up shots should be taken of clothing, or anything unusual about clothing, for example, a label or a missing button, as well as jewellery.

There should be close-up photos of all wounds, as well as other items or evidence on the scene. In short, there should be a close-up photograph of any item described in the docket. There should also be photographs that clearly indicate the position of the body in relation to landmarks at the scene, in case it is necessary for the profiler to return to the scene after the body has been removed.

Nothing should be disturbed until the crime scene photographs have been taken. They should therefore be taken before and after the red beacons are placed next to items of evidence. It is assumed that at this stage only the investigating officer and the photographer have entered the crime scene. After the video and photographs have been taken other members of the investigation team may enter, if necessary. If the profiler is present at the crime scene, he or she should join the investigating officer on the pristine crime scene. It is important for the profiler to see and experience the crime scene exactly as the killer left it, for it carries the imprint of his personality. Once it is disturbed, psychological clues may be lost for ever.

Photos of victims

Apart from crime scene photographs of the victim, the investigating officer should try to obtain a recent photograph of the victim once he or she has been identified. The photographs of different victims will be mounted in the operations room where they may be compared to determine whether there are any common physical characteristics. They may also be released to the media in an attempt to obtain information about where the victims were last seen, and with whom. Members of the public should be encouraged to inform the police if they had any contact with the victim, even just being seated next to her in a taxi, regardless of whether they knew her name.

We should now have all the ingredients for the profile. The following steps focus on drawing up the actual profile.

Step 2: Decision-making process

Homicide type and style

The FBI classifies homicides according to *type* and *style*. The *type* is determined by the number of victims: a single homicide is one victim, double homicide is two victims, one event and one location. The *style* describes whether it is a serial, mass or spree killer at work. This will indicate the specific kind of crime that the profile will focus on, for instance: *Serial killer; organised, lust-motivated*.

Resources available to the profiler in the correct classification of the crime include the SAPS's system of crime classification and the *Crime Classification Manual* (1993) of the FBI's National Center for the Analysis of Violent Crime.

Primary intent

This term is used to describe the main motive for the crime. In some cases the murder may be an ancillary action and not the primary intent. According to the FBI, the primary intent may be criminal enterprise, emotional or sexual. For example, a rapist's primary intent may be the need to establish power and he will kill his victims to prevent them from identifying him, not because he enjoys killing them. Emotional intent may surface in patricide, infanticide, mercy killing, etc.

It is the profiler's task to decipher the motive behind the murder, which can become tricky when psychological motives are investigated.

Victim risk

This is the risk factor to which victims are exposed. For example, prostitutes and street children have a high risk, while a housewife inside a well-guarded home has a low risk. A well-built male has a low risk compared to an elderly woman. Some serial killers will tend to select specific high-risk victims like prostitutes because they are easily available, while others might be compelled to seek low-risk victims for reasons of their own idiosyncratic preferences, or because they are trying to provoke the law or the community.

When the victims are prostitutes, as in the case of the Cape Town Prostitute Killer, the profiler has to determine whether the killer chose prostitutes because he has an idiosyncratic obsession about them, or whether he simply wished to kill women and prostitutes are the most easily available.

The Station Strangler chose schoolboys between the ages of eight and eleven. They may have been street-smart children who often played in the streets, but they were not street children. They all had homes. He was able to talk to them quite comfortably before persuading them to accompany him. Although there are hundreds of homeless children on our streets, he never approached them.

Victim risk is determined by factors such as age, occupation, lifestyle, physical stature, ability to resist, and location.

Offender risk

This term refers to the risk the offender takes of being

identified or caught.

The Nasrec Serial Killer Lazarus Mazingane, took a great risk by parking his vehicle next to a highway off-ramp and murdering his victims on the island between the off-ramp and the highway. Although he killed at night, the area had streetlights and was surrounded by heavy traffic. These factors point to both arrogance and a need for excitement.

During the Station Strangler investigation the police in Mitchell's Plain were very active. Neighbourhood watch organisations were vigilant and any adult male in the company of a young boy was stopped and questioned. The man who was arrested as the Station Strangler, Norman Avzal Simons, realised that things were getting too hot for him, yet he could not suppress the urge to kill again. So he went to the neighbouring Strand thinking he would go unnoticed in this town, since the investigation was focused on Mitchell's Plain. In Strand he picked up two boys, Ryno and Elroy van Rooy, in front of a shopping centre. He made a crucial mistake: he was noticed for the reason that he was a stranger in the community. His attempt at being incognito backfired. His other mistake was his practice of booking himself into a psychiatric clinic before or after the murders, reasoning that no one would look for a killer in a clinic. A nurse who read the profile recognised Simons as a possible suspect, and this led to his arrest. Simons' attempts at lowering his risk factor defeated him in the end.

Apart from indicating arrogance, offender risk can point to intelligence, street wisdom, delusions, desperation and naivety, among other factors.

Escalation

This term refers to the pattern of the murders and includes cooling-off periods.

The Station Strangler had a cooling-off period of almost

three years, and then killed eleven boys in quick succession in the course of one month. A rapid increase in killing can be the result of a major stressful event that confronts the serial killer's self-image to such an extent that one murder does not restore his mental equilibrium. It may also indicate the killer's subconscious need to be apprehended or the need to provoke the law. The need to be apprehended does not mean that the killer will give himself up. It is rather a subconscious cry for help, which the killer will consciously try to ignore. Decreases in escalation can indicate periods when the serial killer is happy, or incarcerated, or absent from the area.

The dates of the renewed killings are compared with the major happenings and movements in a suspect's life. Dates of murders should also be compared with important dates in the suspect's life, such as anniversaries.

Escalation does not only pertain to the dates of the murders, but also to progress in modus operandi. The more the killer practises, the better he gets.

Time for crime

There are four factors to be considered:
- The time the killer spent with the victim before killing him or her
- The time needed to kill the victim
- The time spent after the murder to commit additional acts on the body or to clear up the crime scene
- The time needed to dispose of the body

The entomology reports will reveal when the victim was murdered. This time can be compared with the time when the victim was last seen alive. It is then possible to determine whether the victim was kept captive before being killed. If this is the case, then the deduction may be made that the killer has a hiding place.

Disorganised killers favour blitz attacks and will not

spend time with their victims before the assault. The organised killer may spend some time talking to his victim and accompanying her to the crime scene. This points to planning and a rational mind at work.

It also needs to be established whether the killer later returned to the body and spent time at the crime scene.

Location factors

There are several factors applicable to location. Important locations are:
- Where the killer met the victim
- Where he murdered her
- Where he dumped the body
- Where he dumped her clothing or other effects

Location may also refer to autobanks where the killer drew cash with bankcards stolen from the victim.

Organised serial killers pre-select places where they feel safe and are unlikely to be observed. It is important to note if they digress from this pattern and to establish why. Profilers should become so familiar with their suspects that they should be able to predict the location of future crime scenes. If he is disturbed at his regular spot, the killer will move to a similar place.

Sipho Twala lived in a shantytown that overlooked the Phoenix canefields. While sitting outside his shack, rolling fabric torn from his previous victim's underwear into a ball, he would look out over his 'graveyard' and fantasise about killing his next victim and placing the fabric ball in her mouth. He also practised his knots by tying strips of underwear around cane stems outside his shack.

Step 3: Crime assessment

Reconstruction of the crime

It is important to reconstruct the sequence of events in

exact chronological order. The best way of doing this is to return to the crime scene with the crime scene photographs and walk in the steps of the killer. The profiler endeavours to provide an explanation for every detail of the crime scene, and that is why the initial crime scene notes are so important.

When we were investigating the Cape Town Prostitute case we returned to every scene with the photographs in order to establish the modus operandi and signature of the killer. The following pattern emerged:

When compared with weather records, the dates of death of the victims confirmed that the killer chose rainy nights to pick up his victims. On the afternoons of the days when he decided to kill, he would drive to the farming areas of Philledelphia and Kontermanskloof to select a place where it would be safe to dump a body. There are no lights on these farm roads and a person with no previous knowledge of the area would not have been able to find the side roads on a rainy night. It was clear that he had forced his way through gates, and this he had probably done earlier in the day. That night he would cruise along Voortrekker Road, pick up a victim and then park close by, for instance in an empty parking lot. All the victims were streetwise prostitutes who would not have allowed their clients to take them away from their area, for this would result in potential loss of income for them.

The killer asked the victims to undress. Most of them were found without their skirts and panties. Prostitutes need to conduct their business as fast as possible in order to be able to move on to the next client, so they would remove only the necessary garments. Then the killer would hit the victim in the face – all the victims had facial wounds inflicted with a blunt object. The victim would fall forward and he would pull her across his lap with her face between his legs. He would then strangle her with a ligature. When she was dead he removed the ligature and pushed her back on to the passenger seat. The rain ensured that no one bothered to investigate what might be going on in a steamed-up car in a parking lot at rush hour.

The killer would drive to the spot that he had selected earlier and dump the body. Some victims were just thrown out of the car; others were dragged to a particular place, and others he tried to pose. Then he left the crime scene. The rain would wash away tyre tracks. None of the victims was raped, indicating that the killer was probably impotent.

During the process of reconstruction the profiler attempts to write a general account which will fit the modus operandi revealed at most of the crime scenes. Then a reconstruction of each individual scene is written and any deviations from the general reconstruction are noted and discussed. It is important to find a reason for every deviation – for example, victim resistance – because defence counsel might later argue that one particular crime scene was not part of the series because of deviation from the basic modus operandi.

Every sequence of events is noted chronologically. This precise reconstruction is important in deciphering the killer's fantasy. A killer might change his modus operandi, but his fantasy remains the same.

Once a suspect is apprehended and interrogated his answers can be compared with the crime scene reconstruction.

Crime classification: organised or disorganised?

FBI profilers devised a simple classification system for serial offenders. Table 2 below describes the elements of a crime scene that enable the profiler to classify the killer as either organised or disorganised. Table 3 describes the characteristics of the perpetrator. I found this classification useful, but it is very basic and should not be the exclusive basis for a profile.

Since it is based on research conducted on American serial killers, there may be differences in applying it to South African serial killers. For example, adults still living with parents because of financial problems, is a more common situation in South Africa. Also, fewer South Africans have their own vehicles. Many South African serial killers made use of taxis.

Table 2: Differences at crime scenes

Organised	Disorganised
Planned attack	Spontaneous attack
Victim: selected stranger	Victim: random
Personalises victim	Depersonalises victim
Demands submissive victim	Sudden violence towards victim
Methods of restriction (ropes, handcuffs)	Minimal restriction
Scene reflects control	Scene chaotic
Murder precipitated by aggression	Sexual deeds after murder
Body hidden	Body displayed
Weapon absent	Weapon left at scene
Transports body	Leaves body at scene

Table 3: Personality characteristics

Organised	Disorganised
Average or high intelligence	Below average intelligence
Socially competent	Socially incompetent
Prefers schooled labour	Unschooled labour
High order of birth	Low order of birth
Father in stable employment	Father in unstable employment
Inconsistent discipline	Strict discipline

Controlled mood during murder	Anxious mood during murder
Uses alcohol before murder	Minimum use of alcohol
Precipitating stress	Minimal stress
Lives with partner	Lives alone/with parents
Follows media coverage of case	Minimum interest in news coverage

As far as his personality and modus operandi are concerned, a serial killer can be either organised or disorganised, or show characteristics of both. Elements such as selection of victim, control of the victim, sequence of the crime and modus operandi are the main elements that determine whether a serial killer is organised or disorganised.

If the killer is classified as disorganised the investigating officer knows he must check records at psychiatric institutions and have a psychologist present when interrogating suspects. An organised killer will probably have a job requiring certain skills, he will drive a car and have average or high intelligence. An organised killer may become disorganised over time, but a disorganised killer will never become organised. In instances where there are too many discrepancies, consideration should be given as to whether two killers were working together, one organised and one disorganised.

Staging

This is the term applied to deliberate changing of the crime scene. There may be two reasons for this:

- To mislead the police – the changes will be made by the offender or someone wishing to protect the offender
- To protect the dignity of the victim or his or her family – the changes will be made by a friend or family member who finds the victim

Staging is unlikely to be an arbitrary event carried out by whoever happened to arrive first on the scene; it will be done by someone who had a relationship with the victim. The family of the victim may change a scene to protect the dignity of the victim. This often happens with rape-murders or auto-erotic deaths where victims are found naked or dressed in some outlandish costume. For example, at the murder scene of Marike de Klerk, former South African first lady, a member of the emergency services pulled down her nightgown for the sake of propriety. He did not realise that he could have disturbed forensic evidence. It was a well-meant but irresponsible gesture. The last victim of the Norwood serial killer was forced to undress and was raped. Her body was left lying on her mother's bed where it was found by her mother's boyfriend who covered it with a towel.

A relative who is traumatised by the shock of finding the victim will be further traumatised if the circumstances are bizarre. Relatives have been known to untie victims, re-dress them, remove sex aids and even write false suicide notes – all in the interests of preserving the privacy and dignity of the victim. In the process, they are destroying evidence. It is imperative that the profiler establish whether the person who found the body before the police arrived changed anything on the crime scene.

It is possible for an organised serial killer to attempt to change his crime scene so that it resembles that of a disorganised killer. While an inexperienced detective may have difficulty recognising this, forensic experts, profilers and an experienced detective's attention to detail will recognise it.

In trying to change the crime scene the killer will usually make mistakes. He is stressed, probably in a hurry, and cannot take every detail into account. The investigating officer has all the time in the world to analyse what actually happened at the crime scene. Criminals often have a tendency towards arrogance, thinking that they can outwit the police. In reality, they are no match for a well-trained team of detectives, profilers, crime scene analysts and forensic experts.

The Cape Town Prostitute Killer staged every one of his crime scenes. Although it was obvious from the marks on their necks that his victims had been strangled with a ligature, he removed it and tied their clothing around their necks. He posed some of them with their legs spreadeagled to depict rape, yet rape was never his motive. The fact that he staged every single crime scene in an attempt to confuse the police became his signature.

Place of entry to a crime scene and risk to the offender are important aspects in staging. Here is an example from the FBI files:

A man alleged that an unknown man had attacked him and his wife on a Saturday morning. The perpetrator had placed a ladder against the house and had entered through a window on the second storey after removing the window screen. The husband thought he heard someone downstairs and went to investigate, taking his gun with him. He was overpowered by the intruder, who hit him on the head. Then the intruder apparently went upstairs and killed the wife in her bed. Her nightgown was pulled up, indicating that she had been indecently assaulted. The investigating officer noticed that the ground was still muddy after a recent rainfall, but that the ladder had not sunk into the mud as it would have if anyone had stood on it. Furthermore, the ladder was positioned with the rungs facing the house and the wood was rotten. It was not possible for anyone to have climbed it. There were no muddy footprints in the house. The question was: if murder was the motive, why did the intruder go downstairs when both inhabitants of the house were upstairs? If the motive was housebreaking and the murder coincidental, why did he choose a house with two cars parked in the driveway, a clear indication that the occupants were at home? Why did the husband, who posed a greater threat to the intruder, sustain only minor injuries while the wife was murdered? It did not take long for the detectives to unravel the staging and arrest the husband for murder.

When a crime scene is being evaluated and there is much evidence of offender behaviour but little evidence of motive, the statements of witnesses should be carefully analysed. The investigating officer and the profiler should also look for forensic signs of staging. One of the most important things to check is whether the injuries match the crime. Depersonalisation (eg severe facial injuries) and 'overkill' indicate that the motive was more than just murder or burglary. The victim was the primary focus of the offender.

Another indication that staging has taken place is when the statements of witnesses contradict the forensic reports. Another example from the FBI:

A woman found her husband dead in the bath. It appeared that he had slipped and hit his head while he was turning on the bath taps. The pathological report showed that he had a high level of valium in his blood and that there was more than one head wound. It is unlikely that slipping in the bath would result in more than one bump on the head. His wife had put valium in his food causing him to lose consciousness, and had hired three men to kill him and stage an accident.

One of the easiest types of staging to identify is the staged murder-rape scene. Offenders who had a close relationship with the victim will seldom remove all the clothing in the process of staging. Usually only the skirt is pushed up or the shirt is torn. The pathologist's report will indicate no signs of indecent assault. The offender will usually plan for someone else to discover the body.

Motive

Motive provides the intrinsic reason why the killer committed his crimes. In *Serial Murder* (1988) Holmes and De Burger designed a table which indicates four motives: *visionary*, *mission-orientated*, *hedonistic* and *power/control*. There are three subcategories to hedonistic: *lust*, *thrill* and *comfort*. I find this a rather broad categorisation. The profiler needs to delve deeper and narrow the motive to fit the individual responsible for a specific crime. Like the FBI's organised/disorganised classification, Holmes and De Burger's model is a short cut.

Table 4: Holmes and De Burger's model for classification of serial killers

Serial Murder Type	Visionary	Mission-orientated	Hedonistic			Power/Control
			Lust	Sensation	Comfort	
Factors *Victims*						
Specific/Non-		x	x			x
specific	x			x	x	
Random/Non-	x		x	x		
random		x			x	x
Affiliative					x	
Stranger	x	x	x	x		x
Methods						
Act-focused/Process-	x	x			x	
focused			x	x		x

57

Planned/ Spontaneous	x	x	x	x	x	x
Organised/ Disorganised	x	x	x	x	x	x
Location						
Concentrated/ Dispersed	x	x	x	x	x	x

The idea is to tick off relevant crime scene factors in the extreme left-hand column in order to arrive at a motive depicted in the first horizontal row. Their four categories of classification are:

- Background of behaviour, including psychological, sociogenic and biological etiology
- Victimology, including characteristics, choice and relationship with the offender
- Pattern and method, including process versus deed, planning versus spontaneity, and organised versus disorganised
- Location of the murders, including concentrated or dispersed

Their four category typologies regarding motive are as follows:

- Visionary type – murder on the orders of someone; for example, the voice of God
- Mission-orientated – murder according to a mission; for example, to kill all prostitutes
- Hedonistic type – including three types, namely, lust (sexual), thrill (media sensation) and comfort (financial gain)
- Power/control type – murder to satisfy a need for control over life and death

I cannot agree with the comfort classification. In my opinion a killer thus classified would be an assassin – someone who kills for money. Male serial killers have an intrinsic motive and financial gain is an external motive, although financial gain may be an intrinsic motive for female serial killers (see page 137).

In terms of Holmes and De Burger's classification, American serial killers John Wayne Gacy and Jeffrey Dahmer could both be described as being motivated by a combination of lust and power. They selected men in their late teens or early twenties and both kept the bodies of their victims in their homes. When one delves deeper one finds that Gacy hated his victims and was sadistically motivated. He kept their bodies under his house to avoid detection. Dahmer, on the other hand, was attached to his victims and kept their bodies in his home because he was lonely. A profiler needs to go further than just relying on the Holmes and De Burger classification to establish motive. He or she needs to determine the psychosexual fixation, the results thereof, and the intrinsic meaning that the victims have for the killer, as well as the reason for specific acts.

Crime scene dynamics

This term refers to the relationship between the different crime scenes. The crime scene dynamics will indicate whether the killer is progressing, deteriorating or experimenting, and provide reasons for major deviations such as change in the type of victims selected, change of location and changes in modus operandi.

When we found the first victims of Atteridgeville Strangler Moses Sithole we did not find them in the order of the dates of their death. I made the mistake of being reluctant to link the cases because of major differences in the bondage and strangulation patterns inflicted on the victims. I was concentrating on the differences and ignoring the similarities. Gradually, as the dates of their deaths were established I rearranged them in chronological order as opposed to the order in which they were found. It then became clear to me that the killer had progressed in his methods of bondage and strangulation. Initially he had tied his victims' hands in front of their bodies; later he changed to tying them behind their backs, and yet later to tying them to the neck as well. Strangulation became more 'sophisticated' by the insertion of a stick into the ligature for better leverage.

Other examples of crime scene dynamics are the instances of Sipho Twala transferring clothing from one crime scene to another, and Moses Sithole transferring jewellery.

Step 4: The profile

Finally the ingredients have been gathered, the batter has been mixed, and it's time for the cake to come out of the oven. The criminal profile should describe a personality which will fit the suspect. It is possible that more than one suspect will match the profile, but it should be accurate and detailed enough to narrow down the probabilities to a large extent. The detectives match possible suspects to the profile and disregard those that do not fit it. The intention is to save time and lives.

What should the profile provide for the investigating officer? First of all, it should present facts about the killer's demographics, including gender, age, race, marital status, employment and place of residence.

Next, it should provide information on the killer's background, such as level of education, employment record, military training, driving ability, and so on. It should discuss the killer's personality, including his level of intelligence, mental stability or indications of mental illness, habits, beliefs, and values. Sometimes elements of the killer's appearance can be included; for instance, his height can be deduced from the size of a shoe print. The profile will deal with the killer's interpersonal relationships, including attitude towards sex and towards the opposite or same sex. There should be predictions about the killer's behaviour after the crime; for example, would he keep souvenirs, would he taunt the police, etc.

I added an extra element explaining the killer's psycho-sexual development and fixations which gave rise to his fantasy. This is the kernel of his psychological motivation and interrogation strategies should be based on this crucial element. The interrogation strategy should be set out in the profile. It should be aimed at the individual described in the profile as well as particular items which should be looked for in a house search.

Collateral evidence

Interrogation strategies will not be discussed here as they are the privileged information of the police. The profiler will make recommendations about which sections of the profile may be released to the media.

I would like to elaborate on items looked for in the house search. Ex-FBI agent Roy Hazelwood, who trained me in Dundee, calls this *collateral evidence*. Collateral evidence refers to items that do not directly associate the offender with the crime, but provide information about his sexual preferences, fantasies, interests and habits. It has value as proof of intent and as a source of information. The finding and presenting of collateral evidence during a trial may influence bail conditions, a guilty plea and conviction.

Collateral evidence may at first seem innocent but the profiler and investigating officer will quickly learn to recognise it. It can serve as direct or circumstantial evidence in some cases; for example, underwear taken from a victim can be classified as 'collateral: erotica', and may link the offender directly to the crime.

According to Hazelwood there are four types of collateral material:

- Erotica – that which is sexually stimulating
- Educational – material which provides knowledge about police investigative methods, the judicial process, or psychological information
- Introspective – material that provides the offender with insights into his own behaviour, sexual behaviour and personality
- Intelligence – material that provides information on potential victims, possible future crimes or information gathered by third parties

Some material can be classified in more than one of the above categories. For example, the cover of a detective magazine depicting a half-naked woman can be stimulating (erotica), and the contents of the magazine provide information on investigative techniques.

Erotica

This refers to any material that fulfils a sexual aim for an individual. Investigating officers should not apply their own criteria of what they consider erotic. One may not find a length of rope particularly erotic, but a person with a rope fetish will be sexually aroused when he handles it.

Material considered erotic must be evaluated in the context in which it is found. For example, in the instance of paedophilia a photograph album with pictures of the suspect's own children dressed in appropriate clothing is not erotic, but pictures of other children, even fully dressed, can be erotically stimulating to the paedophile. Underwear belonging to his own children is not significant, but the underwear of other children will have value as collateral evidence. In determining what can be classified as erotica, the following should be considered:

- Does it relate to the crime being investigated or to other paraphilias[1] that do not necessarily pertain to the case?
- Is there an abnormal quantity of the item that cannot be justified for practical purposes? (For example, three sets of handcuffs)
- Was the material hidden or displayed?
- Did the offender go to great lengths and expense to obtain the material? (For example, spend R3000 on pornography)

Common examples of erotica include:

- Items indicating fetishism
- Literature and/or pictures of both an explicit and non-explicit sexual nature
- Literature and/or pictures (not necessarily porno-graphic) depicting a specific type of victim (for example, blondes)
- Sexual toys, such as plastic blow-up dolls, vibrators and sex aids
- Evidence of fantasy – handwritten material, sketches, photographs, tapes or videos
- Evidence of planning of future crimes
- Instruments of crime
- Abused dolls – decapitated, damaged, burnt, bonded, or ragdolls with genitals drawn upon them
- Pictures of humans or animals that have been scratched, have genitals drawn on them or ropes around their necks
- Media references to sex crimes

---

[1] Paraphilia: An umbrella term for any mode of sexual expression in which arousal is dependent upon what are generally considered to be socially unacceptable stimulating conditions.

- Advertisements for underwear, pornography and pornographic videos
- Collections of weapons and police paraphernalia
- Personal items belonging to known victims

Educational

This type of collateral material contains information on committing a crime, whether sexual or otherwise, information on avoiding arrest, circumventing legal procedures, and outwitting psychologists.

Intelligent criminals try to keep up to date on the latest investigative techniques, forensic evidence, legal procedures and psychology. Serial killer Ted Bundy read an article entitled 'Detective magazines: Pornography for sexual sadists' and claimed that it was very accurate. Ed Kemper, another American serial killer, learned by heart the MMPI psychological questionnaire, which contains six hundred questions. During an interview with Roy Hazelwood, a serial rapist said that he had read all of Hazelwood's books.

It might be argued that in writing this book I am 'educating' offenders. However, much of the information presented here has already been published – I am attempting here to set it in a South African context – and there is a wealth of information to be obtained from the Internet. I would not have written this book five years ago when information on profiling was not as readily available as it is now. It also needs to be pointed out that no matter how clever an offender imagines himself to be, he is no match for the combined knowledge, expertise and experience of a team of detectives, profilers, forensic and other experts. Apart from the sophisticated technology at its disposal, the investigation team has time to unravel any attempts the offender may make at deception. Prisons are full of criminals who thought they would never get caught.

Examples of educational collateral material include:

- Fictional and non-fictional books on crime
- Newspaper clippings on sexual or other crimes
- Books, textbooks and articles on psychology
- Published court proceedings
- Detective magazines
- Articles on crime prevention
- Videos or tapes of experts giving lectures on sex crimes

Introspective

This material provides the offender with knowledge about himself – his sexual deviance, behaviour and personality. The FBI was surprised by the number of sex offenders who try to gain insights into their own behaviour, or who try to rationalise it. Paedophiles often try to justify their behaviour. Many sex offenders were found to have attended lectures, group therapy or seminars dealing with the subject of their offence.

Roy Hazelwood once gave a public lecture on the subject of serial rapists in an attempt to entice a suspect to attend. He videotaped the proceedings and no fewer than five serial rapists were identified in the audience, including the one he was looking for.

Examples of introspection include:

- Books or articles about psychopathology or sexual deviations
- Videos or tapes of experts discussing the above subjects
- Self-help and religious books
- Questionnaires about personality types, sexual preferences, etc in popular magazines like *Penthouse*, etc
- Research papers on sexual deviations
- Advertisements, lecture notes or seminars on sexual deviations
- Letters, notes or diaries written by the offender about

his own insights
- Records, accounts or other evidence that the offender had therapy, or was institutionalised, whether voluntary or not

Intelligence

This refers to any material that the offender may make use of in the planning of a crime and includes information which a third party may have gathered about him. For example, a serial killer may keep a press clipping containing an identikit or profile of himself.

Intelligence that indicates the planning of a crime includes the following:
- False vehicle number plates
- Telephone numbers and addresses of possible victims
- Road maps, including hand-drawn maps
- Notes about the movements of another person
- Photographs of a potential victim taken without his or her knowledge
- Written scripts for victims
- Lists of items needed for the execution of the crime

The investigating officer should try to obtain as much information as possible about the offender. The following information may be obtained from a third party like an ex-girlfriend, ex-wife or even a prostitute:
- Specific words he uses during sex
- Favourite sexual practices
- Correspondence
- Places where evidence might be hidden
- Indications of stress factors in the offender's life, such as divorce, unemployment, financial problems, or the death of a loved one

Collateral evidence is not a substitute for direct evidence, but supplements it. The prosecution can use collateral evidence and expert testimony about it to oppose bail, strengthen a case, or as aggravating circumstances.

Norman Avzal Simons kept a scrapbook of newspaper clippings on the Station Strangler, including the profile. Newspaper clippings of the Cleveland Strangler's crimes were also found in the boot of David Selepe's car. In the Donnybrook serial killer case Inspector Theo Goldstone noticed that the suspect, Sipho Twala, had pinned magazine pin-ups of girls in lingerie on the walls of his room. All the girls in the pin-ups were posing with chairs. Surviving victims testified that when Twala raped them he made them bend over chairs. The pictures of the pin-ups were presented in court as collateral evidence.

Feedback

As new information is received by the investigation team the profiler should be notified so that the profile can be updated. Such information will include finding new crime scenes, statements from family members or witnesses, and information from informers. It is important that persons identified as possible suspects are not discussed with the profiler until the profile has been completed. Once the suspect has been apprehended the profiler may not, under any circumstances, amend the profile.

Step 5: The investigation

The profile is the property of the investigating officer. It is usually distributed to the investigation team and care should be taken that it does not fall into the wrong hands. It is the investigating officer's prerogative to decide whether the profile is released to the media. The media will undoubtedly use the profile and the killer may be alerted to the fact that the police have information about him. While the investigating officer has a duty to warn the public about the kind of person his team is looking for, he also has the responsibility of not scaring off the killer which would prolong the investigation and possibly increase the risk of more killings.

The investigation team will use the profile to evaluate and eliminate suspects, which is an important timesaver.

Step 6: The apprehension

After the suspect has been apprehended the investigating officer will use the profile as a guide to the mind of the killer. If he follows the recommended interrogation strategy it is highly likely that the suspect will confess because he feels that he has found someone who understands him completely. This is why including an in-depth psychological analysis of the intrinsic motive of the killer in the profile is so important. The profiler may attend the interrogation at the request of the investigating officer, or may even be asked to conduct the interrogation, provided he or she is a member of the police service.

Senior Superintendent Philip Veldhuizen, who was in charge of the Phoenix serial killer investigation, asked me to interrogate Sipho Twala in the company of one detective because he felt that I had the best insight into the man's mind. It took less than an hour for him to confess. Veldhuizen joined us afterwards and took Twala to a magistrate for a formal written confession.

Superintendent Koos Fourie, who handled the Saloon Killer case in Phoswa, transported the suspect, Velaphi Nglandlamandla, to Pretoria immediately after his arrest so that I could interrogate him. Fourie and the arresting officer Jan Sithole sat in on the interrogation. During the interview Nglandlamandla began recounting a nightmare. I interrupted him and asked Fourie to leave the room with me. I then told him the rest of the nightmare in detail. When we returned to the room I asked Nglandlamandla to continue and he told it exactly as I had related it to Fourie. This was an example of tuning in to his mental vibrations.

Nglandlamandla confessed.

Captain Mike van Aardt, who was in charge of the Jeppe Pyromaniac case, also brought his suspect Norman Hopkirk to me for interrogation. He left me alone with the suspect but watched proceedings from an interleading office. Hopkirk confessed.

Many investigating officers use profiles as a reference document during the trial for it contains all elements of the case. It is the prosecutor's decision whether or not to use the profile. The profile is not evidence; its purpose is to explain the psychodynamics of the crime and how they relate to the suspect. It also explains motive. If the profile is included in the docket the defence counsel will eventually have access to it. If the profiler is called to testify he or she must bear in mind that they will have to substantiate every word of it and must be prepared for cross-examination by the defence. This underlines why it is important that the profile does not contain any speculations.

The prosecution did not ask me to explain the profile during the trial of Stewart Wilken, but the defence lawyers called me as a witness. I was pleased that they had found my profile so objective that they wanted to use it. It is of course the duty of an expert witness to be completely impartial.

After the arrest, or preferably after the conviction, the profiler should check the accuracy of his or her profile. This is not to prove how good you are, but rather how you learn from your mistakes. The best way of doing this is to evaluate all aspects of the case, and to interview the offender and his family – if he and the Department of Correctional Services grant permission. I found offenders to be more forthcoming and honest if I interviewed them shortly after they were convicted. All those I asked, except Norman Avzal Simons, granted me interviews. Simons wrote me letters from prison. Later, because I did not have the time,

I asked students doing master's degrees in psychology at Rhodes University to conduct research interviews with serial killers. Dr Gerard Labuschagne, present commander of the Investigative Psychology Unit, also interviewed serial killers during his research for his degree.

I am often asked by students who want to become profilers what subjects they should study and what the employment opportunities are in South Africa.

The subjects I recommend are psychology, criminology, criminal law, an indigenous language and perhaps sociology. Postgraduate training to master's level is essential, so approximately seven years of academic training is necessary. I have designed a master's degree in profiling, which I hope may be implemented in universities.

Employment opportunities are limited. The South African Police Service employs profilers, but there have been only three in the last ten years. There is work to be found in the private sector but it, too, is scarce. Private investigation companies may employ profilers, who would then have to register with the Security Industry Regulatory Board. Large companies like banks sometimes have their own investigators and might employ profilers to work on white collar crime, rather than violent crime. Students planning to work in this environment should probably include industrial psychology and labour law amongst their subjects at university.

I would also recommend that students try to get as much practical experience as they can. Visits to a mortuary, applying to become a counsellor for Life Line, enlisting as a police reservist, volunteering at a rape crisis centre, a course in photography – all these will provide valuable experience.

Profiling is a profession that requires total commitment. Do not be deceived by television drama series. It is not glamorous work at all. It is in fact gruesome and physically and mentally exhausting, and takes its toll on personal relationships. Profilers need ongoing psychological counselling to help them handle the inevitability of post-traumatic stress. But for those who are prepared to sacrifice virtually everything, including mental stability and interpersonal relationships, it can be both rewarding and satisfying. It was for me.

Serial Killers

DEFINITION

Many people confuse the term serial killers with mass murderers and spree killers. There are several important differences between these categories of homicide that need to be addressed in order to avoid confusion.

A *mass murderer* is defined as one person who kills several victims during one event at one location. There is no cooling-off period and family members may be victims. Barend Strydom, who killed several people on one day at Strijdom Square in Pretoria, is an example.

The spree killer is defined as one or more persons who kill two or more victims during one event, which could have a long or short duration, at two or more locations, with no cooling-off period. Charmaine Phillips and Peter Grundlingh killed four people in June 1983 over a period of two weeks. Their spree started in Durban and they left three more bodies at Melmoth, Secunda Dam and Bloemfontein. Paul Johannes Meyer, who killed seven people including his ex-wife, fiancée and two daughters in Johannesburg in 2004, started out as a mass murderer but developed into a spree killer. Meyer committed suicide shortly after the spree.

In the course of my research I uncovered several shortcomings in different authors' definitions of serial killers. These definitions are presented below in chronological order to show how they have evolved from the simplistic to the more comprehensive.

Leyton (*Compulsive Killers: The story of modern multiple murder*, 1986) merely highlights the element of time in the difference between serial killers and mass murderers by describing serial homicide as murders that are committed over a period of time, and mass murders as murders committed during one explosive event. He attributes the motive for both types of homicide to social failure on the part of the killer. My criticism of his theory is this: if people become serial killers because their ambitions have failed, why are there comparatively few serial killers? Many people's ambitions are unfulfilled.

Cameron and Frazer (*The Lust to Kill*, 1987) classify serial killers as a variation of sex murderers. They define serial killers as men (with a few exceptions) who murder their sexual objects, whether they be women, children or other men. The murders are characterised by sexual assault, rape, torture and mutilation. My criticism of this definition is that the motive is defined as solely sexual.

Holmes and De Burger (*Serial Murder*, 1988) differentiate between a mass murderer as a person who kills many people at one time, and a spree killer as a person (or persons) who kills several people over a short period, whether it be hours, days or weeks. These authors do not define the term 'serial killer', but list the following traits of the perpetrator:

- The central element is repetitive homicide
- They are usually one-on-one murders
- The victim is usually a stranger to the killer
- The motivation is murder and not passion, nor is it precipitated by any action of the victim
- The motivation is intrinsic

These traits are accurate in describing a serial killer, but they omit the 'cooling-off' period and the element of fantasy.

Leibman ('Serial Murderers: Four Case Histories': *Federal Probation*, 1989) defines a serial killer as a person who kills several people, usually in the same geographic area, over a short period of time, which corresponds with Leyton's definition. My criticism of this definition is that a serial killer does not necessarily confine himself to one area and may kill over a long period of time. Russian serial killer Andrei Chicatillo was operative for two decades.

Hollin (*Psychology and Crime*, 1989) considers a serial killer to be a type of mass murderer who kills over a period of time, torturing or sexually assaulting his victims before killing them. Hollin's definition aligns with that of Cameron and Frazer by focusing mainly on the sexual aspect of serial homicide. My criticism is that a serial killer is not a type of mass murderer, and not all the victims of a serial killer are sexually assaulted or tortured before they are killed. David Berkowitz, alias 'Son of Sam', simply shot his victims without interacting with them.

Levin and Fox (*America's Growing Menace – Mass Murder*, 1991) regard serial killers and 'simultaneous' killers as two types of mass murderers. Serial killers are defined as mass murderers who murder victims at different times, while 'simultaneous' murderers are mass murderers who kill their victims in one event. This definition again has much in common with those of Leyton and Leibman. My criticism of this theory is that serial killers are simply regarded as mass murderers, and the authors focus only on the element of time.

Lane and Gregg (*The Encyclopaedia of Serial Killers*, 1992) define mass murder as a deed where several people are killed by the same person or persons at the same geographical site. A spree killing is defined as a multiple murder that is committed over a longer period.

Most of the above definitions focus on the element of time in serial homicide, and ignore other criteria. A robber, for instance, may kill several people over a period of time in the course of his robberies, which means that he will comply with most of these definitions, but he cannot be considered a serial killer. The key is the motive. The robber's motive is greed.

Robert Ressler claims to have coined the term 'serial killer' when he worked for the FBI in the USA. He explained the term by using the example of a television series. As each episode ends on a cliffhanger, viewers are kept in anticipation of the next episode, much as the serial killer anticipates his next murder after committing the previous one. The FBI profilers define a serial killer *as a person or persons who kill more than three victims, during more than three events, at three or more locations, with a cooling-off period in between. Premeditated planning and fantasy are also present.*

After reviewing the different definitions, I propose the following definition of a serial killer.

A serial killer is a person or persons who murders several victims, usually strangers, at different times and not necessarily at the same location, with a cooling-off period in between. The motive is intrinsic; an irresistible compulsion, fuelled by fantasy which may lead to torture and/or sexual abuse, mutilation and necrophilia.

In my definition I have added the criteria of *intrinsic motive*, *sexual abuse*, *mutilation*, *necrophilia* and *irresistible compulsion* to the FBI's definition in order to cover the motivational aspects. A person does not 'qualify' as a serial killer only after he has killed three or more victims, since it is possible for a serial killer to be identified as such and apprehended after his second murder.

The term *irresistible compulsion* in my definition has proved controversial. In South African law a person suffering from an irresistible compulsion – for example, kleptomania – is technically not responsible for his or her actions. Such a person may either be found not guilty on the grounds of mental illness, or be committed to a state psychiatric facility from which he will most probably be discharged in time. Obviously this gives rise to the possibility that a serial killer may be found not guilty of multiple murder, or sentenced to a psychiatric institution and released after a few years when he will most certainly kill again. I would argue that the 'irresistible compulsion' should be interpreted in the sense that the serial killer chooses *not* to resist the urge to kill. All adults have choices in life. The cooling-off periods prove that serial killers *can* control the compulsion, for there are often long periods when they do not kill. Implicit in the term 'irresistible compulsion' is the fact that the serial killer knows the difference between right and wrong, but does not care. Although he knows it is wrong, he still wants to kill, for he becomes addicted to the psychological gratification it provides.

If serial killers are to be condoned because of the psychological irresistibility of their compulsions, this should apply also to people who commit crimes under the influence of drugs or alcohol. This, of course, would be preposterous. Alcoholics and drug addicts know they have a problem, and they also know that help is available if they choose to seek it. It is highly unlikely that adult serial killers, knowing that it is wrong to kill, would seek psychological counselling, but it is not impossible.

CLASSIFICATION OF SERIAL KILLERS

Although serial killers are unique regarding the type of crime they commit, there is consensus in the literature that they can be classified into several different categories. It is the general opinion amongst some authors that the classification of serial killers should be modelled according to a phenomenological description, rather than based on a quantitative study, because there are so few of them and because each one is unique.

Holmes and De Burger employ a descriptive model, which consists of four interdependent classification factors and four category typologies (see page 57).

Leibman differentiates between the *psychotic*, the *ego-syntonic* and the *ego-dystonic* killer:

- The psychotic killer murders as a result of a mental disorder and is out of touch with reality
- The ego-syntonic killer murders without disruption of his ego function. The murder is rational and acceptable to him
- The ego-dystonic killer disassociates himself on a conscious level from the killings – he cannot identify himself with the murder

Leibman considers all serial killers to be ego-dystonic. My criticism of this view has its basis in the fact that serial killers who have even a small degree of an active superego (or conscience) will be ego-dystonic, while those with hardly any superego will be ego-syntonic. Norman Avzal Simons was ego-dystonic and showed some remorse, but the Atteridgeville Strangler, Moses Sithole, was ego-syntonic and bragged about his murders.

FBI profilers prefer the categories *organised* and *dis-organised* in classifying serial killers and do not use Holmes and De Burger's typologies of *visionary*, *missionary*, *hedonistic* and *power-motivated* serial killers. They attribute the following characteristics to the organised serial killer to distinguish him from the disorganised type, but warn that a serial killer could also show characteristics of both categories:

- The murder is planned and effectiveness increases with each murder

- Organised murderers signify psychopathy, while disorganised murders signify psychosis
- The fantasy is the blueprint for the murder
- Victims are selected according to certain characteristics and they are stalked; the disorganised killer murders victims who are often of a high-risk category
- The organised killer will interact with the victim
- Some form of confidence trick is used to gain the victim's confidence
- The modus operandi is adaptable and the killer is mobile
- A weapon is taken to, and then removed from, the scene
- The body will be hidden or destroyed in order to avoid detection
- If a vehicle is used it will be in good working order, to minimise the possibility of apprehension
- The clothing of the victim may be removed or the victim may be mutilated to prevent identification
- False clues may be left at the scene to confuse the detectives
- The organised crime scene is neat, while the disorganised crime scene is chaotic
- The 'trophy' or 'souvenir' taken by an organised killer may be a piece of clothing or other inanimate object, while the disorganised killer may take body parts
- The organised killer will commit sexual abuse or rape before killing the victim, while the disorganised serial killer is more inclined to necrophilia
- The organised serial killer may have short-term sexual relations with a partner, but not a long-term, emotionally fulfilling commitment
- The organised serial killer is confident, attractive and has a superiority complex
- The organised serial killer may be married, while the

disorganised serial killer will more likely be living alone or with parents
- The organised serial killer will probably have a skilled occupation while the disorganised serial killer will have menial employment, if he is employed at all
- A stress factor precipitates the organised serial killer's first murder
- The organised serial killer is more likely to keep newspaper articles about himself and follow the case in the media

In addition to categorising serial killers, FBI profilers also divide serial homicide into four phases, namely:
- Pre-crime phase – the ongoing behaviour of the serial killer (ie the killer's normal daily behaviour, including fantasising about murder)
- The murder – including the selection of the victim
- Disposal of the body – it may be destroyed, dumped or displayed
- Post-crime phase – getting involved in the investigation or contacting the families of the victim

Lane and Gregg (1992) confirm the following aspects of serial homicide, as stipulated by Holmes and De Burger (1988):
- The murders are repetitive, increasing or decreasing in tempo, over a period of time which could be weeks or years and will continue until the offender is apprehended, dies or commits suicide
- The murders are usually one-on-one
- The victim and offender are usually strangers to each other, which includes the possibility that the offender stalked the victim for a period
- Although there may be a pattern regarding modus operandi and victim selection, the motive is seldom

discernible

- Modern technology enables the offender to leave the scene in a hurry before the murder is detected
- There is usually a high degree of aggression and unnecessary violence present and the victim is subjected to unnecessary brutality

The definitions and classification of serial killers have now been discussed, but it is important to review the opinions of other writers on the characteristics and behaviour of serial killers. They all warn that these characteristics are generalised and that not all of them will be present in every serial killer.

FBI profilers describe the early years of the disorganised serial killer as follows:

> As a child, he was a member of a family where the father had an unstable employment record, discipline was strict, alcohol abuse was present and there was a greater tendency to psychopathology in the family history. On the other hand, the father of the organised serial killer probably had a stable employment record and discipline at home during his childhood would have been inconsistent.

Based on their extensive qualitative research, FBI profilers describe the following general characteristics of serial killers:

- Not all come from broken homes or poor families
- Their intelligence quotient varies from below 90 to above 120
- In half the cases there was pathology in the immediate family, or one or both parents were involved in crime
- In more than 70 per cent of cases there was alcohol and substance abuse in their families
- All were exposed to excessive emotional abuse during

their childhood years

- Not one was able to commit to a long-term emotional relationship with a partner
- Relationships with their mothers were described as cold and distant
- In 40 per cent of cases they were subjected to physical abuse as children
- Parental discipline was slack and no boundaries were set for them as children
- More than 70 per cent witnessed or were the victims of sexually stressful events during their childhood
- All grew up lonely and isolated with no one with whom to share their emotions
- More than half their fathers were physically absent during their childhood
- Antisocial tendencies surfaced in most of them at an early age, such as the use of dangerous weapons, abuse of animals, theft and arson
- Their isolation continued during the latency phases (six to twelve years) – they avoided their peers and social gatherings and preferred auto-erotic activities (masturbation) to heterosexual exploration
- Most continued with auto-erotic sexual activities and some developed voyeurism and fetishism during adolescence
- Their fantasies were acted out on animals during adolescence
- Daydreaming, compulsive masturbation, lies, enuresis (bed-wetting) and nightmares prevailed during adolescence
- Their academic achievements were weak, despite the high intelligence of some
- All had a poor employment record and were unable to stabilise in this regard

Lane and Gregg (1992) complemented the FBI list with the following:

- Ritualistic behaviour
- Mental stability that masks mental illness
- Compulsiveness
- Periodic 'cry for help'
- Loss of memory and inability to tell the truth
- Suicidal tendencies
- History of violent behaviour
- Hyper-sexuality and abnormal sexual behaviour
- Head injuries or injuries during birth
- History of alcohol and drug abuse
- Illegitimate birth
- Signs of genetic disorders
- Biochemical symptoms
- Feelings of helplessness and incompetence

Some authors have commented on serial killers' inability to stop themselves from killing. Jeffers (*Profiles in Evil*, 1993) states that because most serial killers are not apprehended, a sudden cessation of murders in an area might be attributed to a total mental breakdown of the killer, institutionalisation, a prison sentence, natural death, suicide or the killer may have moved to another area.

I have found no record, either in case studies or in the literature, of a serial killer who has refrained from killing of his or her own accord. A few have given themselves up, but this is a desperate attempt to abdicate the responsibility of stopping the murders to the police. The serial killer hands himself over so that it becomes the authorities' responsibility to prevent him from killing again. Some of them reason that if the police don't catch them before their next murder, it is the police's fault that someone has died. Many of them have told me they were relieved to be arrested, because they were tired. The relief is temporary.

Stewart Wilken asked me why it took me so long to trace him. Research has indicated that over the years about 350 serial killers have been released from prison worldwide and all of them killed again.

Serial killers have a negative prognosis (ie a negative chance for rehabilitation). It is doubtful if they could ever be rehabilitated because of the lack of opportunity to establish meaningful interpersonal relationships in prison. It takes a serial killer about nineteen years to develop. It would take about the same amount of time for one-on-one therapy to reprogramme their minds, reset object relations and defantasise them. (Object relations is a psychological theory pertaining to one's internal relationship with a parental figure in one's mind, as opposed to the relationship in reality.) Theoretically, a combination of Freudian psychoanalysis, Jungian interpersonal therapy, object relations therapy, transactional analysis and behavioural therapy would be necessary. I don't know of any psychologist who would be willing to commit his or her entire working life to the rehabilitation of one serial killer, or who would take the risk that the killer would not kill again. The practicality of rehabilitating a serial killer is therefore nil, especially because the end result cannot be guaranteed.

Various authors, like Rumbelow (*The Complete Jack the Ripper*, 1988), Levin and Fox (*America's Growing Menace*, 1991) and Ressler and Shachtman (*Whoever Fights Monsters*, 1993) found that some serial killers commit their first murder after a period of isolation. The isolation, whether a prison sentence or institutionalisation, serves as an incubation period for the killer's fantasies. This is also the reason why so many of them kill again after their release. Their murderous fantasies have had years to develop.

THEORIES ON THE ORIGIN OF SERIAL KILLERS

Sociocultural theories

Holmes and De Burger (1988) state the following regarding the sociocultural origin of serial homicide:

> Sociogenic forces, especially in the form of violence-associated learning, are undoubtedly present in the cultural and behavioral background of the serial killer. However, sociogenic theories are also unable to account *directly* for the appearance of serial homicide.

They name two sociocultural sources that are important in the origin of serial homicide. The first is the continuous culture of violence coupled with a continuous change in the relationship between the individual and his environment. The second source is the pattern of early development and interaction within the serial killer's family.

These authors identify the following characteristics of the American culture that are associated with an increase in violence:

- Normalising of interpersonal violence
- Emphasis on personal comfort
- Emphasis on thrills
- Extensive violence
- Magical thinking (the belief that thinking is equated with doing)
- Unmotivated hostility and blaming of others
- Normalising of impulsiveness
- Excessively violent role models
- Anonymity and depersonalising in overcrowded areas
- Extensive and accelerating spacious geographic mobility
- Emphasis on immediate and fast gratification of needs

In my opinion these characteristics also exist within South African culture, especially in the informal settlements, rural communities and crime-infested metropolises. The ongoing political unrest in the province of KwaZulu-Natal is an excellent example of the normalisation of personal violence, hostility and blaming of others and violent role models, anonymity and depersonalising in overcrowded areas. Yet if cultural influences were the only etiology of serial killers, there would be many more of them.

Leibman (1989) also supports the sociocultural theory of the origin of serial homicide. She addresses two elements in a serial killer's early development, namely a cruel and violent childhood and rejection by parents, which correlate with Holmes and De Burger's identification of early developmental patterns as a possible source of serial homicide. She identified the following common social factors in an analysis of the case studies of four serial killers:

- Childhood marked by cruel and violent patterns
- Rejection by parents
- Rejection by a member of the opposite sex during adult-hood
- Confrontation with the law during youth or adulthood
- Admission to psychiatric hospitals

I concur with Leibman's theory in as much as these elements may contribute to a person's becoming a serial killer, but would point out that many individuals are exposed to Leibman's five social factors, and not all of them become serial killers. Her theory therefore does not answer my recurring question as to why a particular individual will resort to serial homicide, while others who have been subjected to the same circumstances do not.

Albert Bandura's theory of social learning states that a child models the behaviour of his parents and the example set by his environment; it can therefore also be regarded as a sociocultural theory which may be applied to serial killers. However, I have not found any record of a serial killer whose father was also one. The intrinsic elements of serial homicide – namely, multiple murder of strangers, torture and in some cases necrophilia and mutilation – are not learned behaviours. In my opinion, these elements are idiosyncratic to the serial killer.

Leyton (1986) is an anthropologist who also proposed a sociocultural theory on the origin of serial homicide. He describes all serial homicide as a type of subcultural political and conservative protest, which implies a social gain of revenge, star status, identity and sexual gratification for the serial killer. He acknowledges that these people kill for pleasure. He regards all serial killers as the 'missionary' type – the mission being a primitive rebellion against the social order to which they would have liked to belong, but were rejected.

Leyton is of the opinion that the victims of serial killers are all of the same social class and this class is usually a higher one than the class to which the serial killer belongs. He regards the sexual motive as a basis for the motive of social revenge. He points out that Ted Bundy, an American law student, achieved the social status which he craved, but he felt uncomfortable with it. To take revenge on the higher social classes, he robbed them of their most precious possessions – their talented and beautiful young women.

Leyton differentiates between serial killers and mass murderers on the basis that while both are rebelling against society, the mass murderer usually ends his own life during the event. He considers the murder of many people in one event to be the 'suicide note' of the mass murderer. The serial killer, on the other hand, wants to live and tries to ensure 'fame' by planning and committing a series of crimes.

My criticism of Leyton's view is that he describes the murder sprees of the mass murderers as 'planned careers'. The mass murderer may well plan the murder as a last despairing cry for help, or out of desperation or revenge arising from a feeling of being duped by his community. However, these murders are not compulsions and may be prevented by counselling. Another aspect of Leyton's theory with which I disagree is his postulate that serial killers kill people of a social class to which they themselves would like to belong. In fact, many serial killers prefer high-risk victims like prostitutes, hitch-hikers and street children, who generally belong to a lower social class. The social rejection to which Leyton refers has validity, but I would interpret it rather as a repetition of the first rejection the serial killer experienced from his parents. Leyton does not refer to any intrinsic psychological motivation in his theory.

FBI motivational model

FBI profilers interviewed thirty-six incarcerated serial killers in the 1980s. The material obtained from these interviews was used as a basis for qualitative and quantitative research on serial and sexual homicide. Based on the information gained from the interviews and the results of their qualitative research, Robert Ressler, Ann Burgess and John Douglas designed the following model to explain the origin of serial killing. The model has five dimensions, each of which will be discussed. They are:

- Ineffective social environment
- Formative years
- Patterned responses
- Action towards others
- Feedback filter

Ineffective social environment

In their description of the serial killer's social environment as a child, the FBI profilers address the dysfunctional family.

As a child the serial killer's social bonding fails or becomes narrow and selective because his caretakers either ignore, rationalise or normalise unacceptable behaviour. They may, for instance, ignore pathological behaviour. An example is found in the case of American serial killer Jeffrey Dahmer's father, who was unconcerned that his child was dissecting animals. (Jeffrey Dahmer was the Milwaukee serial killer who committed necrophilia and who ate the flesh of his victims.)

The FBI profilers found that in about 70 per cent of cases drugs and alcohol were problems in the homes of serial killers' families. There were psychiatric problems, usually linked to aggression, in more than half of the families – in most cases the mother had been institutionalised for a period of time. In half the cases the serial killers' family members were involved in criminal activity, usually of a sexual nature.

It was also found that the family members of serial killers had inconsistent contact with each other as well as dysfunctional interpersonal relationships. This would indicate that the serial killer did not have any close relationships with his siblings as a child. He was a so-called loner.

Many of the families of serial killers were nomadic. Only one third of the cases examined in the research lived in one place for any length of time. About 40 per cent were removed from their nuclear family before the age of eighteen years. They were denied the opportunity to form close relationships with people outside the family because they were uprooted so often. The families also had minimal contact with any community, resulting in extreme loneliness for the killers as children.

The research revealed that in almost half the cases, the father had deserted the family before the serial killer reached the age of twelve years. The FBI profilers concluded that the physical absence of the father did not have as much of a negative effect as his emotional absence. Therefore, even if the father was present, if he had a negative relationship with the child, it had a greater negative effect on the potential serial killer. They cite the example of the father of one serial killer who threw a glass bottle at his son before the boy was one year old. He tried to strangle him when he was four years old and shot at him while he was playing in the backyard as a child.

The FBI profilers propose that serial killers have ambivalent relationships with their mothers. They subconsciously both love and hate their mothers. The mother gives the son contradictory messages, which he cannot decipher. For example, a mother might invite her son to hug her, but freeze when he does, or she might teach him that sex is dirty, yet invite him to rub her body with body lotion.

In their quantitative study the FBI found that serial killers were usually the oldest sons, which means that not only were their parents poor role models, but there were no older brothers or sisters who could substitute as good role models. The parents of serial killers were often divorced and if the mother remarried the son's birth order might have changed due to the arrival of additional stepbrothers and stepsisters. This would be confusing for the child, especially if the situation at home was unstable.

The lack of closeness in family ties is transferred to childhood friendships. As a child the serial killer is a loner who seldom, if ever, has close friendships with other children. Generally their school friends cannot even remember them.

Formative years

Here the FBI profilers focus on the traumas a serial killer was exposed to during his formative years. As a child, he is likely to have been exposed to direct trauma, such as emotional, physical and/or sexual abuse. The direct trauma results in developmental failure because the child's distress is ignored. They describe the developmental defect as the forming of negative social relationships (wrong friends) and a decrease in the child's ability to experience positive affect[1] and emotions. As a result he becomes very desensitised. His interpersonal relations are weak and lack depth, and his role models are defective or lacking altogether.

Witnessing events such as rape, suicide or murder could be considered examples of indirect trauma. The child remembers these images and this destabilises his impulse control. He becomes confused about human responsibility – who is responsible for the trauma? – and so he begins to fantasise about revenge at an early age.

The neglect of serial killers during their childhood is more subtle than one would have expected. The boys were mainly psychologically abused through humiliation, and discipline at home was usually unfair, alien, inconsistent and abusive.

The FBI profilers found that sexual and violent experiences during childhood also have a negative effect on the formation of the personality of serial killers. The quantitative research on the thirty-six incarcerated serial killers provided the following statistics:

* Nine witnessed violent sex as children
* Nine witnessed upsetting sex between their parents
* Eleven witnessed upsetting sex between other family

---

[1] Affect: A general term for feelings and emotions.

members
- Six contracted venereal diseases during adolescence
- Some mutilated their own genitals as punishment for 'bad thoughts'
- Nineteen were punished for masturbating as children
- Some observed homosexual activities between their peers
- The parents of some made derogatory remarks about their genitals
- 43 per cent were sexually abused between the ages of one and twelve
- 32 per cent were sexually abused as adolescents
- 37 per cent were sexually abused when they were older than eighteen years

Within the family, sexual abuse was committed by parents, step-parents, siblings and step-siblings, and outside the family by friends, extended family members or by prison inmates during incarceration either as a juvenile or, later, as an adult.

The FBI profilers found that the adult sexual behaviour of serial killers was visually orientated and that they preferred auto-erotic activities (masturbation). The following results of the quantitative study support this statement:
- About half of the group had a total aversion to sex
- Three-quarters reported sexual problems
- 70 per cent reported feelings of sexual inadequacy

The traumas to which these children were exposed led to the development of fantasies. For example, one of the serial killers had a sexual fantasy between the ages of four to five years which involved an image of needles and knives sticking into his stomach.

Most abused children fantasise as a way of escaping reality. The serial killer's early fantasies are not about escaping from one negative situation to a better one, as are those of other abused children. The serial killer fantasises about aggression, dominance over others, and the repetition of what happened to him, but in his fantasies he is the aggressor and not the victim. The serial killer therefore develops his aggressive fantasies during childhood and discusses them with no one. He becomes committed to his violent and sexual fantasies. The fantasies before the first murder focus on the murder itself, and the fantasies after the first murder focus on improving the way the murder is carried out. The motivation for sexual murder is therefore that it provides the means of acting out a fantasy.

Patterned responses

In this dimension, the FBI profilers postulate that the child's memories of frightening and distressing life experiences shape his developing thought patterns. The type of thinking that emerges develops structured, patterned behaviours that in turn help generate daydreams and fantasies. Their term for the structure and development of thought patterns is *cognitive mapping*.

In the serial killer cognitive mapping is fixed, negative and repetitive and manifests in daydreams, nightmares, fantasies and thoughts with strong visual components. The FBI profilers define a *fantasy* as an extended thought filled with preoccupation, which is anchored in an emotion and exists in daydreams. Although the fantasy is usually expressed in thought, there are also images, emotions and internal dialogue present. As the fantasy reaches a point where it causes unbearable inner stress, the killer is ready to act it out.

According to the FBI profilers the serial killer's thought patterns as a child have the following characteristics:

- Daydreams and nightmares with strong visual components

- Internal dialogue where he rationalises his aggression
- Kinaesthetic arousal levels which accompany the thought patterns
- The themes of the daydreams are dominance, rape, violence, revenge, molestation, power, control, mutilation, inflicting pain on others and death

In their prison interviews with serial killers, FBI profilers found that they do not remember positive childhood fantasies. Although other children may have occasional aggressive fantasies, serial killers have *only* aggressive fantasies and they are totally committed to them and to the secret reality which the fantasy represents to them.

The basis of the aggressive fantasy will already have been acted out during latency (see page 133) in the child's handling of animals, in rehearsals for the murder (eg practising killing, strangling or skinning an animal), or in play. The serial killer will not easily speak about his youthful fantasies because he realises that he still had control over them at that time, but has since crossed the line of reality.

The serial killer is egocentric in his fantasies or play. He regards other children or adults merely as extensions of his own inner world and has no insight into the needs of others or the impact his behaviour has on them.

The personality characteristics of serial killers as children are:
- Social isolation
- Auto-erotic activities – masturbation
- Fetishism
- Rebellion
- Aggression
- Lying
- Self-entitlement

Action towards others

The FBI profilers offer examples of how the fantasies are acted out during the childhood years in the serial killer's behaviour towards other people.

The repetitive patterns, as described in the previous dimension, manifest at an early age. For example, American serial killer Ed Kemper as a child asked his sisters to tie him to a chair. He would then play that he was being shocked to death. When John Joubert was eight years old he fantasised that he was going to kill his babysitter and eat her. As a little boy, he would stand behind her chair and play with her hair with one hand, while stroking a knife in his pocket with the other hand. As a child Harvey Glatman tied a piece of string around his penis, tied the string to a doorknob and swung himself on the door.

Feedback filter

As an adult the serial killer begins to act out the fantasies that have developed during his childhood years, and he measures his performance according to the fantasy. This is what FBI profilers term the 'feedback filter'.

By committing his first murder the serial killer departs from his fantasy world and enters the real world. He justifies the murder and evaluates the mistakes he has made. He reaches a point where he becomes very good at what he does and this is usually when he starts making mistakes, because he gets overconfident.

In summary, the FBI's motivational model emphasises that, as a child, the serial killer grows up in a negative environment where the home atmosphere is characterised by negligence, alcohol and drug abuse and a lack of positive role models. Interpersonal relationships are dysfunctional and the child is emotionally isolated. He is exposed to direct and indirect emotional, physical and sexual traumas, and he starts to develop aggressive and vengeful fantasies, which he acts out in play and towards other children and animals. These fantasies are conscious thought patterns and they condition the child to be able to act them out as an adult by murdering other people. After the first murder the serial killer has departed from his fantasy world and has crossed the boundaries into reality. Each murder provides him with feedback on how to improve the next murder so that it will resemble the perfect fantasy.

I agree in principle that the elements of childhood abuse and the early development of sadistic and revenge fantasies play a part in the origin of serial homicide. I disagree, however, that the motive for serial homicide can be explained on a cognitive level as conscious thought processes. The case studies of most serial killers indicate that they themselves cannot explain why they murdered their victims. Many of them can only ascribe it to an 'impulse' or 'urge' over which they had no control. In my opinion the motivation lies not at a cognitive level, but at a deep subconscious psychological level. The FBI's model has acceptable and logical points but, once again, it does not explain why one man will become a serial killer while his brother, who has been brought up in the same environment, does not.

Systemic theories

The systemic theories on the origin of serial killers focus on how the whole social system, including family environment, the educational system, social structures like churches and welfare organisations, law enforcement, the judicial system and correctional facilities, can contribute to the development of a serial killer. This is in accordance with general systems theory, which focuses on the interaction between the individual and different societal subsystems. Some of the authors who support systemic theories also pay attention to how the system may act to prevent a person developing into a serial killer.

Holmes and De Burger (1988) identify the following elements of a system that may make a contribution in the prevention of serial homicide:

- Components of the criminal justice system, namely police services, courts and correctional services
- The media
- The public

According to Holmes and De Burger these elements of the system should focus on the early identification of violent personalities in an attempt to prevent serial homicide. This statement implies a relationship between that which can prevent serial homicide and that which causes it.

Lane and Gregg (1992) question how much freedom the state, social workers and the police services should have in interference in the domestic activities of families and individuals where abuse is suspected. These authors also consider the defects of the system to be a contributory factor in serial homicide.

The case of Jeffrey Dahmer provides an example of how the system failed to prevent the murder of innocent victims. In 1989 Dahmer was charged with possession of child pornography. During the court case a psychologist described him as schizoid and manipulative, and recommended that he be institutionalised. Dahmer's defence made the following statement during his plea: *We don't have a multiple offender here. I believe he was caught before the point where it would have gotten worse, which means that that's a blessing in disguise ...* (Schwartz, *The man who could not kill enough*, 1992).

At this time Dahmer had already killed five people, but this fact was unknown. Dahmer was sentenced to a year's imprisonment, but he was allowed to go out to work every day. Two years and twelve murders later he was finally apprehended again. In the five years he was on probation, his probation officer suspected that something was wrong, but did not investigate further because the suburb in which Dahmer lived was too dangerous.

In his book Schwartz mentions the two police officers who, on 26 May 1991, ignored the request of a concerned member of public to attend to the boy Konerak Sinthasomphone, who was found naked and drugged on the street. Dahmer arrived on the scene and convinced the officers that it was nothing more than a lovers' tiff and they escorted the under age boy back to Dahmer's apartment. Konerak was murdered a few hours later. The police officers, who are a part of the system, were in this instance negligent in their duty.

I agree in principle that the early identification of certain patterns in the behaviour of children could prevent them from becoming serial killers. I am also of the opinion that society and the system, comprising the family and the authorities, are negligent in failing to identify potential serial killers. The system is geared to react to a serial killer, but not to prevent his development in the first instance.

As a component of the system, the media play a major role in the dynamics of the organised serial killer. Ressler and Shachtman (1993) state that most organised serial killers keep newspaper clippings of their crimes and fantasise about them later. Ressler reported that David Berkowitz only took on the alias 'Son of Sam' after a newspaper reporter referred to him by that name. Ressler blamed the reporter for irresponsibly enticing Berkowitz to murder when he published the names of the counties in which Berkowitz had already murdered and speculated whether he was going to try to commit a murder in each of the remaining counties. In an interview with Ressler,

Berkowitz admitted that the idea to commit a murder in each county only occurred to him after he had read the newspaper report.

Ressler identifies social, environmental, psychological, cultural, economic and stress factors as elements in American culture that contribute to the increase in serial homicide. He singles out the media as an aggravating element. Monty Rissell, who murdered five women in 1978, admitted that he was inspired by the news coverage of David Berkowitz's crimes. Ressler regards the media as a catalyst in the sense that the organised serial killer craves acknowledgement and likes to see his name in print.

Jeffers (1993) refers to Robert Graysmith's book *Zodiac*, which relates the actions of the serial killer dubbed 'Zodiac' who operated in San Francisco in 1986. He was never apprehended. After the publication of the book, a second serial killer calling himself Zodiac applied a similar modus operandi in New York.

I am in complete agreement with other authors that some members of the media have an irresponsible attitude. A journalist broke a story on the front page of a newspaper on the morning we set out to trap the Hammer Murderer in Johannesburg. The killer read the report and avoided his usual haunts. (But, to be fair, it is acknowledged that many journalists act responsibly when covering sensitive cases.)

It is my view that films like 'Silence of the Lambs', 'Seven', and 'Copycat' glorify serial killers as superhuman beings, adding to the myth that serial killers are either raving lunatics or super-intelligent human beings. They are neither. These films provide negative and misleading role models. Several films have been made about the lives of Ted Bundy, David Berkowitz, John Wayne Gacy, Wayne Williams and John Reginald Christie and the most recent, 'Monster', about American serial killer Aileen Wuornos. These films may serve a documentary purpose and in my view are not as harmful as fictional material.

While I agree that there are several systemic factors that contribute to serial homicide, they do not explain its *origin*.

Demonic possession

There is a common misconception that serial killers are possessed by demons. A possible reason for this is that 'normal' people cannot conceptualise that other seemingly 'normal' people are capable of the atrocities that serial killers commit. When asked what the worst act of a serial killer could be, most people are inclined to say necrophilia or cannibalism. They cannot stretch their imaginations to visualise a serial killer masturbating on to the decapitated heads of his victims. The 'normal' person usually will not grasp the symbolism of such an act; the serial killer himself may not be aware of it. People are therefore inclined to attribute such behaviour to demonism.

In his article 'Psychodynamic aspects of demonic possession and Satanic worship' (*Suid-Afrikaanse Tydskrif vir Sielkunde*, 1993), Ivey described the symptoms of demonic possession as follows:

- Radical personality change
- Loss of self-control
- Blasphemy
- Dissociative states
- Voice changes
- Auditory or visual hallucinations of demons

None of these symptoms was evident in recorded case studies of serial killers.

Ivey explains demonic possession, in terms of object relations theory, as the internalisation of the bad object that derives from a disturbed relationship between parents and child. The case study of David Berkowitz illustrates how 'demonism' can be explained as the incorporation of

99

a bad object.

Berkowitz himself attributed his behaviour to demonic possession. He made the following entry in his diary: *There is no doubt in my mind that a demon has been living in me since birth. All my life I've been wild, violent, temporal [sic], mean, sadistic, acting with irrational anger and destructiveness* (Jeffers, 1993).

Berkowitz was the illegitimate child of a mother who abandoned him. He had problems with his adoptive parents. His adoptive mother died when he was fourteen years old and he attempted to locate his biological mother. He succeeded in tracing her but she rejected him. His first sexual experience was with a prostitute, and he contracted a venereal disease.

Although Berkowitz referred to a demon in his diary, there is sufficient evidence that he had the opportunity to internalise the bad mother object. There is no evidence that he ever manifested any of the symptoms of demonic possession put forward by Ivey.

After his arrest, Berkowitz said that he committed the murders in the name of a demon, a six-thousand-year-old man named Sam who lived in the body of his neighbour's dog. He shot the dog before he began to kill. Berkowitz later stated that any dog had the ability to point out his next victim. He was eventually traced as a result of the testimony of an elderly woman who was walking her dog late one night and spotted him with a firearm.

During an interview with Berkowitz, Ressler (1993) confronted him with the fact that the stories about dogs and demons were nonsense. Although Berkowitz had managed to mislead psychiatrists with this story to the extent that they diagnosed him as a paranoid schizophrenic, Ressler did not believe it. Berkowitz indeed admitted to Ressler that the story was a ploy to secure a plea of insanity and that he had committed the murders because he resented his own mother and could not establish a relationship with any woman.

Jeffrey Dahmer's case also provides an example of how a serial killer justifies his acts by believing them to be the work of a demonic entity. Schwartz (1992) reported that Dahmer was fascinated by the devil and enjoyed films such as 'The Exorcist III' and 'Return of the Jedi'. Ressler reported that Dahmer wanted to build a shrine in his apartment with human skulls and a skeleton from which he could draw power. He also bought yellow contact lenses, which he often wore. Although Dahmer was interested in the occult, there is no evidence of demonic possession. Dahmer admitted to an evil influence in his life: *I have no question whether or not there is an evil force in the world and whether or not I have been influenced by it* (Schwartz, 1992).

Based on an extensive review of the available literature, the following conclusions can be drawn about demonic possession as a factor in the origin of serial homicide:

- Serial killers do not manifest the symptoms associated with demonic possession
- People who abduct children and rape or murder them in Satanistic rituals do not have the same intrinsic motives as serial killers
- Satanists belong to covens while serial killers prefer to work alone; although there have been cases of two or three serial killers working together, these instances are rare

Neurological theories

Authors who support neurological theories propose that serial killers suffer from brain damage or injury, which causes them to murder strangers.

In his article 'Forensic Sexology: Paraphiliac Serial Rape (Biastophilia) and Lust Murder (Erotophonophilia)'

(*American Journal of Psychotherapy*, 1990), Money refers to paraphiliac serial rape and lust murder and attributes these two forms of sadism to neurological damage. According to him, the section of the brain that is damaged is the limbic system, which is a complex system of nerves and networks that control basic emotions and drive, including sexual and defensive responses.

According to Money, in the case of sexual sadism, the brain is pathologically activated to transmit the signal for attack coupled with the signal for sexual arousal. He attributes this defect in functioning to a brain tumour or brain injury. The defect is not a continuous phenomenon but occurs intermittently in the same way that epileptic fits manifest.

He states that contributory factors to sexual sadism are inherited vulnerability, hormonal functioning, pathological relationships and syndrome overlapping. Syndromes which overlap may include epilepsy, bipolar disorder, schizoidal preoccupation, antisocial tendencies and dissociative disorders. When the person experiences a paraphiliac attack, his level of consciousness undergoes change. In this state of changed consciousness he may revert to another personality.

Bobby Joe Long, who murdered ten women and raped several others, had suffered several head injuries, the first being at the age of five, when he fell from a horse. He was also injured in a motorbike accident. He suffered from headaches and had outbursts of temper. Long had an insatiable sexual drive. He had intercourse with his wife twice daily and masturbated five times a day. He also suffered from a genetic dysfunction and developed breasts, which were surgically removed.

Although these biological factors support Money's theory, there were other circumstances that influenced Long. He was allowed to share his mother's bed until the age of thirteen. His mother was twice divorced. He married as a teenager and had intercourse with his mother as well as his wife. Both women dominated him. In my opinion, these circumstances may indicate a psychodynamic-related pathology.

Records and case studies indicate that not all serial killers have brain damage and not all of them dissociate during the act of murder, and nor do all people with brain damage become serial killers.

Psychopathological theories

In considering psychogenic[2] factors, it is necessary to establish whether a serial killer can be classified according to the DSM-IV[3] diagnostic categories of mental illnesses.

Schizophrenia

(Schizophrenia is a general label for a number of syndromes with various cognitive, emotional and behavioural manifestations.)

A diagnosis of schizophrenia brings to mind the FBI's description of the disorganised serial killer, which relates more to psychosis than to psychopathy. Schizophrenia commences during the teenage years, a theory which is confirmed by Kaplan and Sadock (*Synopsis of Psychiatry*, 1991). Ressler is of the opinion that a period of ten years is necessary for schizophrenia to take on the characteristics that are found in disorganised serial

---

[2] Psychogenic: Psychological in origin. The term is used as a qualifier for disorders that are assumed to be functional in origin, ie those in which there is no known organ dysfunction.

[3] Diagnostic and Statistical Manual. It is the guidebook of the American Psychiatric Association which is regularly updated. DSM-IV was published in 1994.

killers. This decade will place the operative serial killer in his early to mid-twenties. According to Ressler, an older person's schizophrenia will already have taken on such proportions that he is no longer able to function in society, and will probably be a chronic patient in an institution.

Trenton Chase is an example of a disorganised serial killer who was diagnosed with schizophrenia. Ressler's knowledge of schizophrenia led to an accurate profile and the subsequent arrest of Chase in 1978. His schizophrenia began during his high school years and in 1976 he was committed to a psychiatric institution after injecting himself with rabbit's blood. While he was in the institution, Chase bit off the heads of birds and was often found with blood on his clothing. He believed that he was being poisoned and that his blood would turn to powder and he needed other blood to replace his own. Chase was discharged in 1977 but remained an outpatient. He often killed animals, including his mother's cat. He also set fire to the houses of people he disliked. On the day he murdered his second victim Chase had broken into a house, defecated on a child's bed and urinated on clothing.

Ressler and Shachtman (1993) also refer to the case of Herbert William Mullin who was diagnosed with paranoid schizophrenia. His schizophrenia started during his high school years and he manifested several personality changes. Although most schizophrenics are not dangerous, Mullin was extremely violent. He believed he was committing murder on the orders of his father. His mission was to murder people as a sacrifice to prevent an earthquake in California.

Lane and Gregg (1992) discuss the case of Joseph Kallinger who was diagnosed with schizophrenia and believed he was committing murder in the name of God. He blamed his alter ego, whom he called 'Charlie'. Kallinger spoke in several languages during his trial and foamed at the mouth. He was found to be able to differentiate between right and wrong and was convicted. After he set fire to his prison cell he was transferred to a psychiatric hospital. When he tried to suffocate himself with the plastic cover on his bed he was transferred to the Pennsylvania State Hospital for the Criminally Insane.

Cameron and Frazer (1987) provide further insight into Kallinger's background. In 1975 he killed a woman with a knife after she refused to bite off the penis of a male victim. Kallinger believed it was his mission to relieve people of their genitals. He also fantasised about the mutilation of female victims.

During his youth, Kallinger was operated on for a hernia. When he returned home from hospital, his adoptive parents told him that the doctor had removed a devil from his penis and that it would always remain soft and small. Shortly afterwards he had a daydream in which his penis was resting on the blade of the knife his adoptive father, who was a shoemaker, used for carving the soles of shoes. According to Cameron and Frazer, the combination of symbolic castration by the parental figures, the vision of the knife and the real pain of the operation formed the basis of his delusion.

Kallinger could only obtain an erection when he was holding a knife in his hand. *These events fitted in with what Kallinger later did, and with the notion that he was defending himself against castration anxiety, as well as avenging himself on his parents who castrated him* (Cameron and Frazer, 1987).

Cameron and Frazer also quote Dr Terrence Kay who made the following statement when defending Peter Sutcliffe, the 'Yorkshire Ripper':

A sadist killer can very rarely relate to adult women and therefore is very rarely married; secondly he has a rich fantasy life, dreams about sex and is usually ... very anxious to discuss his fantasies; thirdly such people would stimulate their fantasy with pornography and would be interested in torture, whips and female underwear.

Kay was of the opinion that since Sutcliffe was married he did not conform to these criteria. Sutcliffe tried to present himself as a schizophrenic who committed his murders on God's orders in order to enter a plea of diminished responsibility. Sutcliffe raped Helena Rytka while she was dying and inserted a wooden plank into the vagina of Emily Jackson. He stabbed Josephine Whitaker repeatedly with a screwdriver. He was therefore sadistic and acted out his sadistic fantasies. According to Cameron and Frazer, Kay's defence that Sutcliffe was schizophrenic and not sadistic, held no water. Later Sutcliffe admitted to his brother that he committed the murders because he wanted to rid the world of prostitutes.

Although there is no doubt that some schizophrenics are capable of serial homicide, not all schizophrenics are serial killers and some serial killers only claim to be schizophrenic in order to enter a plea of mental disorder.

Schizoid personality disorder

(This is a personality disorder characterised by an emotional coldness, secretiveness, solitude, withdrawal and a general inability to form intimate attachment to others.)

Case studies indicate that schizoid tendencies are more common among disorganised serial killers than organised serial killers. Reference has already been made to Jeffrey Dahmer's schizoid tendencies. He had no close ties to family members, with the exception of his grandmother; he preferred solitary activities and did not have friends. Schwartz (1992) mentions that acquaintances, neighbours and teachers described him as a loner.

As far as sexual behaviour is concerned, the criterion for schizoid personality disorder is a person who avoids sexual contact. Jeffrey Dahmer avoided sexual contact with live human beings. He tried to turn his victims into zombies by drilling holes into their heads and pouring acid into the holes. He said he wanted to create a sex slave who would comply with all his wishes, without having a personality of his own. Dahmer was unsuccessful in his attempt to create 'zombies' and settled on committing necrophilia with the bodies of his victims. This indicates that he preferred sexual intercourse where no interpersonal relations were possible.

Another criterion for schizoid personality disorder is restricted affect, which Dahmer also exhibited. For most of his trial he was completely expressionless. Schwartz (1992) states that Dahmer stared in front of him and laughed only once about the false news report that he had eaten his prison cell mate. An early acquaintance describes Dahmer as follows: *I felt uncomfortable around him because he was so weird and emotionless* (Schwartz, 1992).

Schizoid tendencies are not found in all serial killers, and not all people with schizoid tendencies become serial killers.

Schizotypal personality disorder

(A personality disorder characterised by markedly eccentric and erratic thought, speech and behaviour and a tendency to withdraw from other people.)

Jeffrey Dahmer also provides us with an example of someone with schizotypal tendencies. He explained the reason for his cannibalism as the belief that the spirits of his victims would live inside him. This is an example of magical thinking. Eccentric behaviour is another criterion of the schizotypal personality disorder which Dahmer exhibited. He wore yellow contact lenses, planned to build an altar of human skulls from which to draw power and did not often wash. He had no confidants, which is yet another criterion for this personality disorder.

Schizotypal tendencies are not found in all serial killers, and not all people who are diagnosed with this disorder become serial killers.

Antisocial personality disorder

(A personality disorder marked by a history of irresponsible and antisocial behaviour beginning in childhood or early adolescence and continuing into adulthood.)

Holmes and De Burger (1988) describe the psychopathic inner structure of the serial killer as follows: *The single most important one of the basic behavioral sources in repetitive homicide is the existence of a sociopathic character structure or personality in the perpetrator and he has sociopathic tendencies and a capacity for aggression and raw violence.*

They emphasise that the typical serial killer is not mentally ill, but that his lack of remorse can be attributed to a psyche that is socially defective. *This sociopathic pattern, originating in early childhood, separates them from the rest of humanity and results in a lack of empathy for it. Yet they are otherwise rational, logical, appropriate, competent, even charming and persuasive.*

All authors seem to agree that several of the criteria for antisocial personality disorder may manifest in serial killers. The criteria manifesting before the age of fifteen, namely physical cruelty towards animals and other people as well as forced sexual relations, are found in many serial killers. Jeffrey Dahmer, for instance, slaughtered and dissected animals as a child.

Some serial killers are also arsonists. Notes on 1400 incidents of arson were found in David Berkowitz's diary.

It is estimated that he carried out about 2000 cases of arson, but it is not known whether this started before the age of fifteen.

Theft before the age of fifteen is another criterion for antisocial personality disorder. The Boston Strangler, Albert de Salvo, already had a criminal record at the age of seventeen for housebreaking. Monty Rissell had raped twelve women and murdered five by the age of nineteen. By the age of nine he had shot his cousin; he was caught driving without a licence at thirteen; and at fourteen he was charged with housebreaking, car theft and two rapes.

An unstable employment record is a criterion for anti-social personality disorder and is commonly found in the case histories of serial killers. According to Ressler, they often have occupations beneath their intellectual or social standards. Dahmer worked in a chocolate factory and Peter Sutcliffe was a truck driver. Dahmer was often truant from work, especially after a murder. In 1991 he was dismissed for being late and for being absent without leave.

Aggression and violence are other manifestations of the antisocial personality disorder and are common characteristics of serial killers. Apart from torturing their victims, they are often involved in fights and woman battering. Albert de Salvo beat his first wife when she refused to comply with his sexual desires. Dahmer's father Lionel reported that his son was often involved in bar fights.

Another characteristic of antisocial personality disorder is the inability to commit to a long-term emotional relationship with a partner. Although some may be married, serial killers as a rule do not have the ability to commit to a long-term fulfilling relationship. Ted Bundy, charged with nineteen murders, was married, but admitted to his inability to sustain the relationship with his wife. He claimed the fact that he was illegitimate contributed to this inability.

David Berkowitz was offended by a newspaper article that referred to him as a misogynist, but later admitted to Ressler that he murdered women because he could not have a fulfilling relationship with them and that he blamed his mother for this.

The criterion of antisocial personality disorder which is most applicable to serial killers is a lack of the ability to feel remorse or guilt. Ted Bundy made the following statement: *What's one less person on the face of the earth anyway; I don't feel guilty for anything; I feel sorry for people who feel guilt; I'm the most cold-hearted son of a bitch you'll ever meet* (Jeffers, 1993). Levin and Fox (1991) cite the case of Clifford Olson who murdered eleven children and at the time of his arrest suggested to the police that he be paid ten thousand pounds for every body he pointed out. He argued that if the police agreed to this, they would be able to clear up unsolved cases and the families could bury the victims. The police agreed to pay the money to Olson's wife. She was paid nine thousand pounds. When he was asked to point out the rest of the bodies without payment, Olson remarked: *If I gave a shit about the parents, I wouldn't have killed the kid.*

Again, not all serial killers are diagnosed with antisocial personality disorders, and not all people diagnosed with antisocial personality disorder become serial killers. Antisocial tendencies are often found in organised serial killers.

Paraphilias

Kaplan and Sadock (1991) describe paraphilias as being characterised by sexual fantasies and intense sexual urges and practices that are repetitive and upsetting to the afflicted person. Paraphilias are considered to be divergent behaviour, which is concealed by the affected person and which disrupts the person's potential for bonding with others. Paedophilia, sexual sadism, fetishism, oralism, sadism, voyeurism and necrophilia are paraphilias which may manifest in serial killers.

The question arises whether serial homicide can be classified as a paraphilia. Elements of paraphilia are present in serial killers but will not necessarily dominate their lives. Another problem encountered when considering whether serial killers can be diagnosed as paraphiliacs, is the criterion that the condition is distressing to the affected person. Ego-syntonic serial killers do not perceive their perversion as offensive. Sometimes they will even attempt to provoke the police with their perversions and generally they do not experience any feelings of guilt.

An example of a serial killer who had a fetish is Jerry Brudos. Brudos already had a shoe fetish at the age of five years. At seventeen he was arrested for ordering a woman to undress while threatening her with a knife. He was detained for nine months in a mental institution and diagnosed as suffering from the early stages of a personality disorder. He often paraded in his wife's underwear and took photographs of himself. In 1968 he murdered a woman, cut off her left foot and threw the body into a river. He kept the foot in a deep freeze and dressed it in different shoes. Apart from committing necrophilia, he also mutilated and kept his victims' breasts.

If the serial killer is offended by his own sexual deviation, as Kaplan and Sadock's definition of paraphilia requires, I would suggest that his ego would defend itself against the offensive impulses by dissociation. He would then be an ego-dystonic serial killer.

Dissociative disorders (Multiple personality disorders)

(This is a general term for those psychological disorders characterised by a breakdown in the usual integrated

functions of consciousness, perception of self and sensory/motor behaviour. Multiple personality disorder is generally included here.)

Carlisle (in Holmes and De Burger) is of the opinion that serial killers have a multiple personality structure. Holmes and De Burger (1988) state:

> Carlisle holds to the position that the serial killer has an overwhelming urge to kill, and that this urge to kill, which some serial killers call their 'beast' or their 'shadow' can take over the complete task of murder. The beasts are only visible to the serial killers, who outwardly appear to be 'nice people'. With some of the serial killers, the person is no longer in charge, only the impulses of the beast.

Cameron and Frazer (1987) analyse the case of Dennis Nilsen who murdered sixteen young men from 1978 to 1983. Nilsen experienced the murders as ego-dystonic. *I seem not to have participated in the killings, merely stood by and watched them happen – enacted by two other players ... I always covered up for that 'inner me' that I loved ... He just acted and I had to solve all his problems in the cool light of day.*

Ted Bundy claimed that his murders were committed by another entity inside him. Lane and Gregg refer to Bundy's statement that an unknown 'urge' hides within the murderer. Bundy confessed to the murders in the third person singular.

Kenneth Bianchi, one of the 'Hillside Strangler' duo of Los Angeles, also maintained that he suffered from dissociative identity disorder. One of his alleged personalities was 'Steve', a violent individual who committed the sex crimes.

I am of the opinion that dissociative identity disorder (multiple personality disorder) develops during early childhood as an escape and defence mechanism against excessive abuse. The abused child fantasises about escaping an unbearable situation and creates different personalities within his psyche to manage the abuse. The serial killer, on the other hand, fantasises about revenge and manages the abuse by acting out the fantasies. The origins of serial homicide and dissociative identity disorder therefore differ fundamentally as different defence mechanisms come into play in each case (escape in the case of dissociatives and revenge in the case of serial killers). No true serial killer will suffer from dissociative disorder.

Normality

Normality is not a DSM-IV category, but the question is often asked whether serial killers are 'normal' people.

Cameron and Frazer (1987) quote the following statement by a psychologist about serial killers:

> Most of them are very normal and very friendly, that you maybe went into a pub to have a drink, and you'd sit there and talk to him and he'd all of a sudden become one of your good friends, you can't look at him and tell that there is something strange about him, they're very normal.

Leyton (1986) comments:

> ... madness is not like cancer or any other physical ailment. Rather it is a culturally programmed dialogue. It should not therefore be surprising that, no matter how hard our psychiatrists search, they are unable to discover much mental disease among our captured murderers (except in the nature of their acts). Therein lies the special horror, for the killers are as 'normal' as you and me, yet they kill without mercy, and they kill to make a statement.

Ressler and Shachtman (1993) indicate that organised

serial killers often exhibit acting out and violent behaviour during their childhood, but this is not necessarily the childhood behaviour pattern of the disorganised serial killer. When he is arrested and his identity is made public, his neighbours, school friends and teachers hardly remember him. *And when his neighbours are interviewed, they characterise him as a nice boy, never any trouble, who kept to himself and was docile and polite.*

The question of whether a serial killer is 'normal' or whether he is mentally ill often arises during their trials. Levin and Fox (1991) discuss the dilemma when a plea of insanity is entered and results in the accused being found not accountable for his actions. Many serial killers have avoided the death penalty by successfully entering a plea of insanity and are institutionalised for the rest of their lives. A psychotic person can, however, still be held legally accountable in the United States of America and sentenced to a prison term. Twenty-seven American states accepted the criteria of the American Legal Society which state the following: *A defendant is not criminally responsible if 'as a result of mental disease or defect he lacks substantial capacity either to appreciate the criminality of his conduct or to conform his conduct to the requirement of the law'* (1991).

Some American states accept the verdict 'guilty but mentally insane' and such a person will receive therapy in prison.

In South Africa an accused may be referred for observation in a state-appointed psychiatric hospital for thirty days or longer. According to Sections 77 and 79 of the Criminal Procedures Act, 1977 (Act no 51 of 1977), the accused may be found to be mentally ill or not mentally ill at the time of the alleged offence, fit to stand trial or not fit to stand trial, to have the capability to appreciate the

114

wrongfulness of the act in question and to act accordingly or not. Most of the serial killers we investigated were found fit to stand trial and sentenced to life imprisonment. The ANC government abolished the death sentence during Norman Avzal Simons' trial, which probably saved his life.

Jeffrey Dahmer attempted to enter a plea of insanity but did not succeed. Schwartz (1992) reports that Dahmer, who showed characteristics of both an organised and a disorganised serial killer, was found guilty and mentally accountable for the murders he committed. The question remains whether the following description of his behaviour, presented by his defence attorney during the trial, is that of a 'normal' person:

> Skulls in locker, cannibalism, sexual urges, drilling, making zombies, necrophilia, disorders, paraphilia, watching videos, getting excited about fish eggs, drinking alcohol all of the time, into a dysfunctional family, trying to create a shrine, showering with corpses, going into the occult, having delusions, chanting and rocking, picking up a road kill, having obsessions, murders, lobotomies, defleshing, masturbating two, three times a day as a youngster, going and trying to get a mannequin home so he could play sex with a mannequin, masturbating into the open parts of a human being's body, calling taxidermists, going to graveyards, going to funeral homes, wearing yellow contacts, posing people who are dead that he killed for pleasure, masturbating all over the place.

Robert Ressler told me that when he asked Dahmer whether he ate the human flesh raw, Dahmer answered: *Mr Ressler, I'm not that sick.* Although their actions can be explained using the tool of psychoanalysis, the majority of organised serial killers are not mentally ill. In my view psychoanalysis provides an explanation for the *origin* of serial homicide, but it certainly does not provide a reason to condone their actions.

Fantasy

(Fantasy is a term generally used to refer to the mental process of imagining objects, symbols or events that are not immediately present.)

MacCulloch, Snowden, Wood and Mills studied a group of sixteen sexual sadists ('Sadistic fantasy, sadistic behaviour and offending', *British Journal of Psychiatry*, 1983). In thirteen of the sixteen cases, sadistic masturbatory fantasies were found to have inspired the sadistic acts. They found that thirteen of the sadists had behavioural 'try outs', where their fantasies corresponded with their sadistic behaviour. In nine cases they found a progression in the contents of their sadistic fantasies.

Prentky, Wolbert-Burgess, Rokous, Lee, Hartman, Ressler and Douglas examined the role of fantasy by comparing twenty-five serial killers with seventeen murderers who committed only a single murder ('The presumptive role of fantasy in serial sexual homicide', *American Journal of Psychiatry*, 1989). The authors hypothesised that the drive mechanism for serial killers is an intrusive fantasy life manifesting in higher prevalence of paraphilias, documented or self-reported violent fantasies and organised crime scenes in the serial homicides. All three of their hypotheses were supported.

Prentky and colleagues (1989) report that Burgess, in a study she conducted in 1986, had found evidence of daydreaming and compulsive masturbation in over 80 per cent of a sample of thirty-six serial murderers, in childhood as well as adulthood.

Prentky and colleagues summarised the research of MacCulloch et al as follows:

While the precise function of consummated fantasy is speculative, we concur with MacCulloch et al that once the restraints inhibiting the acting out of the fantasy are no longer present, the individual is likely to engage in a series of progressively more accurate 'trial runs' in an attempt to enact the fantasy as it is imagined. Since the trial runs can never precisely match the fantasy, the need to restage the fantasy with a new victim is established. MacCulloch et al suggested the shaping of the fantasy and the motivation for consummation may be understood in terms of classical conditioning ... While it is unlikely that the translation of fantasy into reality conforms precisely to a classical conditioning model, it does appear that the more fantasy is rehearsed, the more power it acquires and the stronger the association between the fantasy content and sexual arousal. (1989)

I agree that fantasy is the blueprint for serial homicide. Whereas Prentky and colleagues were unable to explain the lack of inhibition that causes the fantasies to be acted out in reality, I will explain this phenomenon according to Freud's theory of the id, ego and superego. Prentky and colleagues do not support MacCulloch et al's suggestion that the repetitive fantasy can be attributed to classical conditioning, but they themselves do not provide an adequate explanation. In the theory I formulated on the etiology of serial killers, I will explain this phenomenon in terms of Freud's theory on the compulsion to repeat. I call my theory Pistorius' Theory on the Development of Male Serial Killers.

Pistorius' theory on the development of male serial killers

While I was researching other authors' theories on the origin of serial homicide, two questions continued to bother me. The first was: If two brothers grew up in the same adverse circumstances (both were abused, both were exposed to violence and poverty, etc) how did it happen that one became a serial killer while the other did not? The answer had to lie inside the psyche of the individual and not in external circumstances, which might have been contributory but were not causative. The second question that concerned me was that none of the existing theories on the origin of serial homicide were applicable to *all* serial killers. I needed a theory that could be applied to all serial killers.

I found my answer in the psychoanalytical theories of Sigmund Freud. My theory rests mainly upon Freud's theories of the topology of the psyche and the psychosexual developmental phases. I do not claim that this is the be-all and end-all of theories on the origin of serial homicide, but my theory works. I have applied it to more than three hundred case studies of serial killers. It is my hope that it will inspire students to extend their research and come up with even better theories.

Id, ego and superego

Freud formulated a theory on the topology of the psyche, which constitutes the *id*, the *ego* and the *superego* (or conscience). The id is situated in the subconscious, the ego in the conscious and the superego is situated partly in the subconscious, but mostly in the conscious.

The id

The id is the first structure of the psyche, the one with which a child is born. It consists of instincts, urges and needs which are mainly of an aggressive and sexual nature. The sexual instinct (libido) is directed at the function of self-preservation. It is also called the ego-instinct or Eros. Eros does not only encompass sex, but also instincts like hunger, need for affection, and so on, on which a person depends for his existence and survival. The aggression instinct is the death instinct or Thanatos, which can be directed towards the self or towards other people.

The id functions only according to the pleasure principle. It wants its own pleasures satisfied immediately, or it wants the discomfort caused by a need to be relieved by the gratification of that need. The id knows no logic, time, morality or censorship. The id agrees to everything.

Primary process thinking – ie primitive, pre-logical thoughts – takes place in the id. Reality and logic have no part here. It is pre-verbal, meaning that concepts are not yet associated with words but remain vague ideas.

The id is based within the subconscious which is not only the home of aggressive and sexual urges, but everything that is unacceptable to the ego is repressed to the id. It is never quiet within the subconscious, everything there is reorganised, grows, moves and demands acknowledgement in various ways. It reminds me of the witches' cauldron in *Macbeth* – 'double, double, toil and trouble'. The subconscious cannot communicate directly with the ego, because the ego does not want to hear its complaints and demands. And so the subconscious communicates with the ego by way of dreams, symbols and symptoms.

The ego

The second psychic structure to develop is the ego. The ego constitutes the executive personality of the individual. The ego is not present at birth but develops as the child learns to differentiate between himself, other people and objects and cultivates an awareness of the reality surrounding him. An important function of the ego is the reality principle. It has to negotiate with the world outside the psyche. The ego is therefore housed in the conscious.

The ego must maintain the balance between the id and the superego and reality. The id insists on gratification of an instinct or need. The ego checks whether it is realistic to satisfy the instinct or need and takes consequences into consideration. It negotiates with the outside world and the id and the superego until it reaches a compromise. The ego is capable of secondary process thinking, which includes logic, words, evaluation of consequences and time.

The ego has a difficult task maintaining the balance between the id, the superego and reality and gathers itself an army of defence mechanisms to assist it. One of the most important defence mechanisms is repression. When the ego becomes aware of a threatening instinct from within the id because it is in conflict with reality or the superego, the ego represses that instinct or urge or fantasy back to the subconscious and ignores it, or it may employ another defence mechanism to deal with the threat.

Defence mechanisms differ according to their level of maturity. Narcissistic defence mechanisms are very primitive and include denial, distortion, primitive idealisation, projection[4] and splitting.[5] Immature defence mechanisms include acting out, blocking, hypochondria, identification, introjection (unconscious adoption of the ideas or attitudes of others), passive-aggressiveness, projection, regression, schizoid fantasies, somatisation (the manifestation of psychological distress by the presentation of bodily symptoms) and a turning against the self. Neurotic defences are control, displacement, dissociation, externalisation, inhibitions, intellectualisation, isolation, rationalisation,

---

[4] Projection: The process by which one's own traits, emotions, etc are ascribed to another.

[5] Splitting: A defence mechanism in which one deals with conflict and stress by compartmentalising ('splitting') the positive and negative aspects of oneself or others.

reaction-formation, repression, sexualising and undoing. Mature defence mechanisms are altruism, anticipation, abstinence, humour, sublimation and postponement.

The ego is developing continuously, but there are various factors which can delay or retard its development. The id or superego can be so overpowering that one of the two completely dominates the ego. A person whose ego is not continuously exposed to new learning experiences can stagnate. This can happen at any age, but a good example is that of a sixty-year-old person who decides life has nothing more to offer and locks himself up in an old-age home where he is no longer exposed to new experiences. Rigid, opinionated men who rule their families with an iron fist, also suffer from stagnant egos. They literally need to open their minds. The ego learns from experience. A healthy ego can learn from mistakes, failures and pain, but it can also handle success and value happiness. Many parents deny their children these opportunities because of their own neurotic possessiveness and immaturity.

The superego

The superego is the conscience that develops from the ego, starting at about the end of the Oedipus phase at five to six years. There are signs of it during earlier developmental phases, but it becomes an internal force when the child avoids doing wrong through internal conviction and not because he fears external punishment. The superego exists as a result of identification with the parents, mainly the father figure. It represents the moral standards of society, ethics, cultural factors, censorship, conscience and guilt feelings. The superego says 'no' to everything.

The superego holds up an ideal self as a benchmark to measure the ego. Should the ego fail to fulfil the image of the ideal self, the superego punishes it with guilt feelings.

The superego can function from the conscious or the

subconscious. Sometimes we know why we feel guilty, but at other times we don't know why we punish ourselves with self-destructive behaviour. The superego's ideals are often just as far-fetched and unrealistic as the demands of the id.

Table 5: The development of neurotic symptoms in a normal person

ID *SUBCONSCIOUS*	EGO *CONSCIOUS*	SUPEREGO *CONSCIOUS / SUBCONSCIOUS*
Sex and aggressive impulses and fantasies →	← Anxiety	Guilt

Neurotic symptoms
Dreams
Symbols

In the psyche of a normal person, sexual and aggressive impulses and fantasies penetrate the ego from the id. The ego cannot reconcile these impulses with reality or with the superego. They are considered threatening and taboo. Anxiety then forms within the ego and the superego will punish it with guilt feelings. The ego immediately represses the id impulses back to the subconscious. The contents of these destructive fantasies are unknown to the ego. In the subconscious, *fixations* or complexes (psychological short-circuits) form around these impulses, and the impulses will employ other methods to gain acknowledgement, such as neurotic symptoms, dreams and symbols. The more the ego represses, the more the impulses within the subconscious demand acknowledgement. In this process much psychic energy is lost, which prevents the ego from developing and causes depression. As soon as a conflict within the subconscious has been acknowledged and solved by the ego, instead of being repressed, the ego regains the energy it needs to grow and develop. The basis of Freud's psychoanalytical therapy is to uncover the themes within the subconscious through, for example, hypnosis and then to resolve them within a safe and secure therapeutic environment.

Table 6: The development of the serial killer

ID	EGO	SUPEREGO
Sexual and aggressive impulses and fantasies	No anxiety	Virtually non-existent

↓
Acts out destructive fantasies

The serial killer's ego is underdeveloped because of domination by the id. The ego has no need to repress the urges or destructive fantasies from the id, because the ego is too weak to be threatened. The ego is also too narcissistic to care about external reality and the superego is virtually non-existent because of lack of identification with a positive father figure. The ego is free to allow the acting out of the sexual and aggressive fantasies. There is therefore no reason for the development of neurotic symptoms. The ego is aware of the contents of the destructive fantasies and they remain conscious. Serial killers are therefore more normal than most neurotic individuals, which should dispel the myth that they are recognisable as raving lunatics.

Psychosexual developmental phases

Freud postulated that all humans progress through specific developmental phases from birth to adulthood. Although several other psychologists have also formulated developmental phases, Freud's phases focus more on the sexual and aggressive development of the psyche. Since male serial killers are preoccupied with sex and aggression, I found his theory the most applicable.

Oral phase: 0 - 2 years

The oral phase is the earliest phase of psychosexual development where all the child's needs, perceptions and manner of expressing himself are centred around the mouth (lips, tongue, etc). All his needs (hunger, love, etc) are satisfied through the mouth – he sucks and drinks. The substance that gratifies his needs is the milk. An infant's world consists of himself and his immediate surroundings. He puts his fingers, toes, toys, etc into his mouth and so learns to differentiate between objects. He can express himself only through his mouth by screaming, gurgling or crying. The erotogenic zone is the mouth.

Oral sensations include thirst, hunger and touching-pleasure, for example the sensation of the lips when the infant suckles at his mother's breast, and swallows. There are two oral instincts or urges, namely oral erotic (the sucking and drinking stage) and oral sadistic (the stage when the infant bites, spits and cries). Initially the infant is oral erotic – he only sucks and drinks. Later he also becomes oral sadistic – he bites. When an oral need arises, the infant tries to satisfy it either erotically or sadistically to regain a balance (homeostasis). Even at this early stage, there are primitive sadistic fantasies of biting, eating and destruction within the child's subconscious. Eros and Thanatos are already at play. The child is all id at this infant stage.

Too much satisfaction or abstinence – for example the infant gets too much or too little milk – can lead to an oral fixation which will manifest later in his personality. Characteristics of this during adulthood are:

- Excessive optimism – too much milk
- Narcissism – the mother always satisfied the infant's needs at cost to herself – as an adult he thinks that the whole world revolves around him
- Pessimism – especially during depression
- Demanding – demands attention of the mother and later of other people

A person with an oral character is excessively dependent and demands that others should give him everything and care for him. He can be very generous, but there is a subconscious need for the other person to reciprocate. He also expects the other person to boost his self-image. Jealousy and envy are thus also characteristics as an adult. Someone who completes the oral phase successfully can maintain a balance between giving and taking and is not over-dependent on other people.

In analysing a crime scene, I employed Freud's theory in retrospect to commence the psychoanalytical profile of the killer. For example, when I found bite marks on a body, or a body on which the breasts had been mutilated or removed, or signs of cannibalism, I knew the suspect would have the characteristics of an oral personality and there would have been some oral fixation in his infancy.

Bite marks indicate oral sadism, which will probably classify the serial killer as hedonistic lust-motivated. If breasts have been removed or mutilated the suspect was probably rejected by the mother as a baby, or feels subconsciously that he was rejected and is still symbolically seeking the milk (love) he was denied. Cutting the breasts is a symbolic way of getting to the milk. Such a killer was probably not breastfed. I am not postulating that all people who were not breastfed will become serial killers. Of course not. They will find other ways of gratifying this need; eg smoking, drinking, over-dependence on others.

Cannibalism indicates a severe identity crisis, and the killer tries in this very primitive way to incorporate the identity of the victim by physically eating her. The symbolism of incorporating someone's identity by eating their body parts is an excellent example of the pre-verbal and magical thinking processes of the id. Although they are motivated by these primitive processes, they can still function on a cognitive intelligent level in society. The cannibal's trust should be won and he should be acknowledged as a human being, so that he can establish some kind of identity which will enable him to confess.

Stewart Wilken of Port Elizabeth mutilated his female victims' breasts and he ate the nipples at the crime scene. He was abandoned by his biological mother as an infant and was severely abused. He manifests the characteristics of an orally fixated individual in his current adult personality and often regresses to tantrums and childlike behaviour. I talked to him as I would have talked to a disturbed child and he responded to that.

Anal phase: 2 - 4 years

This psychosexual phase is characterised by the development of the sphincter muscle which controls the anal closure reflex. It is the 'potty-training' phase. The erotogenic zone is the anus.

This phase is characterised by an intensifying of aggressive urges and the child derives pleasure from his sadistic impulses. Where he was previously more passive (an infant), he now becomes more active – he has more control over himself and his environment. He learns to

126

walk, he can dress himself and he has control over his own bodily functions. Everyone is familiar with the tantrums of two-years-olds and their need to act independently. This is also known as the *control phase*.

To a child, faeces is the product of his own body. It is something he has produced and he is proud of it. The parent, however, expects him to flush this product down the toilet. A power struggle now ensues between the child and the parent. He is angry with the parent, but on the other hand he also loves the parent and is dependent on him/her for his survival. The child easily gets confused by these ambivalent feelings. If all goes well during this phase, the child learns to individualise and to function independently of the parent.

Anal eroticism refers to the sexual pleasure of defecating – the child can retain his own product or present it as a gift to the parent. Children also equate faeces with babies since they believe that babies are born through the anus, until formal sex education teaches them differently. (When the three-year-old son of a friend of mine was told where babies came from, he asked his mother if he could rather come out of her mouth the next time.)

Anal sadism refers to the expression of aggression and faeces become dangerous weapons of destruction in the child's subconscious fantasies. Children in this phase have fantasies of bombs, explosions and volcanoes erupting. Listen carefully to the explosive noises they make when they play. These are conscious manifestations of subconscious aggressive fantasies and are quite normal.

The child has several defence options against the ambivalence he feels towards his parents. He may feel that he should not get angry with his parent – if he shows anger towards the parent, he may lose the love of that parent, on whom he is dependent for his survival, and he might die. Therefore, he experiences himself as the bad person, rather than considering the parent as the bad person. (This is an example of the objects relations theory.) This usually happens when parents are conditional in their love for the child. Such a child will always suffer from a deep-rooted inferiority complex as an adult.

Another child may fear losing the parent's love and become very compliant and good, just to please the parent. He then develops a pleasing personality, wanting to buy the affection of others and cannot assert himself. He will become a passive-aggressive individual who sabotages interpersonal relationships.

A third option is for a child to acknowledge the parent as the aggressor, but because he fears losing the parent's love, he will identify with the parent and also become aggressive. These children become typical bullies.

A person who fixated in this phase will have the following traits:

- Orderly – he was forced to go to the toilet at specific times
- Hard-nosed – the power struggle with the parent will result in an over-controlling adult
- Stingy – wants to keep the faeces to himself and not share it

Should the child's defence mechanisms fail, he will never be able to deal with ambivalence. One day he will hate a person and the next day he will love that same person. He does not have the maturity to realise that one can be angry with a person while still loving him or her.

Other characteristics of anal personalities are:

- Slovenliness – his environment is as messy as he feels inside
- Anger – he could never control his original aggression towards his parent
- Sado-masochism – he wants to be in control or he wants to be punished because he is angry with the

beloved parent
- Obsessive-compulsive – conscious rituals divert his attention from the subconscious anger and the revenge he experiences towards the parents

Successful completion of this phase is indicated by a person who can function independently, can tolerate ambivalence and cooperate with others without being either complacent or dominant.

An excessively orderly or excessively chaotic crime scene indicates an anal personality to me. Signs of sadomasochism, such as bondage, whiplashes, etc also indicate anal fixation. Signs of obsessive-compulsive rituals will be, for example, re-dressing the victim perfectly, placing the shoes neatly next to each other, making a bow around the victim's neck. If the scene is excessively neat, I know the suspect will dress neatly, and his nails will probably be manicured.

Signs of sadism on the body are significant. Sadism correlates with both the oral and the anal phases. Sadism implies control and the anal phase is a control phase. Such a serial killer can be classified as hedonistic, lust- or power-motivated.

The Station Strangler was a serial killer who fixated in the anal phase. His crime scenes were excessively neat and he tied his victims up. He also sodomised them.

Urethral phase

This is not one of Freud's original phases but was added by his students. This psychosexual phase overlaps with the end of the anal phase and the beginning of the Oedipus/phallic phase. The erotogenic zone is the urinary tube.

Urethral erotism refers to the pleasure derived from urinating and urethral retention is comparable with retention of faeces. Control is also an issue. Many of the anal sadistic characteristics are carried over to this phase. The child experiences his urine as a dangerous poisonous substance or acid, which has the ability to destroy. It often happens that a child who is abused in some manner – physically, emotionally or sexually – at this age, will wet his bed at night. In his dreams he is avenging himself on his parents and trying to destroy them through his urine. (This does not mean that all children who wet their beds are abused! Freud himself urinated on his parents' bed …)

The outstanding characteristics of a urethral fixation are competition and ambition. It may originate from the need to compensate for the humiliation the child feels when he loses control over his urethral functions. A person who successfully completed this phase has pride and feels competent.

If the suspect has urinated on the body, especially the face, it may mean that he is subconsciously trying to destroy the identity (face) of his mother, for whom the female victim is a substitute. He may also urinate on the female sex organs, which means that he feels threatened by women, especially by female sexuality, and is symbolically trying to destroy it. Such a person could have been seduced as a child by an older woman, or he may feel threatened by female sexuality because of his own latent homosexuality. He probably has an intense hatred for women.

Oedipus/phallic phase: 4 - 6 years

Freud considered the Oedipus phase the most important phase of psychosexual development. During this extreme sexual phase, the boy subconsciously falls in love with the mother and he competes with the father for her attention. The opposite happens with the daughter who subconsciously falls in love with the father. The erotogenic zone is the penis.

This phase is characterised by sexual interest, stimulation and masturbation. (Masturbation is natural in all three phases up to now, as the child learns about his/her body. Children should be taught that it should not be done in public or with other people, but they should not be punished or belittled for masturbating.) Both sexes are interested in the penis. The girl may develop penis envy when she sees the boy's penis and realises that she does not have one. She holds her mother responsible for her own 'castration', for she is subconsciously in love with the mother's husband. The boy realises the girl has no penis and develops castration anxiety. He reasons that if the girl has been 'castrated', it is also possible that he could lose his own penis. He fears that the father will 'castrate' him, because he is in love with the father's wife. All of this happens on a subconscious level, but it will manifest in behaviours such as the boy sitting next to the mother and refusing to allow the father near her, hitting the father, etc. It is natural for little boys to be very attached to their mothers during this phase. Fathers may make the mistake of fearing their boys are going to become 'sissies'. Mothers may make the mistake of being so flattered by their son's attention that they neglect their husbands and allow the son to 'conquer' the father figure. It is very important that parents retain their roles as spouses to each other and set loving boundaries for their children.

A man may also feel 'castrated' by a woman who continuously belittles him. This has its origin in the mother rejecting the boy. The boy may also feel subconscious guilt about masturbating, thinking that it will lead to his castration.

At the end of this phase it would be normal for the boy to give up the mother as the object of his sexual attraction and identify with his father; likewise with the girl. According to Freud, identification with the father figure leads to the development of the superego/conscience. The father figure represents society to a child and a positive father figure, who respects society's norms and values, will instil a healthy conscience in his children, by way of example. (Single mothers need not worry; the father figure can be any positive male role model.)

A wide variety of fixations can develop in this phase. The result can be homosexuality, where the boy identifies with the mother instead of the father (Oedipus is, however, not the only reason for homosexuality.) A fixation can also result in the boy marrying a woman who is like his mother. Another result of a fixation is that the boy never regards any man as worthy competition, because he was the victor in the mental battle against his father and his mother favoured him instead of her husband. On the other hand, the boy might lose the battle to such a degree that he will compete with the father figure for the rest of his life, or will try to win the father figure's affection and approval, and he will always feel inferior. Such men have problems with authority.

One of the most important fixations in this phase is castration anxiety which arises from guilt feelings about the boy's aggression towards his father (revenge) and the sexuality directed towards his mother. On a mental level the boy feels that he may be castrated or that he has been castrated.

Someone who has successfully completed this phase will have an appropriate sexual identity and the basis of a healthy conscience.

If I find a phallic instrument such as a bottle, broomstick, candle, etc, forced into the vagina or anus of a female victim, it indicates castration anxiety to me. The suspect fears the woman, who does not have a penis, because this reminds him that he may lose his. He therefore gives her a penis (for example, a bottle) and leaves it behind in the body. He suffers from psychological impotence. A man who rapes feels psychologically castrated and psychologically impotent, though he may be physically potent. The Cape Town Prostitute Killer inserted a bottle into the vagina of one of his victims. The suspect who was arrested (but ultimately not charged because of lack of evidence) reported that he had slept in his mother's bed until he was sixteen. She had many boyfriends whom he detested and he was physically impotent.

The serial killer who commits necrophilia has a serious communication problem. He only feels safe being intimate with a dead person, because a dead person cannot reject or tease or humiliate him.

Latency phase: 6 - 12 years

The latency phase represents a cooling-off of the sexual urges and the ego's development focuses on socialising. There is therefore no erotogenic zone and a lack of interest in masturbation.

During this phase the conscience/superego that was established towards the end of the previous phase develops. The ego grows more mature and individualises and the strengthening of both the ego and the superego gives rise to greater control over the id. During this phase, the one gender ignores the other to a great extent. The child's psychic energy, which was previously sexually orientated, is now directed towards learning and social interaction. It is the primary school phase, where the child learns about the world outside his home environment. He learns to make friends, to share and to accept group norms, and he acquires empathy for other people and incorporates moral standards.

Fixations arise when there is either a lack of control or else too much control over the urges of the id. A lack of control means the child does not channel his energy towards new learning experiences. He remains aggressively and sexually orientated and does not learn to postpone the gratification of his needs. Too much control means the child wastes his energy on the repression of his urges instead of channelling it into learning. The personality is therefore deprived of the opportunity to grow. In both instances the child does not learn to take other people's needs into consideration.

A person who has successfully completed this phase has the ability to tackle new experiences with initiative. Should he make a mistake, he will learn from it without destroying his self-image.

All the serial killers that I researched had father figures who were either physically or emotionally absent during this phase. Therefore they never developed a superego/conscience. Because they never socialised during this phase, they show no empathy towards their victims, treating them merely as objects for their gratification and showing no remorse. The serial killer wants to satisfy his sexual and aggressive needs immediately and has no regard for the consequences or for other people's feelings.

Serial killers are also very lonely during this phase. They do not make friends, or no more than just one friend, and feel excluded by their peers. Their sexuality is not suppressed and they still masturbate – sometimes in the company of that one friend. Some also start to experiment with animal abuse and dissection. They do not perform well at school because their energy is not directed towards learning.

It is dangerous to expose a child to sexual activities during this phase – for example, by seduction, rape, exposure to pornography, or even allowing him to sleep in the same room as his parents.

Although most normal adults suffer from fixations during the first three developmental phases – for example, smokers are orally fixated – what distinguishes us from serial killers is the development of our conscience during the latency phase. Our egos have more mature defence mechanisms.

Genital phase: 12 - 19 years

This phase commences with puberty and continues through adolescence until early adulthood. Sexuality arises again and the erotogenic zones are the genitals of both sexes.

With the onset of hormonal development, the child begins to refocus on sexual aspects. By this time his sexual identity should be established and he should have control over his impulses and be able to postpone gratification. The development of the personality up to this point regresses because of the reawakening of sexual development. (We all know about teenage boys and their hormones!) The child learns to function independently of his parents and learns to have mature, non-incestuous, love relationships.

Conflicts from the previous developmental phases will surface again and the child has another chance to resolve them. Should he fail to do so it may lead to pathology in the adult personality. If the child fails to consolidate his development it may lead to a total identity crisis.

The person who successfully completes this phase is capable of mature sexual relationships and has an integrated personality.

Serial killers and serial rapists are not capable of mature intimate relationships. If they should have an intimate relationship, the partner will also be immature and complacent. It is possible for a serial killer to have a relationship with a woman to whom he acts as a protector. Some may marry and others may masquerade as successful family men, even becoming prominent members of their communities. This type of serial killer is able to distance himself from his actions and maintain normal patterns of behaviour.

The future serial killer has developed established sexual and aggressive fantasies, which he rehearses during this phase.

The pattern of his development is thus:

- A fixation in the first three phases gave rise to the sexual and aggressive fantasy
- No conscience developed during the latency phase to repress the fantasy and failure to learn to socialise enables him to treat other human beings as objects
- Rehearsal of the fantasy in real life during the genital phase, with no conscience to inhibit the acting out

When the serial killer reaches adulthood, he is conditioned by years of repetition of his fantasies, accompanied by the reward of masturbation and sexual gratification. In his fantasies he is omnipotent and powerful – as we all are in our fantasies. The serial killer is a god in his fantasies and he becomes addicted to this feeling. Should anything upset him in the course of his daily life, his inferiority complex will be activated and his mental equilibrium disturbed. By acting out his fantasy, he becomes the master once more and equilibrium is restored. However, reality is never as perfect as fantasy and therefore the serial killer repeats the act, in order to get it right.

My theory can be applied to all serial killers. When I read a crime scene, I could pinpoint the suspect's developmental fixation in terms of Freud's theories and I taught this technique to the detectives I trained. My theory was also incorporated into the interrogation strategies I constructed. It is my view that any theory on the development of serial killers should have a practical value as well, so that society can recognise warning signs (be proactive) and so that detectives can identify and apprehend them (be reactive).

I must emphasise that my theory is an explanation for the origin of serial killers; to say that I understand them does not mean that I condone their acts. They should be permanently removed from society.

Pistorius' theory on the development of female serial killers

My theory on the origin of serial homicide, also described in my book *Fatal Females* (2004), postulates that male serial killers do not kill for financial benefit but to gratify a deep subconscious psychological need. Surprisingly, Dr Eric Hickey, a colleague and a professor of criminology at the California State University, has found that the majority of female serial killers are motivated by financial gain.

In his book *Serial Murderers and Their Victims* (2002) Hickey reports that 74 per cent of female serial killers were motivated at least partially by money, and that 27 per cent of them killed purely for money. *Female serial murderers are more likely to kill in response to abuse of various forms, although this motive appears to be less apparent than greed and desire for money.*

Men who commit multiple murders for financial gain are more likely to be classified as assassins or robbers than serial killers. The difference between robbers and assassins on the one hand, and male serial killers on the other, is found in their motives. Assassins and robbers are motivated by greed. They are not urged to kill regardless of financial benefit, as male serial killers are. Is there such a major difference, then, in the motivations of male and female serial killers, since female serial killers *do* kill for money?

I was puzzled by this question, for at first it did not fit the theory that I had previously developed that serial killers kill to gratify a deep subconscious psychological need. Surely money does not present itself as an internal need, but rather as an external gratification. *For some, the needs for economic and psychological wellbeing are virtually the same*, says Hickey. I decided to research the correlation between the economic and psychological needs of women and this time I found the answer in the motivational theory of Abraham Maslow.

Maslow postulated that human behaviour is motivated by a hierarchy of basic needs. Once lower needs are gratified, the organism – or human – will move towards higher needs. A basic need will dominate behaviour if it is thwarted, or when the organism is deprived of it. Once the need is gratified, it releases its domination of the organism.

Maslow identified physiological needs as the lowest level of the hierarchy. These needs encompass hunger, thirst, sleep and sex. If a person is deprived of one of these needs, his or her behaviour will be directed towards gratifying it. Depending upon the intensity of the deprivation, such a person may put the gratification of all other higher needs on hold, in order to satisfy the physiological needs.

In *Motivation and Personality* (1970, 2nd edition) Maslow explains that if a need has been continually satisfied in the past, the organism will be able to cope better with future deprivation:

> ... those individuals in whom a certain need has always been satisfied (who) are best equipped to tolerate deprivation of that need in the future, and that furthermore, those who have been deprived in the past will react differently to current satisfactions than the one who has never been deprived.

Is it possible to say that those individuals who have been deprived of a certain basic need during crucial childhood years will always yearn for gratification of that need, and no matter how much gratification occurs later, it might just never be enough to fill the void? It is possible to say that the infant's basic physiological needs are mostly gratified by the mother or primary caregiver. If one follows Freud's postulation that children are polymorph perverse (in other words, they are sensually stimulated by body parts other than the genitals), one can also include the mother as the gratifier of the infant's sexual needs. The mother is the one who bathes, strokes and caresses the infant. It is quite clear that early deprivation caused consciously or subconsciously by the mother figure may lead to her son developing into a serial killer.

The second stage in Maslow's hierarchy encompasses the safety needs. These include such concepts as security, stability, dependency, protection, freedom from fear, as well as from anxiety and chaos, need for structure, order, law, limits, strength in the protector, etc. It is also possible to say that traditionally the toddler's security needs are gratified by the father figure, who is recognised as the protector. What I am postulating is that early deprivation by the father figure of a girl's security needs may lead to her becoming a serial killer.

Maslow explains that should these security needs not be fulfilled

the organism may equally well be wholly dominated by them. They may serve as the almost exclusive organisers of behaviour, recruiting all the capacities of the organism in their service, and we may then fairly describe the whole organism as a safety-seeking mechanism.
(Maslow, 1970)

If one bears in mind that female serial killers are willing to kill for money – which is a form of security – the following observation by Maslow seems accurate in explaining their behaviour:

> Practically everything looks less important than safety and protection (even sometimes the physiological needs, which, being satisfied, are now underestimated). A man [or woman] in this state, if it is extreme enough and chronic enough, may be characterised as living almost for safety alone.
> (Maslow, 1970)

If one looks at the history of female serial killers it is often found that they have been sexually abused by a father figure, that there was domestic violence or discord between the parents and often the families were nomadic. If a parent treats a child harshly, the child might fear loss of the parent's love and protection. A girl who has been sexually abused by her father faces a double predicament. First, her basic trust in the father as protector has been broken and, secondly, she fears that if she reveals this secret, she will lose his love and protection. It is understandable that such a child will grow up with a thwarted concept of sexual intimacy and a basic deprivation of her security needs. And it is hardly surprising that female serial killers who were sexually abused are promiscuous as well.

> [Her] safety needs often find specific expression in a search for a protector, or a stronger person on whom [s]he may depend ... The neurotic individual may be described with great usefulness as a grown-up person who retains his [her] childhood attitudes towards the world.
> (Maslow, 1970)

Many female serial killers marry affluent men, whom they identify as protectors who have the means to keep them safe and to 'spoil' them as if they were children. Money therefore becomes a substitute for security. However, the woman's childlike behaviour may frustrate the husband's expectations of a wife, and he might begin to express his irritation. This irritation triggers the woman's childhood fear of rejection by the father figure. She fears that her husband may divorce her and she will lose her security, so she kills him in order to inherit his money – and to gratify her need for security. If the woman is promiscuous as well, the husband may threaten to leave her, or he may become an obstacle to her sexual pursuits. Such women have learned to exercise control over men through their own sexuality. Although she may seem childlike and vulnerable, and therefore very attractive to the kind of man who wants to protect her, she is at the same time a skilled manipulator who will use her sexuality to lure men into her traps, and she will do so without remorse. No wonder some of them are called Black Widows.

Maslow calls the third stage in the hierarchy the need for belongingness and love. He explains the effects that deprivation of this need may have on an individual.

> From these we know in a general way the destructive effects on children of moving too often; of disorientation; of the general over-mobility that is forced by industrialisation; of being without roots, or of despising one's roots, one's origins, one's group; of being torn from one's home and family, and friends and neighbours, of being transient or a newcomer rather than a native.

All the serial killers, both male and female, whom I and my colleagues interviewed complained that they had always felt that they would never really 'fit in'. They all felt like outsiders in a group. They did not acquire empathy for others and because of a lack of identification with the father figure, they never developed a conscience. Since they never feel part of a group, they are able to treat their victims with a callous objectivity that shocks the rest of society.

If a girl is abused by her father, she will become his sexual object. Should one be surprised, then, if she treats her subsequent partners as objects, since this was the role model her father had imprinted upon her? Victims are merely objects who gratify the needs of both male and female serial killers. Once victims lose their usefulness, they will be disposed of.

Maslow also points out that an individual who did not receive love is not in a position to give love. These women often confuse love with sex, which is a lower need. When they receive sex from men, they confuse it with love and they are also more inclined to offer sex, believing that they love. A man who accepts the sex for what it is will be punished by the woman for not reciprocating her 'love'.

The fourth stage in Maslow's hierarchy comprises the 'esteem needs'. Maslow described these as follows:

> These are, first, the desire for strength, for achievement, for adequacy, for mastery and competence, for confidence in the face of the world, and for independence and freedom. Second, we have what we may call the desire for reputation or prestige (defining it as respect or esteem from other people), status, fame, glory, dominance, recognition, attention, importance, dignity, or appreciation.
> (Maslow, 1970)

To men, the above needs are satisfied by wealth.

The fifth and last stage in Maslow's hierarchy is the need for self-actualisation.

> It refers to man's desire for self-fulfilment, namely to the tendency for him to become actualised in what he is

142

potentially. This tendency might be phrased as the desire to become more and more what one idiosyncratically is, to become everything that one is capable of becoming. (Maslow, 1970)

Obviously if an individual is thwarted or deprived in any of the previous stages, he or she will not easily reach this level. However, once an individual has reached this level, he or she can tolerate deprivation of lower needs more easily. For instance, a person may voluntarily go on a hunger strike for a cause that will serve greater humankind. People like Nelson Mandela, Mother Teresa and Mahatma Gandhi are examples.

Maslow's theory on the hierarchy of basic needs led me to hypothesise that while wealth represents gratification of one of the higher needs, namely self-esteem, to men, it represents gratification one of the more basic, subconscious needs, namely security, to women. Wealth makes men feel important and successful; wealth makes women feel safe. The need for security is a much more primitive, subconscious motivation for behaviour than the need for self-esteem.

My theory on the psychodynamics underlying the financial profit motivation of female serial killers may be stated as follows:

Although wealth may seem an external gratification to others, female serial killers kill for money to gratify their deep, deprived psychological need for security. In this sense they do not differ from their male counterparts. Both genders kill to gratify a basic, mostly subconscious, deep psychological need. Most male serial killers combine their murderous acts with sexual gratification. This is as basic and primitive a need to them as security is to women. Sex and money might be two vastly different concepts, but subconsciously both are manifestations of basic primitive needs, depending upon the

143

gender. Serial killers differ from other human beings in that the urgency to gratify this unfulfilled basic need is so great they will kill to preserve it, never grasping that it will always remain out of reach. No matter how many insurance policies the female serial killer inherits, the money will never be enough. The void will never be filled.

Thus my theory on the apparent external difference in the motivations of male and female serial killers (sex versus money) postulates that both genders are intrinsically motivated by the urge to gratify a deep subconscious, basic psychological need.

There are, however, other differences between male and female serial killers. As Hickey so aptly states: *To say the woman cannot be a 'true' serial killer unless she acts like a man, is myopic* (Hickey 2003).

One of the more characteristic differences is that female serial killers are 'quiet' killers. They may go undetected for long periods, probably because people are not inclined to associate a woman with such dark deeds. Kelleher and Kelleher in *Murder Most Rare* (1998) examined a hundred female serial killers and found that it took an average of eight years to apprehend them, while the average period for apprehension of a male serial killer was four years.

Another difference is in their choice of victims. Three-quarters of female serial killers do not kill strangers. *When family members were victims, husbands overwhelmingly became the primary target* (Hickey 2002). Hickey found that 80 per cent of female serial killers used poison as their preferred method of killing.

Female serial killers are also less mobile than their male counterparts: ... *female serial killers were classified as predominantly stay-at-home killers who operate carefully and inconspicuously and who may avoid detection for several years* (Hickey 2002). Keeny and Heide in their article 'Gender Differences in Serial Murderers' (*Journal of Interpersonal Violence*, 1994) are of the opinion that because female serial killers are mostly static, linkage blindness (which refers to the difficulty of linking murders committed over a large geographic area) should not occur. They ascribe the reason for slow detection of female serial killers to the failure of law enforcement and other professionals to recognise that a homicide has been committed and to respond appropriately. They add to this the fact that family and friends may be reluctant to confront female killers with their suspicions. They cite the case of Marybeth Trinning, a New York mother who murdered nine of her children but whose husband did nothing to stop her behaviour, suggesting instead that she seek therapy or take steps to prevent further births.

Keeny and Heide also found that female serial killers tend not to do damage to their victims in the way that male serial killers may mutilate, dismember and exhibit overkill in their murders. Female serial killers are less likely to torture their victims. They apparently do not stalk their victims as their male counterparts do, although some are aggressive in procuring victims by actively seeking out boarding house tenants, or they insure and then kill multiple lovers or partners, or solicit prostitution for the purpose of robbery and murder.

Yet it seems that male and female serial killers do have some personality traits in common: *The women tended to be insincere, amoral, impulsive, prone to exercise manipulative charisma and superficial charm, without conscience, and with little insight, because they failed to learn from their mistakes* (Hickey 2002).

Hickey cites Freiberger who, in her 1997 study, stated that the current classifications for male serial killers do not apply to female serial killers. Kelleher and Kelleher (1998) found that the 'organised' versus 'disorganised' classification developed by FBI profilers in the 1980s was inadequate for female serial killers. They devised a different system of classification, dividing female serial killers into two main groups: those who act alone and those who act in partnerships.

Those who act alone were further subdivided into the following categories:

- Black Widows, who systematically kill multiple spouses, partners or other family members
- Angels of Death, who systematically kill people who are in their care for some form of medical attention
- Sexual Predators, who systematically kill others in clear acts of sexual homicide
- Revenge killers, who systematically kill for reasons of hatred or jealousy
- Profit for Crime killers, who systematically kill for profit or in the course of committing another crime

Killers of this type are often mature, careful, deliberate, socially adept, and highly organised. They usually attack victims in their homes or places of work. They tend to favor a specific weapon, like poison, lethal injection or suffocations (Kelleher & Kelleher 1998).

Female serial killers who act in partnerships are subdivided into the following categories:

- Team Killer, who kills or participates in the killing of others in conjunction with at least one other
- Question of sanity: kills in an apparently random manner and is later judged to be insane
- Unexplained: kills for reasons that are totally inexplicable or for unclear motives
- Unsolved: a pattern of unsolved killings that may be attributed to a woman

Killers of this type tend to be younger, aggressive, vicious in their attack, sometimes disorganised, and usually unable to carefully plan. They usually attack victims in diverse locations. They tend to use guns, knives, or torture (Kelleher & Kelleher 1998).

I would like to expand on the two most common categories of female serial killers, namely the *Black Widow* and the *Angel of Death*.

The Black Widows usually start their criminal careers at the age of about twenty-five years, and target spouses, partners, family members, their children, or anyone else with whom they might have formed a personal relationship. They may kill a person who threatens to expose them. Their preferred weapon is usually poison and the main motive is profit from insurance policies and inheritances. Some of them are attractive and some are 'plain Janes' but their sexual prowess far exceeds their physical appearance. They instil trust in their unsuspecting victims and have an uncanny ability to adopt a chameleon-like persona to suit the specific characteristics a male victim might be looking for in his 'ideal woman'. They are often regarded as dutiful wives and doting mothers, although a few might not be able to conceal their promiscuity and those close to them might observe elements of child neglect in their conduct.

Angels of Death generally commence their criminal careers at the age of about twenty-one years. They operate in hospitals, clinics or nursing homes, where the murders may be disguised as medical fatalities and they have the medical knowledge to choose weapons to facilitate this. They also have easy access to life-support equipment. They enjoy the power they have over life and death and might sometimes also benefit from insurance policies they have persuaded their geriatric patients to cede to them.

Some female serial killers manifest with traits of both the Black Widow and the Angel of Death.

Although not mentioned in Kelleher and Kelleher's typologies, I would like to discuss the phenomenon of

Münchhausen by Proxy. This is a psychological term (also called factitious disorder by proxy) to describe a syndrome in which one individual deliberately exaggerates, invents or induces an illness in someone else in order to get attention. The condition was first recognised in 1977. The majority of individuals afflicted with this syndrome are women.

The general characteristics of people affected by the syndrome are as follows:

- They focus on their victims' symptoms and not on their abilities or personalities
- They like dressing up as medical personnel
- They take over the duties of nursing staff and interfere with doctors' diagnoses and prescriptions
- They try to play off medical personnel against one another
- They express doubts about the nursing staff and physicians' capabilities and attempt to blame them or the hospital for the victims' illnesses or deaths
- They read up on the particular illness and are generally very knowledgeable about medical conditions and medication, although they might not have had formal medical training
- They use appropriate medical terminology
- They insist on certain medications, remedies or treatments and become aggressive when medical personnel do not comply with their wishes
- They might consult several doctors at the same time, or 'hop' from one to another
- They are excited when visiting a doctor and dress up as if they are going on a date
- Initially they are subordinate and friendly towards doctors, but become more demanding and aggressive if they meet with resistance
- They manipulate doctors not to trust their own instincts
- They will withhold food, or supplement the victims'

diets with harmful food, to keep them ill
- They take control of every aspect of their victims' lives
- They are narcissistic and crave attention
- Although they may appear well-dressed and in control in public, at home they are unstable and often threaten suicide
- At home they can become verbally and physically abusive towards the patient, although in the hospital they will feign concern
- They have no insight into their own condition and will deny vehemently that they had anything to do with the victims' illnesses or deaths
- They will unburden their emotions upon their children
- They prefer to find employment in a medical environment

The childhood years of these people will indicate probable sexual abuse by the father figure, resulting in sexual manipulation of men as adults, repressed hostility towards authority and father figures, emotional neglect by parents, and they might have had a parent employed in the medical field.

The FBI's *Crime Classification Manual* (1992) classifies them under Hero Homicides:

- The offender does not necessarily plan the murder, but seeks attention by inducing illness in the victim
- As soon as the victim is removed from the offender's care, the victim recovers
- There have been cases where Münchhausen by Proxy correlates with Angel of Death profiles. When they benefit financially from the death of the victims, they may be Black Widows

Cynthia Lyda of Orlando in the United States was an Angel of Death serial killer, who pleaded Münchhausen by Proxy, and so was Bobby Sue Terrel of Illinois. It would be very easy for a calculating female serial killer to study the phenomenon and feign Münchhausen by Proxy in order to kill her victims, and then plead innocent by reason of insanity.

PROFILES OF SERIAL KILLERS

Case study: The Station Strangler

Background information

Between 1986 and 1994 the bodies of twenty-two young boys, all aged between eight and fourteen years, were discovered in Mitchell's Plain, about twenty minutes' drive from central Cape Town. Desolate dunes extend between Mitchell's Plain and the ocean.

The murders happened in two phases. From 1986 to 1992 ten bodies were discovered in the bush near railway stations surrounding Mitchell's Plain, and in 1994 eleven bodies were discovered in the dunes at Mitchell's Plain. On 19 March 1994, the twenty-second body was discovered near a railway station at Kleinvlei, neighbouring Mitchell's Plain.

The Mitchell's Plain community uses trains to commute to work in Cape Town. Since there are not many recreational facilities for children, they find after-school entertainment at cafes where they play on game machines. Large families occupy small houses and the yards are minute, forcing the children to play in the streets. The children are streetwise and most of their mothers are housewives. There are no apartment blocks in the suburb and the houses are closely boxed in on the streets. Poverty, alcoholism, crime and gang activities are rife in the area.

In the 1986 to 1992 phase the bodies were found by vagrants living in the bush. The community became aware that there was a serial killer operating in the area and the media dubbed him the 'Station Strangler' since the boys had gone missing at railway stations and their bodies were found near railway stations.

In the 1994 phase isolated bodies were at first also discovered by vagrants, giving rise to rumours that the Station Strangler had reappeared. During the last weekend of January 1994, virtually the entire community joined the police in a massive search of the dunes, when the rest of the bodies were found. The bodies were not found in the order of their death. The newspapers printed a list of the names of the boys assigning a number to each. Thus a particular name appeared against the number 14, meaning that this was the fourteenth body found. A few days later another body was discovered. There was a note in his pocket which read: 'Station Wrangler, no 14, Many more to score.'

The last boy was discovered by a passer-by who smelled something bad.

During the 1986-1992 cases, there was only one detective investigating all the dockets but he had retired in 1992 without solving the case. In 1994 a task team of twelve detectives was formed to investigate the case, led by Lieutenant Johan Kotze and under the overall command of Colonel Leonard Knipe. The community assisted the team by providing them with the names of possible suspects.

In February 1994 the suspect left a note at a shopping centre across the road from the police station saying that he was not yet finished. The retired detective who had dealt with the first phase of the killings received a phone call from someone who threatened to kill another fourteen boys. The local television station received a call from a person who said that if they re-broadcast a particular news item, he would make it easy for the police to catch him. The news item showed the community walking in the dunes, searching for bodies. Colonel Knipe received a call from a man telling him to get his detectives out of his graveyard. One of the victims had his mother's telephone number in his pocket and after his death she received silent phone calls.

I joined the investigation team in February 1994, on the first day of my appointment to the SAPS, with a rank equivalent to Captain. I was provided with the case dockets and taken to the crime scenes on a motorbike. I worked with the investigation team for two weeks, interrogating suspects, participating in house searches and meeting community leaders. I was a rookie then and the detectives showed me the ropes of the investigation process and I taught them the basics about serial killers. After the second week I compiled the following profile according to the FBI recipe. This profile was my first and, although it proved accurate, it is not as sophisticated as later ones.

Profiling inputs

Crime scene

Two crime scenes series are applicable. The scene of the first series of murders, committed during the 1986-1989 period, is located in the bushes in the area of the Belhar railway station. One body was found at Mnandi beach in 1992. The bodies in the second series of murders (1993-1994) were found in the Weltevredebos area.

Both areas are situated close to Mitchell's Plain, which is a residential area largely inhabited by Coloured people with a population of about 1.5 million. The socio-economic status is mainly impoverished. Extended family boundaries exist, which means a child could be living with its parents, grandparents or other relatives. Crime is rife in the area.

The areas where the bodies in the second series were found are characterised by dense shrubs growing in the sand. There are also dunes. It is possible for a car to enter the area, but one would have to go on foot to the places where the bodies were found. The areas are mostly desolate, although destitute people may frequent the bush.

The bodies were found in shallow graves, some covered only with branches. They were all lying face down; some of the faces were buried in the sand. Sand had been swept from under the faces to form a mound under the buttocks which were therefore raised. Some of the boys' hands were tied behind their backs. Where possible, the cause of death was established as strangulation. The boys' own clothing was used as murder weapons.

In addition to the letter found in one of the boys' pants, a fresh beer bottle was found next to one of the decomposed bodies and a wine bottle containing liquid was found next to another. Although both bodies were badly decomposed, the label on the beer bottle had not yet faded, indicating that it had been left there long after the murder was committed. This indicates that the killer returned to the bodies to drink and relive his fantasy. It is unlikely that any other person would have done so without informing the police of the presence of the body.

A set of dentures, a piece of billiard cue, and a penknife were found next to two of the 1994 victims; their ownership was not established.

Victimology

None of the boys were street children. Although a few were problem children, they all had homes and all attended school.

Forensic information

Most of the bodies were badly decomposed. Sodomy could be established in some of the 1987 cases as well as some of the 1994 cases.

The cause of death was strangulation. It is uncertain if necrophilia was committed. One of the 1994 boys had a fractured skull and one of the 1986 boys had stab wounds in his neck but there were no other signs of mutilation on the bodies. The severed ear of one of the boys could be attributed to animal activity. No semen was found.

Preliminary police report

It is believed that the 1987, 1992 and 1994 murders were committed by one man.

The earlier series of murders remains unsolved. Previous suspects were brought in for questioning again.

The 1994 bodies were discovered by wood cutters. Thousands of uniformed policemen were brought in to search the bush for bodies. The search was filmed by the SABC news service and broadcast on television.

The community has set up a neighbourhood watch and they are also cutting out the bush in one of the areas. (This area happens to be a nature reserve.)

The community is suffering from hysteria and any suspicious-looking character is pursued. Some residents believe that the Strangler is using the sewers that run underneath the area and are searching them for more bodies. The person leading the search is also regarded as a suspect. The community burns motor cars and besieges houses and police stations if they believe the Strangler is there.

Crime rate

Name	Missing	Found	Period between murders
Jonathan Claasen	30-9-1986	3-10-1986	
Yussuf Hofman	29-12-1986	7-1-1987	3 months
Mario Thomas	?	23-1-1987	?
?	?	9-4-1987	±3 months
Freddie Cleaves	25-6-1987	26-6-1987	±2 months
Samuel Nqaba	24-8-1987	25-8-1987	2 months

?	?	1-10-1987	±2 months
Calvin Sapiro	5-2-1988	8-2-1988	±4 months
Denver Ghazu	28-3-1989	11-11-1989	1 year 1 month
Jacobus Louw	23-10-1992	27-10-1992	3 years 7months
?	?	13-1-1994	±2 years 2 months
Jeremy Benjamin	13-12-1993	25-1-1994	
Marcelino Cupido	20-12-1993	27-1-1994	7 days
?	?	27-1-1994	
Elino Sprinkler	5-1-1994	20-1-1994	
Neville Samaai	7-1-1994	27-1-1994	2 days
Fabian Willowmore	10-1-1994	27-1-1994	3 days
Owen Hofmeester	10-1-1994	27-1-1994	Same day
Donovan Schwartz	11-1-1994	25-1-1994	1 day
Jeremy Smit	24-1-1994	26-1-1994	14 days
?	?	27-1-1994	
Elroy van Rooy*	11-3-1994	19-3-1994	2 months

*Elroy van Rooy's particulars were added to the profile during the feedback

Periods when murders ceased:
February 1988 to March 1989: 1 year and 1 month
March 1989 to October 1993: 3 years and 7 months
October 1992 to December 1993: 1 year and 1 month

The victims are easily lured by the offer of money or food or a lift. Victims trust the killer, who controls them easily – which gives rise to the theory that he may be wearing a uniform, or be a social worker, priest or teacher. Two boys were taken on one day – either they were knocked unconscious or the killer had an accomplice, who would have been intimidated by him. The killer leaves no clues; controlled emotional state and criminal sophistication are present.

Decision process models

Homicide type and style: Serial killer
Primary intent of murderer: sexual and power, intrinsic motivation

Victim risk

High-risk victims: boys between eight and fourteen years, picked up at railway stations or game arcades/cafes; boys from poor families, easily lured by money or food; no street children.

The extended family environment means that a boy may inform his mother, with whom he is currently staying, that he wishes to live with his grandmother for a period. The mother will allow the boy to leave for the grandmother's house, without checking whether he arrived safely. It would not be unusual for a boy to be absent from home for a few nights and for his mother to assume that he was visiting friends or relatives. Boys hang out at game arcades, often travel alone by train or sometimes assist taxi owners and ride with them.

Many of the so-called social workers take food to school children. Such a person would immediately have an audience of five hundred children who will know him as the man who brings them food. The following day he need only approach a boy wearing the uniform of the school and the boy will willingly accompany him.

Offender risk

Should the offender be wearing a uniform of some sort, he will not be taking a risk by abducting the boys. It is believed the boys accompany the offender willingly.

During January and February (1994) any man seen with a boy was regarded with suspicion – therefore, lately, the risk will be high. Most of the boys were abducted during the daytime.

The area where they were sodomised and killed is remote. There is little chance that the killer would be surprised while committing the act. He could also have used an accomplice who kept a lookout for him.

Escalation

The murders escalated to one every few days during December 1993 and January 1994. According to police knowledge, the last murder was committed on approximately 24/25 February 1994. Several threats of 'fourteen more to come' have been received.

Previous cooling-off periods (years) may be due to incarceration in prison or a mental institution or the killer may have moved to another area or province, where he may have killed as well.

Quietness since 24 January may be due to the following: the killer has moved out of the area (and could have committed murders elsewhere); the killer is lying low because the investigation is getting too close; it is difficult to find victims and he is waiting for the hysteria to abate before he strikes again.

Time factors

It takes about ten minutes or less to drive to the killing fields. It takes about ten to twenty minutes to walk to the crime scenes.

Only one boy (and possibly the two unidentified boys) was killed after it became public knowledge that a serial killer was on the loose. Therefore none of the victims suspected they were in the presence of a killer. (Unless they were forcefully abducted and then it would have been noticed.) The victims could have walked with the killer to the sites where they were killed.

Since the killing fields are so desolate the killer would be able to spend time with the victim without being seen. He may also have had an accomplice to keep watch for him or to restrain the children.

Location

The victims were lured from railway stations and game arcades during the day. It is therefore apparent that the killer knew he would not be suspected; the children seemed to trust him.

The killer probably drove to the edge of the bush and then walked. There are no indications that the boys were sodomised elsewhere and that the bodies were later dumped. All indications are that they were sodomised and killed at the place where they were found.

Crime assessment

Hypothesis

The killer chooses a victim spontaneously, provided that he falls within the category eight to fourteen years. The victim is usually alone (except for the two friends on one occasion). The killer approaches the boy and lures him with some kind of promise – for example, money or a lift home. The killer and victim get into the killer's car and proceed to the bush. At this stage the killer may either walk with the boy to the site of the murder, or the he may knock the boy unconscious and carry him. The killer undresses the boy or the boy undresses himself. The boy is pushed to the ground. A mound of sand is gathered under the boy's buttocks. The killer ties the boy's hands behind his back with his own clothing and ties the clothing around the boy's neck. He either sodomises the boy first, and then strangles him, or sodomises him while strangling him. The boy's face is pressed into the ground. Sand is pushed up next to the boy's face, burying his face in the sand. Some boys are re-dressed, but their underpants are left next to the body. The killer covers the body with bushes or branches and leaves the scene.

In terms of the 'organised-disorganised' classification of serial killers, this killer is organised. No murder weapon is taken along, but seldom are any clues found – the note, the beer bottle and the wine bottle contained no fingerprints. Since no semen was found, the killer probably uses a condom. He will also use gloves. As far as can be assessed, no souvenirs are taken.

There is a hypothesis that the killer uses an accomplice to restrain the boys, especially in the case where two boys were abducted and killed right next to each other. The clothing of one was used to kill the other.

No excessive force is used to control the victim unless it seems necessary.

The accelerated rate of crimes from December 1993 to January 1994 indicates planning and confidence on the part of the killer. Serial killers may go on this type of spree after a period of incarceration or a precipitating event.

The motivation of the killer is intrinsic. There are no connections between the boys other than race, sex and age. They are not from the same school or church, etc. It is possible, however, that they all remind the killer of the boy he once was. An intrinsic motivation could be that he himself was sodomised and this is his revenge upon the community. Sexual fantasies will also play a role in his motivation.

Regarding crime scene dynamics, it seems that the boys were left in a position such that they would easily be found. The killer went back to one of the bodies and left a note to communicate with the police. He expected the bodies to be found. He is playing his own game, and once the bodies have been found he invites the police to participate in his game. He feels no distaste about touching the bodies – they were re-dressed after the murder. There are no mutilations. The killing field is his own personal domain, which he knows well. The fact that he returned to body Number 14 to leave a note, and returned to drink wine and beer at other crime scenes, indicates that he remembers exactly where he left them. He will resent people disturbing the bodies or trampling over his domain.

He has paedophilic and psychopathic tendencies. He can manipulate and feels no remorse (eg, drinking next to the corpses).

Organised serial killer

- The murders are well planned and show increasing effectiveness – in 1987 the boys' hands were tied next to the body, whilst in 1994 their hands were tied behind their backs
- There are more signs of psychopathy than psychotic signs – no mutilations, no mess at the crime scene
- Victims are selected according to a specific category: Coloured boys between eight and fourteen years and no street children
- The killer talks to the boys to lure them away – there is an element of personalisation present
- The killer uses some ploy to lure the victim. He may be wearing a stolen police uniform
- There is no murder weapon – the boys' own clothing is used to restrain and strangle them. No traces of semen were found – he probably uses a condom
- Bodies were left in a remote area where it was difficult to find them
- A car was probably used to drive to the killing fields
- There is no evidence of necrophilia
- The killer probably lives with others, or his neighbours are often home – it is believed that he did not take the

children first to his home
- The killer probably has middle-class employment; for example, policeman, teacher, priest, social worker, etc – he finds it easy to influence children. He is free during the afternoons, or works shifts
- The phone call to SAPS *radiospoor* after the television news coverage of police searching the killing fields for bodies indicates that the killer watches the television news coverage of the case. Also, a note was placed at the correct body number 14, after the newspapers named the wrong body number 14. This indicates he follows newspaper reports as well. He gets excited about the press coverage

The profile

Age: 25-37	Most serial killers are in the 20-25 age group. The Strangler has been active for a period of nine years, which will put him in an older group.
Race: Coloured	The activities of a white man operating in the Mitchell's Plain area would have been noted. The children would more willingly go with a Coloured man than a white man. He could, however, be a white man who grew up with Coloured people. Serial killings are usually intra-racial.
Language: Afrikaans and English with a Coloured accent	Children will easily trust a man who speaks with the same accent they do. Most of the children speak Afrikaans. The note found on victim Number 14 was written in English.
Residential:	The children were taken direct to the killing fields. The killer did not risk taking them home to sodomise because there could be other people there. It is possible that he lives alone, but that neighbours would notice strange behaviour or sounds.

Employment: Not an office job; he could be unemployed but was previously employed. Could be wearing a uniform. Suggested job: teacher, police-man, fire brigade, security, priest, social worker (children's homes)	The killer was free to move around during the day when he abducted the children. He knows the area where the murders were committed very well and must have had time to move around there. Most 1987 bodies were found near railway stations. He may have been a railway policeman who later joined the police force. He will be in a position to earn money – it is believed the children were lured with money. Suggested employment: people whom the children will trust and who will not arouse suspicion.
Marital status: Probably single	Acts of paedophilia suggest the killer would have difficulty in maintaining a personal relationship with a woman. May have a gay relationship with a man, but not a lasting one.
Appearance: Neat and average	Perfectionistic tendencies: the note of number 14 was placed on the correct body number 14 after the press named the wrong body as the fourteenth victim. Victims are not mutilated and there is no mess at the crime scenes. A neatly dressed person will be able to persuade children to accompany him. No one saw the killer operate – he has the ability to be inconspicuous – his clothing and appearance will not stand out in a crowd. He chooses only schoolboys, who are clean. No street children, who would be dirty. Perfectionism is also indicated by the fact that he leaves no clues.
Intelligence: Average to above average	The murders are organised and planned. There are no signs of degenerating intelligence. The killer is playing a game with the police – he leaves notes and makes phone calls. He must perceive himself as a man who can outwit the police.
Car: Probably not a new expensive model	The hypothesis is that he used a car to drive to the bush. A car could have been used to offer the boys a lift from the railway stations. This may be his own car, or a borrowed one. Several suspicious cars were seen at the crime scenes.

Record of arrest: Possible prison term during 'quiet periods'. Possibly recently released	Psychopathic tendencies may have manifested in theft, burglary, etc. May have had a prison sentence or been institutionalised for sodomy or paedophilia. Serial killers tend to murder after an incubation period during which their fantasies 'brew'. The dramatic rate of murders – 11 boys within a month – indicates that there was probably an incubation period or some precipitating event. The murder of boys is an act of revenge against the community – there could be anger towards the community and the police because of his imprisonment.
Social: A loner; introverted type who prefers the company of children. Interpersonal relationships with adults are not good. May trust one person to confide in or brag to	The killer hangs out at game arcades – where the children are. He feels in control in the company of children. Serial killers work alone, although there are indications that this one might have had an accomplice. The accomplice will be a 'skollie' type – a degenerate – who is manipulated and controlled by the killer. The accomplice may hero-worship the killer and identify so closely with him that he will not give him away. He may also keep quiet because of fear that he will be implicated in the murders. The killer might boast of his deeds. The fact that he has not yet been caught will boost his ego.
Social: Underlying aggression towards father figure or representatives of father figure like the police or community	The hypothesis is that the killer was sodomised by his father or a father figure when he was a boy. There would then always be resentment towards such a figure. Both notes to the police indicate a taunting attitude. The phone call to the previous detective who worked on the 1986-1988 cases also indicates a taunting attitude. He is trying to punish the Mitchell's Plain community by showing them how helpless their boys feel – just as helpless as he felt when he was sodomised and no one helped him.
Emotional: Controlled emotions but there is an underlying rage	So far the killer has made no mistakes by which he could have been caught out. His emotions are controlled and he might even

	be in a position to distance himself from the crimes. He shows no remorse. Strangulation is particularly sadistic because the victim dies a slow death. The killer can tighten and loosen the ligature and watch the victim fade in and out of consciousness. He uses only enough violence to control the victim. Only one boy had a fractured skull. He is not out of control. The killer might experience an emotional high because of the media attention he is receiving – therefore he might boast.
Sexual: Inadequate sexual relationship with a woman, possible homosexual tendencies	A man with a normal sex life would not have to relieve his urges by sodomising and killing children. He could have tried to relieve these urges in a homosexual relationship, but the fact that he killed these children recently shows that the relationship did not fulfil his needs.
Sexual: fantasies	Serial killers have fantasies, which are acted out in real life.
Sexual: Hatred for boys	The killer hates boys who remind him of himself when he was a victim. By sodomising and killing them he is conquering his own fears. He is establishing to himself that he is no longer the victim – the boys are now the victims – and he is the one in control of the situation, like the father figure was in control.
Pathological behaviour: There seem to be more psychopathic tendencies than psychotic tendencies	This serial killer is organised, he plans the murders, leaves no clues and does not mutilate the victims. Taunting the police indicates a psychopathic nature. He is manipulative; he managed to lure the boys. He is not subtle and leaves his victims in the position that he wants them to be found.
Post-offence behaviour: Communications with the police.	The killer might want to be caught. To him this is a game he is playing with the police. It is no longer a private fantasy he is acting out. By communicating with the police he has opened his game to other players, provided they play

according to his rules. He left a note with one of the victims. A fresh beer bottle with no fingerprints and a wine bottle were found next to two decomposed corpses, which indicates that he returns to the crime scenes. He might have a mental map or an actual map of where the bodies are and which number is in which place. Someone phoned the first detective who worked on the case (who has an unlisted number) and threatened to kill fourteen more boys and to leave the next body on his doorstep. (This former detective now works at a bottle store.) The message on both notes found – the one on the victim and another received during February – also promises fourteen more bodies. *Radiospoor* received a telephone call from a man asking that the SABC news clip be re-broadcast, after which he would make it easy for the police to find him. The man has access to television. It is believed he may wear a police uniform or at some stage was physically present during police investigations. All people offering help are viewed as suspects. A telephone call was made to Colonel Knipe telling him to 'get your fucking detectives out of my graveyard'. One of the victims had his mother's telephone number in his pocket. This mother has received silent phone calls. A second mother has also received silent phone calls.

The following profile was released to the press:

The Strangler is probably a Coloured man between the ages of 25 and 37. He is bilingual. We believe he is single, although he could be divorced. The Strangler probably lives with other people, or he might rent a room. If he lives alone, his neighbours will easily be able to monitor his movements.

The Strangler is an intelligent man who dresses neatly. He may be the sort of person who prefers to wear a tie. His appearance will not attract any attention. If he is employed at the moment, we believe he has a middle-class job like a policeman, a teacher, a priest, or he works for some charity organisation. He might also be pretending to be in one of these jobs. He is free to move around during the afternoons and might frequent game parlours or railway stations, where he hunts for his victims.

We believe he uses a car, which may be his own or one that he borrows.

The Strangler could have a previous record of arrest for sodomy of boys, theft or burglary. He may have been in prison. The periods that he was either in prison or an institution or moved away from Mitchell's Plain are the following:

February 1988 to March 1989

April 1989 to October 1992

October 1992 to December 1993

The Strangler is a loner, who prefers to keep to himself. He prefers to talk to children rather than to adults. He has an underlying aggression towards any authority figure, which will not manifest directly. He might make use of an accomplice, who will be intimidated by him. The accomplice might not be aware that this man is the Strangler, or the accomplice may be afraid that he will be implicated if he comes forward with information. He might boast to someone that he is the Strangler, or that he has done things no one knows about, or that he knows more about the case than the police.

Emotionally, the Strangler exercises tight control. He may have acted strangely during the period 13 December 1993 to 25 January 1994. He may be able to distance himself from the killings and he shows no remorse.

He enjoys the media attention and might videotape news flashes or keep a scrapbook of newspaper cuttings.

The Strangler will have an inadequate sexual relationship with either an adult male or female. He was probably sodomised by a father figure when he was a boy and the victims remind him of this traumatic experience. He is punishing the community because he felt helpless when he was sodomised and no one helped him.

The Strangler will not stop until he is apprehended or until he gives himself up. He is playing a cat-and-mouse-game with the police.

The public is requested to come forward with information regarding anyone who fits this profile. Any person who fits the profile and suddenly changes his behaviour – for example, dresses differently – should be regarded as suspect. The public is urgently requested to bring any information to the caravans at the Mitchell's Plain Police Station and not to take the law into their own hands under any circumstances.

A substantial reward is offered for any information that might lead to an arrest and conviction.

Outcome

The profile was released to the media on 25 February 1994. We were inundated with calls and eventually processed in the region of two thousand suspects.

On 19 March 1994 we discovered the body of Elroy van Rooy, a child abducted in the neighbouring Strand, in the vicinity of the Kleinvlei Station. Mrs Fouzia Hercules, a friend of the Van Rooy family, noticed the man walking with Elroy and his cousin and she reported this to the police when she heard that Elroy had gone missing. Ryno van Rooy, the cousin who accompanied Elroy and the Strangler to the station, but then left, came forward as well. Both of them drew up identikits, which were released to the press. A nurse at a private mental institution thought the identikit looked like a patient and he seemed to fit the profile. She phoned the detectives. The suspect, Norman Simons, was kept under surveillance for a day or two and finally arrested on 13 April 1994.

Norman Avzal Simons was a twenty-seven-year-old Coloured man and a primary school teacher. He dressed neatly. Earlier on the day he abducted Elroy he joined the police reservists to help with the Strangler investigation. He hoped to get a uniform. He was a homosexual who lived with his mother and sister in a house in Mitchell's Plain. He owned a car. He spoke seven languages, including Afrikaans, English, Xhosa and French. He was very intelligent and played classical music on the piano. He had no previous arrests and worked as a volunteer at NICRO, an institution that assists rehabilitated criminals to re-enter society. He was a loner and an introvert with no long-lasting relationships. He preferred the company of children whom he often took swimming at the beach or bought ice-cream. He was sodomised by his older brother between the ages of eight and fourteen. He was diagnosed with borderline personality disorder, which incorporates psychopathic tendencies. At a much later stage a friend came forward and admitted that he had helped Simons lure the children and that he had seen the two boys in Simons' car. This accomplice was killed in a gang fight shortly before the trial commenced. Simons had boasted to his sister that he had killed the boys. He hid away at the clinic before and after the murders, reasoning that this would be a plausible alibi. During the periods when there were no murders, he was studying and he described these as the happiest times of his life. His boyfriend had rejected him, which was the precipitating event just before the December 1993 to January 1994 murder spree.

I made a crucial mistake in the profile by not recognising the signs of undoing on the crime scenes; the profile also provided too many options. At that stage I had been working for the police for only fourteen days and had not yet been trained by the ex-FBI profilers. Having been thrown in at the deep end, I used the theoretical knowledge I had acquired during my research on serial killers, I learned about crime scenes from the detectives on the job, and I trusted my gut instincts. The profile was accurate enough for the nurse at the psychiatric clinic to recognise the suspect.

I was not allowed to participate in the interrogation. Simons confessed to killing the boys, and blamed his brother's spirit living inside him for the murders. He pointed out the crime scenes. He was only charged with the abduction and murder of Elroy, because of lack of evidence in the other cases. He was found guilty on both charges and sentenced to ten years for abduction and twenty-five years for murder. He appealed and his sentence was changed to life imprisonment. The death penalty was abolished just before his trial ended. No similar murders occurred after his arrest.

I spoke to him shortly after his arrest, when he was being taken to Valkenberg Psychiatric Hospital for an interview with Dr Toviah Zabow. Simons and I sat alone in the car for a while. We did not talk about the murders, but rather about his love for classical music, his love for his pupils, and his wish to visit Denmark. When one of the detectives joined us in the car, we switched to French. I also spoke to him in French during the trial. Our conversations were about general issues. I visited him once in prison shortly after his conviction, but he said that he was too upset to talk to me. Then he unexpectedly gave me a hug. He wrote to me from prison for a while. I never wrote back.

Psychoanalytical profile

Simons was one of the case studies I included in my doctoral thesis, *A psychoanalytical approach to serial killers* (1996, DPhil Psychology, University of Pretoria). This analysis of his development and explanation of his motivation was not included in my profile, as I had not completed it at the time of drawing up the profile, but I explained the basics of it to the investigation team. I would like to expand on the psychodynamics of Simons' personality as an example for profilers who may wish to apply Freud's theories. Since all the resources I refer to were public documents during the trial, confidentiality is no longer an issue.

Personal background of the subject

Norman Avzal Simons was born in Cape Town on 12 January 1967 to a Coloured mother and a Xhosa father. He never knew his biological father and only met his stepfather in 1982. Simons had an older sister and later acquired an older stepbrother and an older stepsister. His mother was a domestic worker and his stepfather a driver. His older stepbrother was a Rastafarian and an alcoholic and was murdered in 1991.

Simons led a nomadic life as a child. At a pre-school age he was sent to live at his aunt's home in Queenstown and adopted a Xhosa lifestyle. At the age of five he started primary school in Queenstown. He failed grade nine and at the age of fifteen he returned to his mother's home in the Cape, where he continued his schooling. He had to adapt to a Coloured lifestyle while living with his mother. He failed grade 12 in 1987. He was a volunteer teacher from 1986 to 1988 and attended a teachers' college from 1989 to 1992. In 1992 he was appointed as a teacher at Alpine Primary School in Mitchell's Plain. Simons sometimes lived at his mother's home, sometimes at a friend's home and sometimes he boarded at children's homes.

He was a Christian, but converted to Islam in 1993 (when he took on the name Avzal) and converted back to Christianity in 1994.

He spoke seven languages, played classical music on the piano and was a volunteer at NICRO, an organisation which assists rehabilitated criminals to re-enter society.

He was recognised as a community leader and was loved by his pupils to whom he often gave sweets.

He was admitted to Groote Schuur hospital, Valkenberg psychiatric hospital and Kenilworth psychiatric clinic at intervals between 1991 and 1994. The diagnoses varied between several personality disorders and depression.

Psychosexual development phases

Oral phase (0-2 years): Medical records state that there were no problems during his birth and that he was breastfed for eleven months. He was a healthy baby although quiet, and reached all the usual milestones at normal ages.

Anal phase (2-4 years): No information is available about this phase, but the deduction can be made that potty training was managed by a surrogate mother figure since he was not living with his mother at this time. There are no references to any complications during this phase in his medical records.

Oedipus phase (4-6 years): No information is available on this phase.

Latency phase (6-12 years): Medical records state that he remembered not having any friends at primary school. He received sex education during grade 1.

Genital phase (teens): According to medical records he alleged that he had many friends. He did not participate in sport, but achieved B-average grades. He 'discovered' masturbation at age fourteen to fifteen and described it as a 'funny' experience. The records state that he recalled feeling guilty about it and that it felt like 'killing somebody'.

The oral, anal and Oedipus phases are collectively regarded as the pre-genital phases and I will discuss them before elaborating on the latency and genital phases.

Being sent away from his birth mother constituted an object-related rejection in Simons' fragile emerging ego during the oral and anal phases. The 'good mother' made way for the 'bad mother'. He said he had encountered a witch within his traditional rural Xhosa upbringing, whom he believed cast a spell on him. The family he lived with was financially deprived and the home was overcrowded. His later perfectionism points to a fixation (a psychological short circuit) during the anal phase. The fact that he returned to the correct victim number 14 to alert the police of its correct order, and the fact that his crime scenes were so neat, point to obsessive-compulsive neurosis, which would have arisen during the anal phase.

Being moved from one town to another will have resulted in instability and caused a feeling of 'not belonging'. Simons was an outsider from the beginning. Although not strongly formed, Simons still had a superego. This means there must a been some good father figure with whom he identified during the Oedipus phase. The father figure is also represented by the community and as an adult Simons immersed himself in community work. His superego thrived in the company of the detectives, whom he regarded as 'good fathers' and it was to them that he confessed.

During the latency phase a child's sexual urges are repressed and he needs to socialise with others to learn empathy. Simons had no friends in primary school and did not develop empathy, which meant that he was able to treat his victims as objects. Furthermore, he had been subjected to severe sexual abuse in a phase where sex is naturally taboo to children. Simons described the first of these incidents in his own words:

> My brother and his girlfriend were drunk. The problem was that we were sharing a bottom room of the maisonette. They had sex and I got an erection. I closed my eyes with that erection or movement from the opposite bed. I was

fast asleep when suddenly somebody's hands were around my body. My big brother was busy sodomising me. He told me not to tell anybody about the happening. At once, during penetration, I told him to stop because I was hurt. I cut him off. He innocently went to sleep without a guilty conscience ...

He told the detectives that his brother had tied him up on the occasions when he was raped.

Like all children, Simon must have developed sexual and aggressive fantasies during his pre-genital years. His superego was too weak to repress or sublimate these fantasies and he was therefore able to act them out as an adult.

By the time Simons reached the genital phase, he had all the psychosexual developmental attributes of a serial killer in the making. He was a rejected outsider, unable to empathise and he had been sexually abused. A child's ego will repeat a trauma in order to master it. The child, a passive victim, will identify with the active aggressor when he repeats the act, in order to master it. In Simons' case, the passive-active role reversal was taken a step further. Eros and Thanatos, the life and death instincts, became dangerously intertwined. Simons did to his victims what had been done to him. They *became* him and in a sense he was committing psychological suicide every time he murdered one of them. To preserve his sanity and authority, his Eros, he had to become the aggressor, releasing Thanatos, the death instinct, upon the victims who represented him. He became his brother, as is evident in his transference of blame for the crimes.

Id, ego and superego development

As explained earlier, a serial killer has a dominating id, a very weak ego and virtually no superego to inhibit his murderous impulses.

Simons blamed sexual abuse by his older brother when he was between the ages of eight to fourteen as well as an 'amafufunyana' or 'bad mother witch' who influenced his pre-school life, for the murders.

Explanation of Simons' id: Unacceptable impulses from the id are denied recognition by the ego. In psychological terms, this is called repression. Since they arise from the subconscious, they seem alien and intelligent ego-dystonic serial killers will often attribute them to external forces or possession. (Ego-syntonic serial killers identify themselves with the killings and usually have no trace of a superego or conscience, while ego-dystonic serial killers dissociate from the murders because of a faint trace of superego/conscience. Yet the superego is not strong enough to curtail the id's impulses.) Simons called these id impulses the 'spirits' inside him and made several references to them in his confessions and other communications with the police.

Explanation of Simons' ego: The incorporation of the 'bad mother object' would have severely retarded the development of the ego at an early age. Simons suffered from severe identity crises. He was born a Coloured, grew up with his extended Xhosa family and Xhosa traditions and then had to revert back to a Coloured culture. He had a religious crisis, being first a Christian, converting to Islam and then back to Christianity. He had a sexual identity crisis in having to admit that he was gay. All these identity crises would weaken the ego.

Explanation of Simons' superego: Simons had himself admitted to a psychiatric clinic for the first time when he was twenty-four years old, after he had already killed nine children during the previous six years. This indicates a struggling superego crying for help. However, the id continued to dominate and the later admissions to clinics were an attempt to avoid detection. It is clear from this that his beleaguered and depleted superego struggled for domination over the murderous id impulses and the weak ego. Excerpts from letters he wrote provide an insight into the way his fledgling superego progressively gained temporary ground over the dominating id.

Voices, my brother's voices, Kill because I kill you. Me emotionally ... Brother did it. Brother is whispering to me ... It is a power. It is not me. We walked until the end. Free at last. Free at last it is finished. Life has conquered over death ... The voice said to be strong, be strong. I could not resist it. I spoke to brother in quiet times. Told him he was destroying my future. The theme I chose is peace with myself, the church, no peace brother is too strong. I haven't done it. The spirit of the evil is within me. Let this moment pass me by. Evil spirit still remains. Evil spirit remains with my people. The forces talked. I am sometimes boss. Brother is dead. He remains within. The spirit had opened in me. Satan in me.

At the end of the second letter he admits to himself that he is capable of doing wrong, which shows that the superego is gaining dominance over the id:

At a stage the urge/voices/spirits came up to me to walk to Johannesburg for killings. I stopped the journey that wasn't even started. If I may describe these feelings, they were: at times audible (can hear), talking inside my belly/stomach and ears, destroying, gave me hell, no joy, had no feelings as such. At the scenes the spirits/persons within are strong to commit these deeds. They are very dominating and serious. I can always have the whole world at other times ... I could never give utterance to these forces/feelings ... According to what I am commanded, I'll speak to the kids. The innocent kids would listen to me and carry out the instructions. At times it seemed that these forces were carried over to the kids in order for them to listen. My personality then changes and I'm now capable of doing the wrong.

In the third letter the superego has grown very strong, as a result of his identifying with the detectives as positive father figures:

Help is there. Why did I not previously seek help? While I am writing these pages I am going through emotional turmoil, but I will keep at it. It is an internal struggle and I am not going to fight it alone. I am giving utterance to my feelings in this prison cell where I am today. The true Avzal Norman will never live on. No more bending to any forces, help is at hand. After eight years of emotional wandering, I feel today, 1994-04-17 at 20h40 very relieved. The truth must come out ... FORGIVE ME IF I CAN'T SPEAK FOR MYSELF, FORGIVE ME FAMILIES, FRIENDS AND SOUTH AFRICA. I'M DOOMED.

During the pointing out of the crime scenes Simons made a confession in which it was clear how the superego had gained prominence and domination over the id. No further reference was made to the 'spirits', and he took responsibility, as illustrated by his use of the word 'I'. [The confession may not be reproduced here due to a pending court case.]

Simons later admitted that he never really heard voices in the way that schizophrenics would. During his awaiting trial period, his lawyer refused the detectives access to him. This period of incubation without the presence of the superego 'father figures' (the detectives) was enough for the id to regain dominance over the superego once more. He did not have access to victims and therefore had no outlet for his brooding fantasies. It came as no surprise to me that when he came to trial, he pleaded not guilty. The id had triumphed over the fledgling superego.

Ten years later Simons is to face charges relating to other victims. He still claims his innocence.

The psychological insight into Simons' development should be understood as an explanation for his actions. It is in no way a condonation.

Case study: The Phoenix Serial Killer

I have included this case study to demonstrate how my skills as a profiler had developed since drawing up my first profile during the Station Strangler investigation. The cases were three years apart, during which time I had been involved in eight other serial homicide investigations and I had received some formal training from ex-FBI profilers. Gaining hands-on experience is essential for a profiler.

Background information

Phoenix is a suburb of Durban, one of South Africa's major port cities. It encompasses major sugar cane fields sprawling over the hills, and is bordered by formal residential neighbourhoods as well as informal settlements of corrugated iron and cardboard shacks. One of the informal settlements overlooking the rolling green cane fields is KwaMashu.

At harvesting time the cane fields are burnt. During February, April and May 1997 labourers burning the fields were horrified to come across the bodies of three decomposed, burnt women. The cases were assigned to different detectives at the Phoenix police station. Four more burnt bodies were discovered during June and when another was found in July, the Phoenix police realised they had a serial killer on their hands. They called Superintendent Philip Veldhuizen, second in command at the Durban Murder and Robbery Unit. He had completed both my courses on the investigation of serial homicide. As a matter of fact, one of his officers, Superintendent Allan Alford, had completed the course just a week earlier. They contacted me.

I arrived at their unit on 14 July 1997, bringing my colleague, Inspector Elmarie Myburgh, with me. Elmarie had recently been transferred to my unit and I wanted her to gain experience. I was impressed by the fact that Veldhuizen had already set up an operations room and appointed an investigation team. Two members of Phoenix Detective Services were included in the team, as was Sergeant Bushy Rambadhursing, who had attended my course a few years earlier. Veldhuizen had collected all the dockets and asked for all other dockets of rapes or murders in the area to be forwarded to him. There were three additional murders, committed in June 1994, July 1995 and August 1995.

We went at once to the mortuary to attend the autopsy of body number ten and the following day we visited the crime scenes. I commenced the profile, but my work was interrupted for a week when I had to return to Johannesburg for the Wemmer Pan serial killer investigation being conducted by Captain Piet Byleveld of the Brixton Murder and Robbery Unit. During my absence Veldhuizen and his team had sent the police dogs into the cane fields and eight more bodies were found within two days. Because the dogs found the bodies before the fields were burnt, we had more evidence. One victim's sister came forward and gave a description of the killer, as she had seen him when he accompanied her sister into the cane fields.

I handed the Wemmer Pan case over to Elmarie and returned to Durban on 28 July to complete the profile.

Profiling inputs
Crime scenes

Crime scenes are discussed in the order that they were

found, and not in the order in which the victims were killed. The crime scene of Victim 1 was pointed out by the victim who had survived the same attack. Victims 2 to 11 were mostly found by cane cutters. Victims 12 to 18 were found on 23 and 24 July 1997 by the police dog unit.

Victim 1: Gabisile Buthelezi: 12 years
Murdered: 23 June 1994   Found: 23 June 1994
Last seen: 23 June 1994
Crime scene: sugar cane plantation: field 271
The victim was found lying on her stomach. Her hands were tied behind her back with a rope and her feet were tied with a piece of torn shirt. She was strangled with a rope and a scarf. She had been raped.

The suspect lured the two young girls into the cane fields where he assaulted them. He tied up one of the girls and then tied up, raped and strangled Gabisile. Then he untied the first girl, raped her, tied her up again and strangled her. She did not die and managed to escape after the suspect had left. Her statement has been retaken.

Victim 2: Unidentified: approximately 25 years
Murdered: 30 July 1995   Found: 2 August 1995
Last seen: Unknown
Crime scene: sugar cane plantation: field 431
The suspect assaulted the victim on the head with a blunt object. There were five wounds to the forehead and her skull was fractured. She died from her head wounds. He undressed her and posed her body so that she was crouching on her knees with her buttocks raised. She was still wearing her panties. He committed *ukuzoma* (a Zulu custom of penetrating between the thighs instead of the vagina. This is done to preserve virginity and to avoid pregnancy and contracting diseases). The suspect strangled her with his hands while committing *ukuzoma*.

No clothing or jewellery were found at the scene.

Victim 3: Unidentified: approximately 25 to 30 years
Murdered: 19/20 August 1995 Found: 21 August 1995
Last seen: Unknown
Crime Scene: sugar cane plantation: field 241
The victim was found naked, lying on her stomach on an opened-out cardboard box. Another opened cardboard box had been placed over her body and covered with sugar cane leaves.

The suspect assaulted the victim on the right side of her face with a blunt object. He probably also committed *ukuzoma* while manually strangling her. There was a wound on the right side of her stomach running towards her back, probably inflicted when he cut her clothing off with a knife.

The fact that the victim was covered indicates feelings of guilt. He probably knew her. Her clothing was found scattered in the cane fields, but the panties were missing.

Victim 4: Unidentified
Murdered: Unknown   Found: 17 February 1997
Last seen: Unknown
Crime scene: sugar cane plantation: field 301
The victim was found lying on her stomach. Her hands were tied behind her back with a piece of cloth and her feet were tied with a piece of green cloth. She was wearing a dress. Her shoes and jewellery were missing. As there are no photographs available, it is difficult to reconstruct this crime scene. The body was badly decomposed, so no smears were taken.

Victim 5: Unidentified: approximately 25 years
Murdered: Unknown   Found: 30 April 1997
Last seen: Unknown

Crime scene: sugar cane plantation: field 431
The victim was lying on her right side. Her blouse was pushed up and she was wearing a pink bra. She was strangled with her panties, which had been torn or cut. She was not bound and was probably unconscious when he committed *ukuzoma*. Her skirt and shoes were missing. The body was badly decomposed and no smears were taken.

Victim 6: Unidentified
Murdered: Unknown   Found: 27 May 1997
Last seen: Unknown
Crime scene: sugar cane plantation: field 673
The victim was lying on her back and her hands were tied in front with a piece of cloth. She was wearing black panties and a blouse. Her feet were tied with the same cloth as her hands. Her handbag and shoes were placed next to her body. There were skeletal remains only and therefore no smears were taken.

Victim 7: Unidentified
Murdered: Unknown   Found: 4 June 1997
Last seen: Unknown
Crime scene: sugar cane plantation: field 243
The body was close to the main dirt road running through the cane fields. Only charred remains were found since the field was burnt the day before the body was found. It seemed as if the victim was lying on her stomach with her hands tied behind her back. Her tackies were found on the scene.

Victim 8: Unidentified
Murdered: Unknown   Found: 9 June 1997
Last seen : Unknown
Crime scene: sugar cane plantation: field 673

The victim was lying on her stomach and her hands were tied behind her back. Her feet were not tied. She had been gagged and strangled with cloth. Her upper torso had been pressed between two cane stems, probably to restrict her movement. A jersey and blouse covered one arm. The body was badly burnt.

Victim 9: Unidentified
Murdered: Unknown   Found: 18 June 1997
Last seen: Unknown
Crime scene: sugar cane plantation: field 671
The victim was found lying on her stomach. Her hands were tied behind her back with strips of canvas cut from a sack and her feet were tied with the same material. The gag around her mouth and neck was made from her bra and T-shirt. She was still wearing her dress.

The suspect probably knocked the victim unconscious, ripped her dress open in the front, cut her bra off and then plaited the bra and strips of T-shirt into a gag. Her panties had first been pushed into her mouth. He committed *ukuzoma* while strangling her. Her legs were bound tightly together to facilitate *ukuzoma*. The body was badly decomposed.

Victim 10: Hlengwe Theresa Mfeka: 24 years
Murdered: Unknown   Found: 20 June 1997
Last seen: 14 April 1997
Crime scene: sugar cane plantation: field 671
The victim was lying on her stomach. Her hands were tied behind her back with strips of petticoat. Her feet were also tied with strips of petticoat. The torso was squeezed between two stalks. Again the suspect had plaited an intricate gag and wrapped it around her face and neck. He committed *ukuzoma*. The victim was wearing only panties. Her clothing and shoes were missing from the scene. The body was badly decomposed.

Victim 11: Unidentified
Murdered: Unknown   Found: 12 July 1997
Last seen: Unknown
Crime scene: sugar cane plantation: field 462
The victim was naked and was lying on her back. Her hands were tied behind her back with plastic hessian strips. Her feet were tied with strips cut from her bra. The suspect had plaited the intricate gag from her panties and bra. He committed *ukuzoma* while strangling her. Her legs were bound closely together to facilitate *ukuzoma*. Her shoes were found twenty centimetres from her feet. Head wounds indicated that the victim had probably been knocked unconscious. The rest of her clothing was missing from the scene. The body was badly decomposed.

Victim 12: Unidentified
Murdered: Unknown   Found: 24 July 1997
Last seen: Unknown
Crime scene: sugar cane plantation: field 461
The victim was lying on her back. Her hands were tied in front of her with a piece of petticoat and were also tied to her left thigh. She was strangled with the same type of cloth. A ball of material made from a piece of petticoat had been forced into her mouth. Her feet were tied with a strip of her dress and her panties. She was wearing a polka dot dress and the front buttons had been undone. In her right ear was a sleeper earring and a gold stud with a blue stone. The second sleeper was found under her head, but no second stud with a blue stone was found. Her shoes were missing. The body was badly decomposed.

Victim 13: Banothile Nompumelelo Dube
Murdered: Unknown   Found: 23 July 1997
Last seen: 7 July 1997
Crime scene: sugar cane plantation: field 461

The victim was lying on her right side on top of a floral skirt. She was wearing a dark jersey. Her panties had been ripped, with one piece remaining on her right buttocks. Her buttocks were exposed and her knees drawn up. Her hands were tied in front of her with a rope and her feet were tied with the same rope. There was a ball of material in her mouth, probably made from victim number 15's petticoat. *Ukuzoma* must have taken place from the rear as with the previous victims. Two blue Kembruck sandals were found at the scene.

Victim 14: Nokuthula Zothile Cele: 29 years
Murdered: Unknown   Found: 24 July 1997
Last seen: 2 July 1997
Crime scene: sugar cane plantation: field 461
The victim was found lying on her back. She was wearing only her bra. Her panties were torn and were around her right ankle. She was lying on top of a pink overall coat and her petticoat. Her slip-on sandals were found at the scene. She had been gagged and strangled with a cloth, which appeared to be made of strips of petticoat which did not belong to her. Her hands were not bound. Her body was badly decomposed.

Victim 15: Unidentified
Murdered: Unknown   Found: 24 July 1997
Last seen: Unknown
Crime scene: sugar cane plantation: field 434
The victim was wearing a blue and white dress and a blue and white striped jacket and a petticoat and she was lying on her stomach. Her legs were tied with strips of bra and floral material (which matched the floral material of victim 14). Her legs were pressed between two cane stems. Her hands were tied above her head, in front, with the floral material and a piece of bra. She had been gagged with the

floral material and a piece of bra, which was also wrapped around her neck and tied in a knot on top of her head. There was no ball of material in her mouth. Her buttocks were raised, but covered by her skirt. An extra pair of panties, which had been cut, was lying next to her. Her shoes were found on the crime scene, and a muti bottle, a blue plastic bag containing a wash cloth, a rosary, a purse and a newspaper was found next to the body. He had lifted up her shirt to cut off her bra. A pair of black panties and a handkerchief were found in the left pocket of her jacket. It seems as if both pairs of panties belonged to her. The body was badly decomposed.

Victim 16: Unidentified
Murdered: Unknown   Found: 24 July 1997
Last seen: Unknown
Crime scene: sugar cane plantation: field 434
The victim was lying on her right side. Her blue gown was pressed up to expose her breasts and she was lying on her bra. She was wearing a petticoat, but it had been disturbed. Her red shirt was low down on her torso, but unbuttoned and pulled to the right. A purple skirt was lying near her head. Her hands were not tied. Her feet were tied with a strip of her panties and part of a scarf. Part of the scarf also covered her face. A black beret was lying next to her face and her empty handbag was placed over her face. A muti bottle and a green, yellow and white muti string were found on the scene. The victim was wearing an earring. A yellow plastic bag, a transparent plastic bag and a blue plastic bag were found on the scene as well as a cigarette butt, a shoulder pad from the red shirt, strips of panties and a white cloth with a possible semen stain. Chewed sugar cane was also found on the scene. Blood was leaking from the vagina and the anus was exposed, but covered with the gown. The body was blistered.

Victim 17: Staff Pumzille Gumede: 21 years
Murdered: Unknown   Found: 23 July 1997
Last seen: 16 July 1997
Crime scene: sugar cane plantation: field 434
The victim was lying on her stomach. She was wearing a pink sleeveless top and a grey skirt with a black belt. A pair of peach-coloured panties was lying on her head. Her beige bra was intact. Her sandals were found on the scene. A black purse was lying next to her neck, the contents of which led to her identification. Her hands were tied behind her back with strips of petticoat. She had also been strangled and gagged with strips of petticoat and a ball made of petticoat fabric was pressed into her mouth. More strips were lying next to the victim. Her feet were not bound. A small mirror had been smashed on her head and splinters were lying beneath her face. Two small balls of tissue or toilet paper were lying behind her and a further two pieces were lying next to the mirror. It seemed as if one of her eyes had been gouged out.

Victim 18: Unidentified
Murdered: 20/21 July 1997   Found: 24 July 1997
Last Seen: Unknown
Crime scene: sugar cane plantation: field 434
The victim was lying on her right side with her knees pulled up. She was wearing only her petticoat. Her hands were tied in front with a piece of black scarf. Her feet were also tied with the scarf material. Her hands and feet were then tied together. A pair of blue panties was lying on top of her body. She had been strangled with a piece of her black bra. The killer had fashioned the cup of her bra into a small ball, presumably to place in her mouth, but he did not use it. The rest of the scarf and her red slip-ons were lying next to the body. A face cloth covered with a shiny liquid was found at the scene.

Victimology

The victims in case 1 were two girls aged eleven and twelve. One escaped. Victim 9 was about sixteen years old. The rest of the victims were black women between the ages of twenty and thirty years. It appeared that some of the women were on their way to cut cane in the fields when they were approached by the suspect. Some witnesses' statements also indicate that the suspect offered the victims employment.

(Photographs and descriptions of each crime scene completed the victimology report, which I cannot reproduce here.)

Forensic information

Cause of death

The cause of death in most cases was ligature strangulation using underwear, rope or clothing. Victim 2 died as a result of head injuries. Victim 3 was strangled manually. Some of the bodies were burnt and the cause of death could not be established.

Wounds

Post-mortem reports indicated head wounds in most of the cases. Victim 3 had a cut mark running from her stomach to her back. This was probably caused when the killer cut her clothing from her body. Victim 17's eye appeared to have been injured.

Pre- and post-mortem sexual acts

The victims in case 1 were vaginally raped. It seems as if in the other cases the suspect committed *ukuzoma* – a Zulu practice which is described on page 179. The suspect prefers to commit *ukuzoma* from the back, often binding the legs so tightly that the thighs touch each other. He is trying to avoid picking up a disease and probably also to avoid leaving semen in the vagina, which he knows can be traced.

Post-mortem reports

Most of the post-mortem reports indicate that the bodies were in a state of decomposition or burnt.

Preliminary police report

Background information

All the bodies were found on Cornubia Estates, which is the name of a Huletts Tongaat sugar plantation in Phoenix. The plantation consists of 1200 square hectares of cultivated sugar cane fields. It is bordered by KwaMashu, an informal settlement; Phoenix, a predominantly Asian suburb; Glen Anil, a predominantly white suburb; and Avoca Hills, a predominantly Asian suburb. The roads bordering the plantation are the N2, R102 and the KwaMashu highway.

The plantation is divided into different fields spread over a number of hills. There are several fire breaks and footpaths. Pedestrians use the footpaths to walk from one neighbourhood to another. There is a dam in the plantation and construction is taking place to one side.

Who found the bodies

Victim 1 was reported by the surviving victim. Victims 2 to 11 were found by cane cutters and cane thieves. Victims 12 to 18 were found by police dogs on 23 and 24 July 1997.

Surroundings

The victims were mostly found about fifteen to twenty

paces inside the fully grown cane fields. The cane is more than two metres high and no one would have been able to observe the murders taking place.

Time of crime and ratio

No.	Murdered	Last seen
1	23.6.94 Thursday	23.6.94 Thursday
2	30.7.95 Saturday	30.7.95 Saturday
3	19.8.95 Saturday	
4	Beginning 1997 January	
5	Beginning 1997 April	
6	Mid 1997	
7	Mid 1997	
8	Mid 1997	
9	Mid 1997	
10	14.4.97 Monday	14.4.97 Monday
11	Mid 1997 June	
12	Mid 1997	
13	Mid 1997	
14	2.7.97	
15	Mid 1997	
16	Mid 1997	
17	16.7.97	
18	24.7.97	

Since so few of the bodies have as yet been identified no pattern can be established. Entomologists have collected insects from the most recently found victims to try to establish a date of death.

Fourteen of the victims were, however, killed within the first six months of 1997 and the suspect is believed to have been active since 1994. Dockets pertaining to similar cases in other areas are still being evaluated at the time of drawing up this profile.

It is believed that the murders are committed during the day. The cane fields are infested with snakes and rats, which makes them dangerous, especially at night. Women will be unlikely to walk through the cane fields at night and cane thieves will operate by day.

Statistical analyses

- Race: All the victims were black women
- Age:
  10-20 years: No 1 and No 9
  20-25 years: most of the victims
  25-30 years: No 13 and No 14
- Cause of death:
  Head injury: No 2
  Manual strangulation: No 3
  Ligature strangulation: All the remaining victims
- Weapons: blunt instrument such as a rock to knock victims unconscious
  Clothing or rope to strangle
  Knife to cut clothing
- Raped: victim 1 was vaginally raped. Probably *ukuzoma* was committed on the remaining victims
- Assault: most of the victims had head or face injuries
  Victim 3 had a cut from the right side of her stomach to her back
- Position of the body:
  Stomach: Nos 1,3,4,7,8,9,11,15,17
  Back: Nos 6,12,14
  Right side: Nos 5,13,16,18
  Kneeling: No 2
- Clothing:
  Fully clothed: Nos 1,4,6,9,12,15,17
  Naked: Nos 3,7,11

190

Only panties:	Nos 2,10
Only bra:	No 14
Only petticoat:	No 18
Lower body exposed:	Nos 5,13,16
Upper body exposed:	No 18
Shoes on the scene:	Nos 3,7,15,17,18
Shoes on feet:	Nos 6,9
Shoes missing:	Nos 2,4,5,8,10,13,14,16
	(No 1 was barefoot)
Clothing on the scene:	Nos 3,13,14

No 8 was badly burnt but had a sleeve covering one arm

- Bondage:

No bondage:	Nos 2,3,5
Only hands:	Nos 6,7,8,10,17
Only feet:	Nos 14, 16
Hands and feet:	Nos 1,4,9, 11,12,13,15,18
Gagged:	Nos 6,8,9,10,11,12,13,17

Decision making process

- Type of crime and style: Serial killer: organised, power-lust motivated
- Primary intention: Power
- Victim risk: The victims have a high risk by walking through the cane fields alone. They are gullible and can easily be lured by promises of employment
- Suspect risk: The suspect has a low risk. A black man talking or walking with a black female is not regarded as suspicious. The cane fields are relatively desolate and the height of the cane provides excellent cover. The suspect quickly overpowers the victim and assaults her to render her unconscious. The suspect would there-fore not be heard or seen
- Escalation: It is difficult to calculate the escalation since the dates of death are mostly unavailable. It

would be fair however to say there is a marked increase in murders since May 1997

- Time of crime: The suspect probably kills during the day. Women will not walk alone through the cane fields at night because they are too dangerous. The suspect spends a long time in the company of the victim when they walk through the cane fields. He will spend ten to twenty minutes on the crime scene as indicated by the bondage activities and the plaiting of the gag, as well as undressing the victim. When the victim is dead he will probably just pick up the clothing and leave immediately.

Crime assessment

Reconstruction of the crime

Pre-crime behaviour

The suspect will select a specific type of female, usually between the ages of twenty and thirty years. They will not be in the company of a male but might be in the company of other females. The suspect will then move in and strike up a conversation with the female. He will use some ploy to gain her confidence, probably offering her employment, offering to accompany her or to assist her with cane cutting. He will then accompany her to the cane fields, making reassuring small talk.

Selection of the crime scene

An analysis of the crime scenes indicates that the suspect chooses mature cane fields, where the cane is at least two metres high. There will be a footpath or a firebreak for him and the victim to walk along on their way to the specific field he has selected. On the crime scene itself there is an embankment behind him, and when he exits the field the view in front of him will be of the surrounding hills.

Modus operandi during the crime

The suspect will lure or drag the victim about fifteen metres into the cane field itself. Once inside the cane field he has entered his comfort zone. He will pick up a rock and attack the victim and he will also bash her head on the ground several times. The wounds are usually inflicted on the head. The victim falls down, unconscious or dazed. The suspect then undresses the victim. It is assumed that the less clothing the victim was wearing, the closer to death she was at that stage. The suspect will then position the body so that either the upper torso or the legs are pressed between two cane stems. He will then turn the body on to its stomach. He will sit on the victim's buttocks while he cuts strips of clothing. He ties her hands behind her back and turns her over. He lifts up her legs and ties them together, with the knot at the front. He then drops the tightly bound legs. He folds a piece of the bra or the panties into a wad or ball and places this into the mouth of the victim. Then he plaits the gag and ligature, usually using the bra and material from the clothing. He wraps this around the victim's mouth and around her neck. The suspect then unzips his pants and penetrates his penis between the thighs of the victim from the back (this is called *ukuzoma*), at the same time as he strangles her. Once the victim is dead, the suspect usually removes some of her clothing from the scene. He will also search her handbag and remove any form of identification, if she had any on her.

Post-crime behaviour

Since many of the crime scenes are situated in close proximity to one another, especially the last seven, it is likely that the suspect will revisit old crime scenes, where he might masturbate. After each murder he feels relieved and might drink or visit a shebeen. He may carry strips of the victim's clothing in his pocket to excite him. He may masturbate with the clothing and practise tying knots at home. It is believed that he may take clothing from one victim home, fold strips of it into a wad or ball and have it in his pocket when he selects his next victim.

The suspect will definitely read newspapers and watch television to gain intelligence about the investigation. He might also befriend a policeman to try and obtain information.

Reconstruction of each case

Keeping the above modus operandi in mind, the differences in each crime scene will now be discussed. Reasons will be given for these deviations. The differences should, however, largely be considered as variations on the same theme. There are more similarities than differences. There can be many reasons for the differences; for instance, resistance from the victim, experimentation, progression in techniques, time factors, disturbance, etc.

Case 1

There are three main differences in this case: (1) there were two victims involved (2) the victims were younger than the others and (3) the victims were raped and no *ukuzoma* was committed.

These differences can be explained as follows. The suspect was walking along the road when he noticed two young girls approaching from the opposite direction. Serial killers react to an urge. It could be that this urge had been building up for some time, perhaps due to incarceration of some form, and that he was desperate to relieve it. He thought it would be easy to overpower two young girls at the same time. Their size and not their age is the important factor. The suspect generally engages in *ukuzoma* instead of vaginal penetration to avoid contracting a venereal disease. He considered the girls to be virgins, which would eliminate exposure to disease and he therefore raped them.

Case 2

The main difference in this crime scene is that the victim was not bound and was left in a kneeling position. There was also no ligature, but signs of manual strangulation were present.

The post-mortem report indicates that the cause of death was a severe head injury. The suspect usually assaults the victim with a blunt object to render her unconscious. With this victim, he struck too hard and killed her. She was now an object whom he could pose in any position. Since she was already dead, there was no reason for him to use a ligature on her neck. However he still needed to feel empowered and therefore still wrapped his hands around her neck while he committed *ukuzoma* to enact his fantasy.

Case 3

The main difference in this case is that the victim was covered with a cardboard box and leaves. Also she was not bound, was manually strangled and had a wound on her stomach.

The fact that she was not bound could be explained by the post-mortem report that she had a head injury. The deduction has been made that the closer to death the victim is, the more clothing he will remove since she has become no more than a dummy to him.

The stomach wound may be explained by the suspect having cut the victim's clothing from her body with a knife. He also strangled her manually. He realised that she was dying from the head wound and wanted to kill her himself. There was no time to make a ligature.

Case 4

There are no crime scene photographs available but according to the description of the crime scene in the docket, the case corresponds to the general modus operandi.

Case 5

The main difference in this crime scene is that the victim was not bound. Crime scene photographs are not available, but the fact that the victim was lying on her right side can be attributed to sexual experimentation. In several other cases the body was also found lying on the right side, so this is not a major deviation.

Case 6

The main variations in this case are that the victim was lying on her back, her hands are tied in front and there is a gag in her mouth.

These differences can also be attributed to sexual experimentation. The rest of the scene corresponds with the general modus operandi. The gag is a development of the sexual fantasy of power by bondage.

Case 7

The main variation in this case is the fact that the body was left close to the main dirt road running through the cane fields. The rest of the scene corresponds with the general modus operandi.

The suspect could have felt he was losing the victim's confidence and therefore decided to attack her sooner than he would have liked to. He took a bigger risk in killing her close to the main road, where he could have been disturbed. If he killed her at a weekend there would have been less pedestrian traffic since the cane cutters were not in the fields.

Case 8

The case shows no major deviations from the general

modus operandi. This is the first scene in which he pressed the torso of the victim between two cane stems to restrain her. It shows progression in technique.

Case 9

This case fits the general modus operandi.

Case 10

This case fits the general modus operandi.

Case 11

This case fits the general modus operandi.

Case 12

The main variation in this case is the fact that the victim was lying on her back and her hands were tied in front. However, it corresponds exactly with case number 6. There are no other deviations from the general modus operandi.

Case 13

The only variation is that the victim was lying her right side, which corresponds with case number 5.

Case 14

The only variation in this case is that the victim was lying on her back and was not bound.

Case 15

The case corresponds with the general modus operandi.

Case 16

The variations here are that the victim was lying on her right side and her hands were not tied, although her feet were. This corresponds with cases 5 and 13.

Case 17
The case corresponds with the general modus operandi.

Case 18
The case corresponds with the general modus operandi.

Organised versus disorganised serial killer

The killer is an organised serial killer for the following reasons:

- The murders are planned – the victims and crime scene locations are carefully selected
- The suspect personalises the victims – he has conversations with them to gain their confidence
- He demands a submissive victim and uses methods of restraint – he binds and gags them
- The crime scenes reflect control – the suspect is careful not to leave evidence behind
- The murder is precipitated by aggression – he inflicts head wounds on the victims
- The bodies are hidden (in the cane fields)
- Weapon – the suspect uses the victims' clothing and the rope that they are carrying to bind the cane. He removes the knife he uses to cut the clothing

SERIAL MURDER TYPE	Vision	Mission	Hedonist			Power
			Lust	Thrill	Comfort	
FACTORS :						
VICTIMS						
Specific /		X	X			X
Nonspecific	X			X	X	
Random /	X		X	X		
Non-random		X			X	X
Affiliative /					X	
Strangers	X	X	X	X		X
METHODS						
Act focused /	X	X			X	
Process focused			X	X		X
Planned /		X	X		X	X
Spontaneous	X			X		
Organised /		X	X		X	X
Disorganised	X			X		
LOCATION						
Concentrated /	X	X	X		X	
Dispersed				X		X

As indicated from the table above, the suspect is motivated by power. There is also a slight element of lust. Victims are specifically selected, and are unknown to him. There is a strong element of fantasy at his crime scenes and he spends a long time there, especially when he makes the gags. This indicates that the crime process is focused. The whole process of selecting a victim, conning her into accompanying him, tying her up and then committing *ukuzoma* and strangling her, is important to him.

The profile
Demographics
Race

The suspect is a black man of Zulu origin. Serial killers usually kill intra-racially. According to the statements of the witnesses in cases 1 and 10, he was described as a Zulu man, but he had an outlandish accent.

Age

The suspect will be between thirty and forty years. He has been active for several years and his crime scenes show definite progress and experience. The fact that he has not moved his crime activities to another area after it was announced that the police were looking for him shows arrogance and the confidence of an experienced killer.

Marital status

The suspect could be divorced. He does not have the ability to maintain a long-term relationship with a woman. He would probably prefer to live without a woman.

Home

The suspect is well acquainted with the area. He is a local and probably lives in KwaMashu although he has travelled to other parts of the country. He has a place where he can shave and change his clothing.

Employment

The suspect is probably unemployed and makes a living from crime. He has psychopathic tendencies and will therefore not rely on earning an honest salary. His financial status changes rapidly. His employment record will be inconsistent.

Educational level

The suspect will have a high school education. He is of average to above-average intelligence. There is an element of criminal sophistication about his deeds. He is streetwise.

Vehicle

There is no indication that the suspect uses a vehicle in his crimes. He will probably be able to drive, given his age and the fact that he has travelled. If he owns a vehicle it will probably be a stolen one, as he would not have enough cash to buy one.

Appearance

The witnesses in cases 1 and 10 have given a description of the suspect. His hair was cut and he had a two-day-old beard and a grown moustache. He wore tinted sun glasses. This indicates that he is concerned with his facial appearance and is vain. He had no scars on his face.

His clothing is old, but fits well. One garment was torn. He does not have the appearance of a well-dressed, over-neat person, but he is not shabbily dressed either. To him clothing should be functional. He is not a fancy dresser. He is a practical man.

He walks straight and upright and keeps his hands in his pockets.

He is not a hygienic person who will wash every night. He probably washes every second night. There is a faint odour of perspiration about him. His nails are dirty, but not bitten.

He avoids eye contact and shifts his eyes when talking to others.

Previous criminal record

He will have a previous criminal record. He is a psychopath, who does not believe in earning an honest salary. He will probably have been in prison for theft. Because of his age, he will have progressed from mere burglary to more serious crime such as car theft or illegal weapon trading.

The reason that he commits *ukuzoma* is to avoid infection, but it could also be that he has knowledge of DNA and avoids leaving semen on the crime scene because he is aware that it could link him to the crime. He may therefore have previously been charged with rape.

Since he is clearly aggressive he may have been charged with assault.

Given his financial status he may have been involved in fraud, but not the type that an experienced white-collar criminal would be involved in.

Habits

He probably smokes, drinks and gambles.

Emotional temperament

He is aggressive and self-confident. He has a macho attitude and demands respect. He has a short temper and will use physical aggression to solve an argument.

He is a great manipulator of people and can easily appear to be friendly. He will maintain only superficial friendships and only as long as he can personally benefit from them. He can act acceptably in a social sense and people who have not been taken in by him, will probably like him. He does not have any true friends, only partners in crime. He holds grudges and is unforgiving.

He is easily slighted and will take insults to heart. He justifies his own actions and will not apologise. He tolerates no opposition and considers himself to be superior to other men. He thinks he is a leader and is arrogant. His superiority complex masks a deep inferiority complex caused by rejection. He will not admit this easily. He feels superior to the detectives and will arrogantly provoke them. He has no respect for the law.

He has to have his basic needs immediately gratified and will experience outbursts of anger and frustration if he does not get his own way at once.

He does not learn from his mistakes in the sense that he may be rehabilitatable. He only learns from his mistakes to improve his crimes.

Attitude towards women

The suspect detests women. He has a deep hatred and contempt for them. He sees them merely as objects to be used and discarded. To him, women are inferior beings, not worthy of attention. However, he sees them as easy prey and will conduct himself very charmingly until he has gained their confidence. Thereafter he will turn very aggressive and vent all his anger and aggression upon them. He has no sympathy or mercy for them.

He feels it is his right as a superior man to force them to have sex and that they should not refuse him. He prefers to have sex from behind so that he does not have to look into their eyes and acknowledge them as humans. Even when he has consenting sex with a girlfriend he will prefer this position. If he has sex from the front, he wants to see the fear in their eyes.

He was probably belittled by a woman in his adult life. It could have been a girlfriend whom he wanted to marry, who rejected him or cheated on him and this triggered the murders. He may give this as a reason for hating women and killing them. This should however be regarded as a trigger for a deeper fixation which has its origin in his childhood.

Childhood years: Psychoanalytical development

The suspect's two main characteristics are that he detests women and is obsessed with power. He also has psychopathic tendencies as an adult.

A man who detests women to such an extent has been rejected by his mother, which will result in a fixation. A serial killer has a weak ego and is dominated by the id – either because his mother over-fulfilled his id's needs and his ego never differentiated from hers, or because she rejected him during the oral phase. Had the suspect's fixation taken place during such an early phase, the crime scenes would have been more disorganised and mutilation of the breasts would have occurred. We can therefore deduce that he went through normal oral phase development and the mother probably over-gratified his needs as a baby.

A man whose ego did not differentiate from his mother's feels impotent towards women. He fears their mysterious power. He overcompensates by trying to dominate them and demands that they are submissive. The suspect's fixation must then have taken place in a later phase.

He is motivated by power. This is a characteristic of the anal phase. He is addicted to feeling omnipotent. A child feels omnipotent if he can dominate his mother during the anal phase. His mother must therefore have continued to be submissive or over-gratifying during this phase. The suspect therefore fixated on power during the anal phase. This still does not explain his hatred of women which was certainly caused by a major rejection.

The rejection by the significant female – which could be a mother or a surrogate mother – must therefore have taken place during the Oedipus phase, when the boy subconsciously falls in love with the mother. During this phase he must have been either consciously rejected by the mother, or subconsciously rejected: for example, she died, or he was removed from her care, etc. He does not suffer from castration anxiety – there are no foreign objects inserted into the victims' vaginas – but he fears intimacy with women, because he was so dependent upon his mother and this made him feel powerless.

He murders women because he fears losing his ego to their power. By murdering them he has the ultimate power over their lives or deaths, which is the opposite of the situation when his mother had the power of life and death over him.

Although his female victims may represent or look like the adult woman who rejected him in his adult life, he is symbolically murdering his mother and thereby trying to differentiate his ego from hers. This is a subconscious process.

If we interpret the symbolism on his crime scenes, we will find that:

- He binds hands and feet – he prevents women from touching him because it is too intimate and he fears intimacy
- He gags them – he prevents them from talking to him and belittling him and he demands them to be submissive. Also, he regards them as mere objects who cannot talk
- He turns them on to their stomachs – they are not allowed to look at him because he fears them and he does not want to acknowledge them as humans
- He cuts their underwear – female underwear represents their mysticism, it is lacy and soft

The suspect's father was either physically or emotionally absent during his childhood. He did not socialise nor did he learn social and ethical values during the latency years, which is why he is able to treat his victims as objects. His father's discipline was inconsistent. He either had no relationship or else a bad relationship with his father, and no replacement father figure. The relationship between his father and mother was also not good. The father could have been a criminal as well.

The suspect was either an only child, or he had no brothers. He probably grew up in rural KwaZulu-Natal and was exposed to violence, perhaps faction fights. As a child he was involved in physical fights, lied often and stole and destroyed property. He probably ran away from home before the age of fifteen. He never had close intimate relationships with other children and considers friendship a weakness.

Sexual fantasy

The suspect is motivated by power – he uses bondage. He wants a completely submissive partner whom he can dominate. The partner becomes an object who has no identity. He will not even talk to the partner during sex because she is not human to him.

His fantasy has progressed. It will be described as it is at the current moment. The fantasy is acted out on the crime scene, but reality is never perfect. It will be pointed out at which crime scenes the reality failed him and how he rectified it.

The fantasy exists as follows:

Selecting a victim and conning her into accompanying him is part of his fantasy. While he is walking with her and making small talk he is already anticipating how he is going to kill her. He notices her clothing and imagines how he is going to use it to bind her. He enjoys the anticipation he experiences while he is walking with her. The urge is building up inside him. When he reaches a spot where he feels safe he will enter the cane fields. He will lure her in, or drag her in forcibly, or threaten her with his knife.

When he walks into the cane field, the leaves of the sugar cane rustle loudly in his ears blocking all other sounds, including her voice, from his mind. His actions become automatic and animal-like. He strikes the woman hard with a rock to render her unconscious or dizzy. He wants her to become an object. In cases 2 and 3 he struck his victims too hard. The victim in case 2 was already dead before he undressed her. The victim in case 3 was dying. This disappointed him and therefore he did not tie them up.

The bondage is very important to him. It makes him feel powerful. In the first case he first tied up the victim who survived and then tied her friend up and raped and strangled her. Then he untied the surviving victim and raped her. Then he tied her up again and strangled her. It was not necessary for him to have tied her up the second time for he was strong enough to strangle her with his hands. This indicates the important part the bondage plays in his fantasy.

Several issues play a part in the bondage, which would explain why some women are gagged and others not, and why the hands and feet of some were not tied.

If the victim is dead, as in case 2, he is disappointed. He wants to strangle them himself – there is no greater power than the power over life and death. It makes him feel like God. Although he was disappointed, he still had a sexual urge and therefore undressed her. The body was still warm. He could therefore pose her in a kneeling position. Since she was dead there was no point in binding her. Simply having sex/*ukuzoma* was not enough. So he compromised by strangling her manually although she was already dead.

In the case of number 3, he also hit his victim too hard. She was dying and so he undressed her quickly. But he had no time to bind her before she died. Again, he compromised by committing *ukuzoma* and strangling her manually.

If he considers a victim to be not submissive enough, he will gag and bind her. The resistance and personality of the victim may therefore play a part in the extent of the bondage.

His urge and the time factor also play a role. The urge almost reaches a climax while he is cutting the strips of clothing with his knife. If he feels the urge is going to climax too soon, he will omit tying the hands and feet, or will only tie the feet to save time. This also plays a role in the amount of clothing he removes.

The ultimate fantasy is to render the victim unconscious, without killing her. He will remove a certain amount of clothing, depending upon the urgency of his sexual need at that point. He likes to open a shirt or dress from the front and cut the bra off. He turns the victim on her stomach. He sits on her buttocks while cutting the strips of clothing. The sexual urge is almost unbearable by then and the anticipation is extremely high. He ties her hands behind her back, turns her over and lifts up her legs and ties her feet very tightly. He wants the thighs to be tightly together for ultimate pleasure when he penetrates between them. Then he drops the legs and turns her over again. He constructs the gag carefully, using underwear and different strips of garments. He considers this his masterpiece – no less than a work of art. The wad or ball of material is carefully folded and placed in the mouth of the victim. Then he wraps the ligature around her mouth and neck. He unzips his pants and inserts his penis between her thighs. He has sex while strangling her. The ultimate experience will be that he climaxes when she takes her last breath.

He might take some of the clothing with him and practise folding the gag. He will masturbate while doing this. He might also use items of previous victims' clothing on future victims. He might carry strips of clothing in his pocket and feel them to remind him of his pleasure. He also has the knife in his pocket and likes to play with it for the same reason. This is why he keeps his hands in his pockets when he talks to women. He might return to the crime scenes and masturbate, although this is unlikely because victims are so readily available. He can just kill another.

Mental disorder

The suspect will not suffer from a mental disorder. His crimes are too organised and well-planned for the actions of a disturbed person. He is sane and knows what he is doing.

He may, however, have a personality disorder, such as antisocial or narcissistic personality disorder.

Part of the profile was released to the press during July 1997. The last body was discovered on 5 August 1997. Two condoms containing body fluid were found at the scene. In the mean time Philip Veldhuizen had also found a docket from April 1996 of a woman who was raped in the area. The suspect in this case was identified as Sipho Agmatir Twala, but he was not charged because the victim, Mrs M, failed to turn up for the trial. The semen in the condoms found at the last scene matched the DNA in Mrs M's rape case. We had identified our suspect.

I arrived back in Durban on 11 August 1997. By then Bushy Rambadhursing had located the address of the suspect in KwaMashu. We arrested him in the early hours of the following morning. He lived in a three-room shack with his mother and sister. He had a wonderful view of his killing fields from there. His room was filled from floor to ceiling with female clothing. Several female watches were lying next to his bed. Outside his shack we found strips of clothing tied to cane stems; he was practising his knots.

I interrogated Twala in the company of Captain Nathaniel Kwyema. His rights had already been read to him and I started by introducing myself as a psychologist. Then I related his sexual fantasy, as detailed in the profile, to him in the third person singular. When I had finished he admitted that he was the man in the story, but added that I had made one mistake. He placed the folded wads of material into his own mouth first before he put them into the victims' mouths, to make sure that they would fit.

Twala said he killed the women because his girlfriend had told him that she had aborted his child and after that she left him.

Twala fitted the profile perfectly. He was a Zulu man and although he did not know his exact age, he guessed it to be between thirty and forty. He was traditionally married to his girlfriend, but she had left him, implying a traditional divorce. He lived in KwaMashu and spent time in the cane fields on a daily basis. He had been a truck driver and had therefore visited other parts of the country. At the time of his arrest he was unemployed and made a living from stolen sugar cane.

I made a mistake about his educational level. He only completed grade 2. His intelligence had never been officially measured, but he was not unintelligent. He did not own a vehicle.

His appearance and clothing as well as his hygienic habits fitted.

He had been an ANC cadre and involved in illegal gun-running. He was acquitted on the rape charge because the victim did not show up in court. He had been sentenced to a prison term for vehicle theft and had been involved in several fights, but no assault charges had been laid.

He smoked, drank and gambled now and then when he had money.

I interviewed his mother and sister who confirmed his emotional temperament. His aggressive outbursts scared them. They described him as moody and dangerous. They tried to keep out of his way and never dared to ask him questions as to his whereabouts or the female clothing he had in his room. They were typically submissive towards him.

His attitude towards women was confirmed. The adult

girlfriend had rejected him. He admitted he chose victims who reminded him of her. He admitted to taking clothing home and folding the wads of material. He admitted carrying the wads in his pocket when he approached the victims and that this had excited him. He committed *ukuzoma* to avoid leaving semen behind on the scene; however, he later found this frustrating and wanted to penetrate the women vaginally. He decided to use condoms and had forgotten to remove them from the last murder scene. He admitted offering his victims employment and thus was able to persuade them to accompany him.

As a child his mother was over-protective towards him. He did not know what had happened to his father.

He confirmed that the sexual fantasy was completely accurate, apart from the detail of placing the wad in his own mouth first. He told me that I knew his heart and his mind very well.

After Twala had admitted to the murders, Philip Veldhuizen joined us in the interrogation room and Twala took great pleasure in demonstrating upon the uncomfortable Captain Kwyema how he had tied the women up. He enjoyed boasting in front of the detectives, expressing his superiority towards them. As they understood his needs and did not confront him, they gained an excellent first-hand demonstration and were able to testify to it in court. Twala confessed that he had watched us processing a crime scene from a distance and returned to it after we had removed the body. He had read about the investigation in the newspapers, but was convinced that he would never be caught.

Sipho Agmatir Twala was arrested within six weeks of commencing the investigation and was sentenced to 506 years' imprisonment. I testified on the profile at his trial. My testimony went unchallenged by the defence's expert psychologist. Ex-FBI profiler Robert Ressler sent a fax of congratulations regarding the speedy arrest and was of the opinion that the profile was 99 per cent accurate. I attribute the success of our investigation to teamwork.

In compiling the profile of the Phoenix killer, I relied upon my training, experience and sixth sense. Without realising it, I first wrote the reconstruction of the crime scenes in the first person singular, as if I was experiencing them myself. I changed it to the third person after Philip Veldhuizen pointed this out. I had managed to enter the mind of Sipho Twala and it had a devastating mental effect upon me. My delta brainwaves functioned in overdrive during this case.

Pyromaniacs

DEFINITIONS

Although pyromaniacs and arsonists both set fires, the main difference between them is their motivation: pyromaniacs are psychologically motivated, while arsonists may be motivated by money, ideology, concealing a crime, anger or revenge.

According to Kaplan and Sadock in *Synopsis of Psychiatry* (1991) the elements of pyromania are deliberate and purposeful fire setting on more than one occasion, tension or affective arousal before setting the fires; and intense pleasure, gratification, or relief when setting the fires or seeing the fires burn. Freud viewed fire as a subconscious symbol for sexuality and believed that pyromaniacs set fires to relieve their sexual tension. The fire becomes a substitute for sex. Some pyromaniacs report no sexual tension, but rather an uncontrollable urge, preceded by tension headaches, palpitations and an almost trancelike state when watching the fire.

The onset of pyromania occurs during childhood and it often goes hand in hand with bed-wetting and cruelty to animals. The children often play truant, grow up to become delinquents and are prone to alcoholism. They have a below average intelligence level, and resent authority figures.

My training as a psychologist provided me with an insight into the mind of a pyromaniac, but it was ex-FBI agent Robert Ressler who taught me how to profile arsonists and provided me with research material on the subject.

TYPOLOGY OF ARSONISTS

Arsonists vary, mostly on account of their different motives. The following types of arsonist are listed in the FBI's manual *The Firesetter: A Psychological Profile*:
- The typical male arsonist
- The adult revenge fire setter
- The jealousy-motivated adult male fire setter
- The would-be hero
- The volunteer fireman solitary fire setter
- The fire 'buff' fire setter
- The pyromaniac
- The excitement fire setter
- The typical female fire setter
- The child fire setter
- The adolescent fire setter
- The schizophrenic fire setter

A discussion of the profiles of each of these is beyond the scope of this book. I would, however, like to concentrate on the pyromaniac because this will be applicable to the case study I would like to discuss.

THE PYROMANIAC

FBI arsonist profilers describe pyromaniacs as seemingly motiveless. *Offenders said they set their fires for no practical reason and received no material profit from the act, their only motive being to obtain some sort of sensual satisfaction.* They feel compelled to set the fires although they might receive no financial benefit from it. Pyromaniacs have something in common with serial killers, who describe an irresistible impulse to murder. David Berkowitz, alias Son of Sam, set countless fires.

FBI profilers Lewis and Yarnell compiled the following characteristics of the typical pyromaniac:

Age:	Between sixteen and twenty-eight
Gender:	Male
Race:	Predominantly white
Intelligence:	Ranges from mentally defective to genius
Physical defects:	Frequently present
Bed-wetting:	Present in some
Mental disorders:	Psychopathy as well as psychotic disorders were identified within this category: the compulsive urge also appears to reflect an obsessive compulsive pattern of behaviour
Academic adjustment:	Poor educational adjustment, underachievers
Rearing environment:	Pathological and broken environment with inconsistent discipline and parental abuse and neglect
Social adjustments:	Socially maladjusted, severe problems in developing and maintaining interpersonal relationships
Sexual adjustment:	Sexually maladjusted and inadequate
Employment history:	Unskilled labourers if employed
Personality:	Misfit, feeble person, physical coward, inadequate, self-conscious, introverted, reclusive, frustrated and aloof, obstinate towards authority, no ambition
Criminal record:	Delinquency, burglary, theft

Source: *The Firesetter: A Psychological Profile*, FBI Manual

CASE STUDY: THE JEPPE PYROMANIAC

Background information

Jeppe is a sub-economic neighbourhood close to the centre of Johannesburg. No one would willingly want to bring up a child in this environment. Housing consists mainly of overcrowded apartment blocks and houses, all desperately in need of repair. A community centre provides relief in the form of entertainment and soup kitchens provide food to those who cannot afford to find it elsewhere. Gangs rule the streets, and in the privacy of their homes most of the residents are involved in crime of some sort or other. Shops are interspersed with seedy bars. Litter and household garbage are dumped in the park.

Early on Saturday morning, 30 August 1997, children found the scorched body of a thirty-five-year-old white man in the park. A burnt-out mattress covered his body, but not his contorted face. Everyone gathered around as the police began processing the scene. Three days later, on Wednesday 3 September 1997, a resident of a retirement village adjacent to the park noticed a shoe lying outside one of the residential units. Then he saw that the door of the unit was open. Inside he found the burnt body of a sixty-nine-year-old white man.

The cases were assigned to Captain Mike van Aardt, a detective at the Jeppe Police Station. Van Aardt had not been trained in serial homicide, but he had heard about me. He sounded hesitant on the phone when he asked for help. I invited him to come and see me and asked him to bring the crime scene photographs and all other available information. They were some of the most gruesome photographs I had ever seen.

The body on the first crime scene had head wounds and had been strangled and set alight. His pants were pulled down and his underpants torn off. He was lying on his back. His limbs were contorted as a result of the muscles shrinking in the heat of the fire. His face was bloodied and contorted. His wallet and shoes were missing. A lighter and spectacles were found on the crime scene. The burnt-out remains of the mattress was on top of him. Van Aardt explained to me that the mattress could have been lying on a rubbish dump in the park. A brick was also found near the body.

At the second crime scene the man was lying on his stomach in his bedroom. He had a knife wound in the heart, his throat had been slit and he was covered with a burnt duvet. Photographs taken after the duvet was removed revealed that his pants had been pulled down and his underpants torn off. The scene was a bloody mess. The bed had also been set alight. One shoe and possibly a television were missing. A brick and bloodstains were found outside the unit, indicating that the attack must have been initiated in the garden.

The crime scenes were situated about three hundred metres apart. There is a wall around the retirement village and it is situated adjacent to the park. Apartment blocks overlook the park.

Van Aardt returned to Jeppe and a short while later I provided him with the following profile:

Profiling inputs

Crime scene analysis

There were two crime scenes, which correspond on the following elements: both victims were adult white males; the pants of both men had been pulled down and their underpants torn off; both victims had been burnt. The first victim had been assaulted on the head with a brick and strangled with a strip of cloth, and the second was stabbed in the heart with a knife and his throat had been slit. Both murders were committed in the early hours of the morning, just before sunrise. Differences in the crime scenes were the age difference between the victims and the fact that the first murder was committed in a park and the second within a residence.

Physical evidence

A cigarette lighter and spectacles were found at the first scene. Apart from the broken brick, no other evidence was found at the second scene. Fingerprints and DNA samples were taken at both crime scenes. The forensic results have not yet been released.

Pattern of physical evidence

Bricks were found at both crime scenes. There was no other pattern of physical evidence.

Position of bodies

At the first crime scene the victim was discovered lying on his back in a park. His pants had been pulled down and he had been strangled. A mattress that had been discarded in the park was placed on top of him and set alight. In the second incident, the elderly victim was lying on his stomach in his room. He was covered with a duvet and set alight. His pants had also been pulled down.

Weapons

A brick and a strip of cloth were used in the first incident and the body was set alight. In the second incident a brick was used, but the fatal wounds were inflicted with a knife. The victim was also set alight.

Victimology

Both victims were white men of low socio-economic status.

Jeppe CAS 1209/8/97

The victim has been identified as thirty-five-year-old William Crichton. He was employed at a local hardware store. He was divorced and lived with his parents. He was an alcoholic, but did not use drugs. He knew the other victim, but everyone in the neighbourhood knows everyone else. He had not been paid on the day of his murder. He was not homosexual.

Jeppe CAS 146/9/97

The victim was identified as sixty-nine-year-old Clarence Albert Pretorius. He lived in the retirement village next to the park. The retirement village consists of free-standing double units, each with its own entrance, but with a shared bathroom. He suffered from insomnia and was in the habit of smoking a cigarette outside his unit during the early hours of the morning. He preferred sexual relations with black women and was not homosexual.

Forensic information

Cause of death

| Jeppe CAS 1209/8/97: | Strangulation |
| Jeppe CAS 146/9/97: | Wound to the heart and throat cut |

Wounds

| Jeppe CAS 1209/8/97: | Assault to the head with a brick and burns |
| Jeppe CAS 146/9/97: | Stab wound to the heart, throat cut and burns |

Pre- or post-mortem sexual activities

In both cases the pants of the victims had been pulled down and their underpants torn off, which indicates a sexual motive. The fact that both bodies, as well as the bed in the second case, had been set alight, indicates the possibility of pyromania. Pyromania is a sexual disorder in which a person becomes sexually aroused by arson. The fire is a substitute for sex.

Pre-mortem sexual activities may have been indecent assault on the victims. Fondling the sexual organs as well as the anuses may have taken place.

In post-mortem sexual activities the suspect may have masturbated over the bodies before setting them alight; or he may have masturbated at or close to the crime scenes after setting the bodies alight, while watching the fire.

Forensic results have not yet been released.

Post-mortem results

No anal tears were found in either victim.

Preliminary police report

Background

The incidenct occurred in a low socio-economic neighbourhood. Gang activities are rife. The crime scenes were situated about three hundred metres apart. Housing in the area consists of apartment blocks, houses and a community centre. Soup kitchens cater for poverty-stricken residents.

Jeppe CAS 1209/8/97

Children discovered the body at six o'clock in the morning. The park is full of garbage and it is assumed that the mattress had been discarded there by a local resident.

Jeppe CAS 146/9/97

The body was discovered at about six o'clock in the morning by one of the other residents in the retirement village. The village is situated next to the park and consists of free-standing units. Each unit is divided into two separate quarters, with a communal bathroom. Each resident has his/her own entrance. The woman who shared the unit with the victim smelled fire during the early hours of the morning and knocked on the bathroom door. She heard voices, but did not investigate. Another resident heard a loud noise during the early morning hours, but did not investigate either. He later found the shoe of the victim and noticed that the victim's front door was open. He entered the unit and found the victim. The retirement village is enclosed within a wall. Domestic staff quarters are located in the yard, but separately walled. Discarded building material, including bricks, is piled close to these quarters.

Police observation

Extensive enquiries have been conducted in the neighbourhood and the investigating officer patrols the area during the early morning hours.

Time of crime

Both crimes were committed during the early hours of the morning, just before sunrise. It must have been light enough in the park for the offender to have spotted the mattress. He did not spend more than twenty minutes at the crime scene, but may have observed the scene and the fire from a distance.

Crime tendencies

Gang activities are rife in the area. Drug peddling, burglary and car theft are common problems. Alcoholism, domestic violence, child abuse and neglect, as well as cruelty to animals, will be common in households.

Decision making process

Type and style: Serial homicide, disorganised, visionary-lust. Primary intent: The primary intent is sexual, although the sex act manifests indirectly.

The offender seems to be a visionary-lust motivated serial killer. A visionary motivated serial killer has specific victims, but they are randomly chosen. They were at the wrong place at the wrong time. The victims are strangers to the offender, although he might previously have met them or seen them. The murders are spontaneous, not well planned and are centred in one area. The deed of murder is more important than the process which would have included victim selection, planning, disposal of the body and escape. The offender has a low level of intelligence and will probably tend towards a mental illness or disorder. The crimes committed in this series fulfil these elements.

A serial killer motivated by lust will introduce a sexual element to the crime and will act out forcible sexual fantasies. There is a sexual motivation to the crime, but the visionary motive takes precedence.

Victim risk

Both victims had a high risk. In the first incident the victim was most probably on his way home after visiting a pub. Forensic results regarding his blood alcohol content are outstanding, but according to his family he drank regularly. It can be assumed that he was under the influence of alcohol and therefore an easy target. He may already have been lying on the grass in the park when the attack commenced. The second victim was an elderly man who smoked outside his room. It would have been easy to overpower him.

Offender risk

The offender has a low risk. The crimes were committed

during the early morning hours when most people are waking up and preparing to go to work. He approaches his victims, who are probably not suspicious of him, and launches a blitz attack once he is within reach. Thus he prevents them from calling for help. Although residents of the apartment block across the street have a view over the park, the offender knows they are still indoors and probably still sleeping. He knows the residents of the retirement village will either be sleeping, or too scared to confront him. There is a risk that he may be caught red-handed, but he knows there is enough opportunity to escape, or that he will be able to overpower any other elderly person who confronts him.

He probably lives in the immediate vicinity of the crime scenes, where he can easily get rid of his blood-soaked clothing.

Escalation

The murders were committed on the Saturday and Wednesday mornings, within a period of four days, at the end and beginning of a month. No murders have since been committed, but more may take place at the end of September and the beginning of October. The murders were most probably triggered by an incident in the offender's life. It is suspected that he may have lost his job.

Time for crime

The offender does not spend more than twenty minutes at the crime scenes, but may observe the fire from a distance.

Location factors

The two crime scenes differ in that one was out of doors and the other inside a residence. In the second incident, however, the victim was attacked outside and then dragged into his room. The crime scenes are three hundred metres apart. The suspect is well acquainted with the area.

Crime assessment

Reconstruction of the crime scenes

Jeppe CAS 1209/8/97
The offender was already in the park when the victim arrived. He noticed that the victim was inebriated and immediately decided to kill him. He picked up a brick and approached the victim. The victim evidently did not fear him and allowed him to approach. He assaulted the victim on the head with the brick until the victim lost consciousness. He picked up the rag and strangled the victim. He pulled down the victim's pants, tore off his underpants and indecently assaulted him. He may have masturbated over the body. He robbed the victim of his wallet and shoes. He dragged the mattress over the body and set it alight. He stepped away and watched the fire and may have masturbated again. He left the scene and discarded or washed his clothing.

Jeppe CAS 146/9/97
The offender was roaming within the walls of the retirement village, probably with the intent of burglary. He spotted the victim smoking under the tree and saw another opportunity for murder. He approached the victim who did not show signs of fear. Once he was close enough, he stabbed the victim with a knife. He dragged the victim towards the unit, but the victim struggled. The offender picked up a brick and assaulted the victim. The victim attempted to flee, but the offender caught him from behind at the door of the unit and slit his throat with the knife. He pulled the victim's pants down and tore

off his underpants. He probably masturbated over the body and indecently assaulted him. He pulled the duvet over the body, picked up a spray can containing poison and sprayed it over the bed. First he set the bed alight and thereafter the victim. The only motivation for these actions would be the sexual arousal of observing the fire. If he stole the television, he would have placed it in the scullery before setting the fire. He probably watched the fire from a distance before he went home to rid himself of his clothing.

The spray can exploded in the fire and this caused the loud noise heard by one of the other residents. It was not a gunshot.

Organised versus disorganised killer

The offender is disorganised in the execution of the murders.

The victims belong to a specific category, namely white men of low socio-economic status, but this category is extensive and there are no other similarities between them. They were chosen randomly.

The offender used a blitz attack and attempted to overpower his victims as quickly as possible. No discussions or personalisation of the victims took place. The weapons were weapons of opportunity that were present on the scenes, apart from the knife. It is likely that the offender carried a knife at all times for self-defence and not specifically for murder.

There are no indications that the murders were carefully planned. The crime scenes reflect chaos. There is an element of sexual fantasy being acted out, but this fantasy is not as sophisticated as in the case of organised killers.

The offender commutes by foot and lives and works in the same area. He probably lives with his parents, possibly an elderly mother.

The fact that there was little evidence on the crime scenes and that the knife was removed from the scene, indicate that the offender would not have the very low intelligence normally expected of disorganised killers. His intelligence level is probably between ninety and a hundred and ten, which is average. The lack of evidence may point to a degree of criminal sophistication, indicating previous incarceration.

The above elements are generally regarded as those applicable to a disorganised killer. On a scale of one to five, where one is very organised, two is organised, three represents a mixture, four represents disorganised and five represents very disorganised, the offender would score four.

Staging

Staging is the term that describes a situation in which the offender changes something at a crime scene to mislead the police. In this case the offender may have stolen the television and the wallet to disguise the motive as burglary. There are no other indications of staging.

Motivation

The motivation is sexual. The fire is a substitute for the sex act. The murder is secondary, because the methods employed to kill the victims differ. One was strangled and the other was stabbed and had his throat slit. The offender wanted the victims dead in order for him to indecently assault them, to masturbate and to set them on fire.

The fire is the signature of the offender. A signature is any characteristic the offender leaves behind on the crime scene, which is unnecessary to the crime. Both victims were already dead and it was unnecessary to burn them, nor was it necessary to burn the bed in the second instance. The offender did not burn the victims to conceal evidence. The mattress was not covering the first victim's face in order to conceal his identity. Should there have been semen on the bed, it would have been on top of the duvet, and the duvet was burnt in any case. Therefore there was no reason to burn the bed as well, except that the offender was aroused by fire. This is typical of pyromaniacs.

There are two sexual elements at play, namely pyromania and homosexuality.

The profile

Demographics

Race

Serial homicide is usually intra-racial. In this case there are no indications that the suspect does not belong to the same race as the victims. Both victims were comfortable about allowing the suspect to approach them. The elderly victim in particular would have shown fear if a man of a different race approached him at that time of the morning. It is possible that the suspect was an acquaintance of both victims, since most people know everyone else in the area.

It must be noted that the elderly victim's room was close to the domestic workers' quarters. Surplus building material had been dumped there. There is a remote possibility that a man of another race might have been visiting the domestic quarters and attacked the victim as he was leaving.

Gender

The suspect is an adult male, probably homosexual.

Age

In the case of adult victims, the age of the suspect is

usually in the same age group. However, in this case there is a considerable age difference between the victims. Research on arsonists indicates that they are usually between fifteen to twenty years old, but arsonists who set fire to other people are usually older than twenty-five. In this case the suspect would be between the ages of twenty-five and thirty-seven, most likely twenty-seven years of age.

Residence

Disorganised killers usually live in the immediate vicinity of the crime scene. The suspect will live within a half kilometre range of the scenes. He probably lives with his elderly mother, who has no control over him. Other family members will have no interest in his comings and goings. He may stay out until the early morning hours without raising suspicion. He is also able to rid himself of or wash his bloodied clothing without notice. No questions will be asked if he arrives home with a stolen television set.

Marital status

The suspect will be single and is most probably homosexual. He is in a position to roam around in the early hours of the morning on a weekday, without being missed.

Employment record

The suspect was most likely fired from his job shortly before the first murder. The murders were committed close to pay-day. He could have stolen a few rands from the first victim. The second murder was committed early on the Wednesday morning. The suspect would not have had time to return home, wash or hide his bloodied clothing and still be on time for work. He is therefore most likely unemployed.

Educational record

The suspect will probably have secondary education up to grade ten. It is likely that he will have attended a hostel, reformatory or orphanage. He probably has below average to average intelligence.

Vehicle

The suspect does not use a vehicle and probably has never earned enough money to buy or maintain a vehicle or to afford petrol. He will walk most of the time, or use public transport.

Previous criminal record

The suspect will probably have a criminal record for burglary, theft, arson, indecent assault or sodomy. He has probably been sentenced before and spent time in prison where he acquired some criminal sophistication, but not extensively.

Habits

The suspect will probably smoke and use alcohol. He is nocturnal, which means he prefers to sleep late during the day. He will have disturbed eating and sleeping habits. He is slovenly. He likes to roam about at night, but does not have the finances to afford nightclubs or restaurants.

Appearance

The suspect will have a dishevelled appearance. His clothes are old and dirty and his shoes will be down at heel. He is reserved and will not maintain eye contact. He will have an unusual 'walk' in order not to attract attention, but this will have the opposite effect. His hands are rough and his nails and hair will be unkempt and dirty.

Emotional temperament

The suspect is a lonely, reserved, shy person who is uncomfortable in the company of others. He is very self-conscious and has a total lack of self-confidence. His family regards him as reclusive and surly.

He has a problem with authority and will be obnoxious when confronted with authority. He will usually seem passive and lazy.

The suspect is impulsive and his frustration tolerance is low. He cannot deal with stress in any form and has temper tantrums. He is demanding and insists that his needs be attended to immediately. He will often direct his anger upon himself and will probably have attempted suicide several times. He will be the kind of man who mistreats animals and kicks doors.

He takes no responsibility for his actions, shows no empathy for others and has no ambition. He regards himself as a rejected failure and selects victims who pose no threat.

Sexual orientation

He fears women and will probably not have had a long-term intimate relationship with a woman. Apparently he prefers men, but he does not have the interpersonal skills to cultivate a relationship. He can't afford male prostitutes and therefore he overpowers and murders his victims.

The suspect is probably impotent and sexually naïve. He fondles the victims' genitals, but cannot penetrate. He is sexually aroused by fire, which is a substitute for sex. He will masturbate on the body or on the crime scene. He knows the fire will destroy the semen on the scene.

The suspect has aggressive sexual fantasies. He will probably keep a small souvenir from each victim and masturbate with it. He will masturbate daily. Because love is missing from his life, masturbation will have a consoling effect on him.

Childhood years

The suspect grew up with a dominating mother. His father was emotionally absent, possibly an alcoholic and a criminal. It is likely that the suspect is an only child.

His mother was domineering, but submissive. She over-protected the suspect, which castrated him psychologically. She continues to treat him like a child. She will not express any physical affection. It is possible that either parent or another family member suffered from schizophrenia.

The suspect will probably have suffered from bed-wetting and may still do so. It is likely he was sodomised in an institution as a child and again later in prison. He will have set fires as a child and have been cruel to animals. His academic achievements were poor and below average.

He was a lonely child without friends. He was reserved and not physically strong. He did not participate in any sport. To compensate for his weaknesses, he developed omnipotent fantasies as a child in which he destroyed other people. These fantasies are more important than reality to him and most of the time he lives in this dream world.

Pre-crime behaviour

The murders were not pre-planned but were spontaneous, spur-of-the-moment acts. Some incident triggered the suspect's already poor self-esteem, which triggered the murders. His frustration tolerance is so low that the murders and arson provided emotional relief for his stress. Before the murders he would have roamed the area aimlessly, just to avoid going home. He will probably be a peeping tom, for this makes him feel powerful. People do not know they are being watched, which makes him feel superior.

Post-crime behaviour

Immediately after the murder the suspect will masturbate and watch the fire. Then he will return home to wash or destroy his clothing as it will be covered in blood and will reek of smoke. He will hide these activities from his family. Thereafter he will go to sleep and bath when he wakes up. He will probably return to the crime scenes to watch the activities surrounding the discovery of the bodies and the processing of the crime scene.

The suspect will be interested in the investigation. He might contact the investigating officer and offer assistance, but since he is a reserved person who has a problem with authority he is more likely to make anonymous calls. The investigating officer may wish to attach a tracing device to his phone.

The suspect will visit the retirement village and discuss the murder with other residents. Perhaps a member of his family lives there.

If posters are distributed about the murder, he will keep one. The fact that he is suddenly the centre of attention and that a detective is searching for him will have an empowering effect on him. He is not used to this and may begin to brag about the incident, just to enjoy people's reaction, but since he is reserved the bragging will not be boisterous.

Mental disorders

Visionary and disorganised killers tend to be psychotic,

but this suspect is intelligent enough to leave virtually no evidence. He is therefore not so mentally disturbed as to be totally irrational.

Schizophrenia is eliminated, since he was rational enough to take precautions and avoid arrest. He knows the difference between right and wrong.

It is likely that the suspect will suffer from a personality disorder. This is not a mental illness, but indicates a defect in the individual's personality and his interpersonal relationships.

Several personality disorders are a possibility, of which the most likely are:

Group A
• Paranoid personality disorder
This person has a long-standing distrust of other people. He refuses to takes responsibility for his own emotions, is aggressive, hostile and irritable. He interprets the behaviour of others as intentionally detrimental to him. In other words, he believes others are intentionally out to defraud and deter him. This is an illusion. He will defend himself by taking revenge on these imagined enemies.

• Schizoid personality disorder
This person is very uncomfortable and fearful in the company of others. He is reserved and introverted. He prefers solitary activities and cannot function in a group. He becomes anxious when others approach him or pay him any attention. He appears cold and unfeeling. He avoids sexual and physical contact and functions within his dream world. He cannot easily express his anger overtly and will find other ways to express it. He might later develop schizophrenia.

Group B
• Avoidant personality disorder

This person is very sensitive to rejection and will therefore prefer to avoid people. He has a great need for friendship, but is too shy to make friends because he fears rejection. He lacks self-confidence and will refer to himself in a derogatory manner. He interprets the comments of others as hostile, rejecting and humiliating. He will always try to please others, which in itself is irritating.

(An interrogation strategy and list of items to be searched for in the suspect's home were included in the profile.)

Scarcely three weeks after the second murder, on 27 September 1997, another murder was committed. This time the victim was fifty-year-old Alex Landsburg, who lived in an apartment in Pretoria. Photographs of Alex's and Clarence's crime scenes were almost identical. A major difference in the murders was, however, that one took place in Pretoria and the other in Johannesburg, yet for someone used to walking, the fifty-odd kilometres would not have been very difficult. Another difference in Alex's crime scene was that there were sex toys involved.

There were forty-seven stab wounds on Alex's half-naked body. Clothing had been thrown over his body and set alight. His bed was also torched. The investigating officer, Inspector Claassen, pressed the redial button on the phone and a Mrs Venter in Kimberley answered. She told Claassen that her son, twenty-six-year-old Jan Adriaan van der Westhuizen had phoned her and confessed that he had killed a man and was planning to flee to Durban. It did not take Claassen long to realise that Alex's vehicle was missing.

Mike van Aardt and I contacted Superintendent Philip Veldhuizen of the Durban Murder and Robbery Unit. A month later, on 21 October, Jan van der Westhuizen was arrested in Durban and brought back to Gauteng. Van Aardt brought him to me the following day.

Van der Westhuizen told us that he had murdered Alex because Alex had picked him up in a gay bar and tried to force sex upon him. He vehemently denied having any knowledge of the Jeppe murders, despite the fact that he frequented that neighbourhood. Neither Van Aardt nor I believed him. He fitted the profile perfectly.

Van der Westhuizen was kept in custody at the Pretoria West police station, from where he escaped on 20 November. He hitch-hiked to Johannesburg and was picked up by a motorist who promised him work if he would meet him at a particular shopping centre the next day. That night the motorist read about Jan van der Westhuizen's escape and realised he had given a lift to a dangerous killer. He phoned the police who went to the shopping centre the following day and rearrested Van der Westhuizen. Mike van Aardt brought him to me a second time. Again, he remained adamant in his denial of the Jeppe murders. I still did not believe him. Van Aardt, however, decided to search for another suspect. Jan van der Westhuizen became an awaiting trial prisoner.

A year later, in May 1998, Mike van Aardt phoned me. Someone in Jeppe had tipped him off about a murder that had taken place in 1992. Close to the other scenes, a black man had been assaulted with a broken glass bottle. His pants had been pulled down, but he was not burnt. Van Aardt traced the docket and finally tracked down twenty-seven-year-old Norman Hopkirk who was in prison serving a sentence for theft. He booked him out and brought him to me.

Hopkirk confessed to me that he had attacked the unidentified black man in 1992. The man later died of his injuries. He also killed William and Clarence, but had avoided detection. Shortly after Clarence's death, he was arrested for theft and sent to prison without anyone knowing about the murders he had committed. He was,

235

however, in prison at the time of Alex's death. Norman Hopkirk fitted the profile perfectly as well.

I chose to discuss this case to illustrate my mistake of being convinced a suspect was guilty because he fitted the profile perfectly. Since pyromania is so rare and since Jan van der Westhuizen fitted the profile to a tee and admitted to spending time in Jeppe, I could not believe that another pyromaniac, who fitted the profile equally well, could be on the loose in the same area. My mistake almost resulted in Norman Hopkirk getting away with three murders. Had it not been for Mike van Aardt's persistence, more people might have died after Norman Hopkirk's release.

Outcome

Norman Hopkirk was sexually molested by his father and cousins as a child. The family was very poor and would often find themselves on the street. Shortly after Norman Hopkirk's birth his father deserted the family. Although the parents were reconciled later, their marriage was fraught with conflict. The father drank and the mother was overprotective towards her son.

Hopkirk was placed in several hostels and later in a reformatory, because his parents could not control him. He had set fires as a child. He was sodomised at these institutions. He liked to wander around alone at night from a very young age. He was more often than not truant from school. As a child he would often bash his head against a wall until it bled. He had below-average intelligence. He admitted to having aggressive fantasies in which he was the destructive hero, and had committed many thefts as a child, but was never caught. He completed grade ten and then worked at an abattoir in Johannesburg in 1992. His alcoholism led to the loss of his job. He committed theft and burglary. At this stage his father was also arrested.

Hopkirk lived with his mother in Jeppe, in an apartment overlooking the park. He was a bystander when the police processed the scene and actually stood right next to the police photographer. On the night of the murder he had met William in the park and asked him for a cigarette. He knew Clarence by sight as his girlfriend's parents lived in the retirement village. He had visited her one night and spotted Clarence lighting a cigarette under the tree. Hopkirk admitted to me that in both cases it was the flame of the cigarette lighter that triggered his murderous impulse. He was taking vengeance on his victims for the sodomy he had suffered as a child. He returned home after the murders and watched the fire from the balcony. Norman Hopkirk was sentenced to two life sentences and a further twenty years for the first murder. Ironically, he trained as a welder in prison, because he liked the blue flame.

Jan Adriaan van der Westhuizen had a similar profile. He had never met his biological father. His mother described him as hyperactive, a school dropout and a car thief. She feared that he would set their house on fire. As a child he often set himself on fire. He was arrested for car theft in grade eleven, and set the Kimberley prison on fire. He escaped after being admitted to hospital. He admitted that he would hustle himself as a male prostitute and that was how he met Alex. He killed Alex because he reminded him of the men who had sodomised him as a boy. He was sentenced to thirty years.

Both men fitted the profile:

Race, gender and age:	Both were white men: Van der Westhuizen was twenty-six and Hopkirk twenty-seven
Marital status:	Both were single. Van der Westhuizen was a male prostitute.

	Hopkirk slept with women, but never had a long-term intimate relationship with a woman
Employment:	Both were unemployed and did menial jobs when they could find them
Education:	Both had below-average intelligence levels. Hopkirk completed grade ten and Van der Westhuizen grade eleven
Vehicle:	Neither had a vehicle and both preferred to walk. Both often hitch-hiked
Criminal record:	Both had been arrested for theft
Habits:	Both smoked and abused alcohol. Both were nocturnal
Appearance:	Both were dishevelled and avoided eye contact. Both walked with a slouch
Emotional:	Both were lonely, reserved individuals who had problems with authority. Both directed their anger at themselves and both had attempted suicide
Childhood:	Both grew up in dysfunctional, poverty-stricken families with domineering mothers and emotionally absent fathers. Both were sexually abused as boys. Hopkirk's father was an alcoholic with a criminal record. Van der Westhuizen did not know his father. Both wet their beds. Neither had friends. Both became delinquents and both had omnipotent fantasies
Mental disorder:	Both men were pyromaniacs who were sexually aroused by fire. Both suffered from avoidant personality disorder.

Norman Hopkirk and Jan Adriaan van der Westhuizen could have been cosmic twins. I learned a valuable lesson from this case: It is possible for two killers fitting the same profile to be operating at the same time and employing a similar modus operandi. One should never be overconfident that a suspect is guilty just because he fits the profile. A profile describes a personality type, not an individual, no matter how accurately it fits.

Rapists

DEFINITION OF RAPE

Rape statistics in South Africa are among the highest in the world. The organisation People Opposing Women Abuse (POWA) released the following statistics regarding rape and abuse in South Africa in 2004:

- A woman is raped every twenty-six seconds
- One in every four women is in an abusive relationship
- Every sixth day a woman is murdered by her partner
- A minor is raped every twenty-four minutes
- A child is molested every eight minutes
- A child is assaulted every fourteen minutes

Profiling can make a serious contribution to counter these crimes and the Investigative Psychology Unit of the South African Police Service (SAPS) has profiled several serial rapists successfully over the past ten years.

In 2004 the Criminal Law (Sexual Offences) Bill was presented to the portfolio committee for Justice and Constitutional Development. In this bill the proposed definition of rape reads as follows: *Any person who unlawfully and intentionally commits an act of sexual penetration with another person, without such person's consent is guilty of the offence of rape*. The bill also makes provision for sexual assault. Marriage or any other relationship is no excuse for forcing sexual relations upon another without that person's consent. If the victim is in any way forced, coerced or tricked into sex, it is unlawful.

Having sexual relations with a person who is asleep, in an altered state of consciousness, drunk, under the influence of drugs or mentally disturbed is also regarded as being without consent.

It will also be illegal to expose any person to pornography or a display of sexual relations without such person's consent. It is illegal to have sex or any sexual relations with children under the age of eighteen and it is illegal to display any sexual relations or expose children to pornography.

The bill also make provisions for beastiality, incest and the sexual violation of a corpse. The previous act did not make provision for men being raped, but that has been rectified.

TYPOLOGY OF RAPISTS

The FBI designed a practical typology of rapists that is acknowledged all over the world. Knight and Prentky ('The developmental antecedents and adult adaptations of rapist subtypes', *Criminal Justice and Behavior*, 1987) divided rapists into two groups, namely power rapists and anger rapists. Both these groups are further divided into two groups, which gives a total of four types of rapist. There is a fifth group, namely the impulsive rapist, who will rape when the circumstances of another crime offer him the opportunity to do so. It is important to remember that the characteristics described in each of the four groups are very general. A rapist of a certain typology will therefore not necessarily have all the elements of that group and some elements may overlap.

Table 7: FBI typology of rapists

Power-motivated rapists	Anger-motivated rapists
Compensation rapist	Anger retaliation rapist
Power assertive rapist	Sadistic rapist

Power motivated rapists

This rapist needs to exert power and control over his victim. Physical aggression, threats and intimidation are used to force the victim to submit. He has inadequate interpersonal relationships, both on sexual and social levels. The rape makes him feel adequate. He plans the rape and uses just enough violence to control the victim.

Rape is the means whereby he confirms his virility, identity, mastery, strength and dominance. It defies his inferiority complex, feelings of rejection, helplessness and vulnerability.

The two types of power-motivated rapists are:

Compensation rapist

The compensation rapist is also called a power confirmation rapist. The aim of this rapist is to confirm his power. He wants his victim to confirm his power as a man to him, because he can find no other confirmation. He will often ask her questions about her own sex life and about his ability as a lover.

This rapist is ego-dystonic – he cannot identify himself with the knowledge that he is a rapist. He feels guilty after the deed and will be concerned about the victim and ask her forgiveness, or apologise. He will try to make conversation with her. In his normal life he is the kind of person who will go out of his way to help other people in order to be accepted and to gain approval.

This rapist is motivated by sex and not by aggression.

The rape compensates for an inadequate self-image. The rapes are compulsive and routinely repetitive, as he needs continuous confirmation of his manliness.

During the rape his sexual arousal level is quite high and there is a high possibility of premature ejaculation. The rape will therefore not be extended, but rather short in duration. The rapist will probably attempt to arouse the victim sexually by foreplay. He fantasises that she is enjoying his advances. He is likely to contact the victim after the rape and try to make a date to see her again. If the victim offers resistance during the rape, he may flee, but he may also increase violence to regain control over her.

Power assertive rapist

This rapist tries to confirm his virility, mastery and dominance. In contrast to the compensation rapist who needs the victim to confirm his power to him, the power assertive rapist wants to assert power himself.

This rapist will only use aggression to attain his goal. Aggression in itself is not the main aim of the rape. He believes it is a man's right to force a reluctant woman to have sex with him. He has double standards – he believes women who are promiscuous, who wear provocative clothing and who flirt, deserve to be raped, while conservative women do not.

Anger-motivated rapists

The primary aim of these rapists is aggression and not sex. The attack is characterised by unnecessary violence and the sexual activities are aimed at humiliating the victims. Sex is the mode by which the aggression is expressed.

Generally this rapist despises women and shows anger towards them. His relationships with women are conflict-related and he might get physically abusive. The rapes usually follow a confrontation with a known woman, after which he transfers his anger to a stranger. The victim might be the same age or older than the rapist.

Anger retaliation rapist

This rapist uses aggression to express his anger. He wants to avenge himself on all women and will humiliate his victim by forcing her to have oral and anal sex as well as other offensive acts.

The rapes are inconsistent and unexpected. The anger increases after a confrontation with a known woman, causing an explosive tantrum which is diverted to a strange woman.

These rapists are also known as transferred aggression rapists. The rapes are very violent and may seem out of character if the rapist's personality is taken into consideration. He usually has good social interaction skills and an active interpersonal life. He achieves a high level of success in his social and work life. On closer inspection, it is obvious that he has problems in his dealings with women, especially regarding his emotions in relationships. If he has an outlet for his aggression, he is capable of warmth, friendliness and love; however, his normal attitude towards others is usually cold, distant and overcontrolled. He is active, self-assertive and independent and he is not able to play a submissive role in a relationship.

He is irritated by women who have strong mothering characteristics at the expense of their other feminine characteristics. His specific anger towards such a woman is transferred to a stranger. He wants to hurt, humiliate and belittle the victim. He experiences and expresses anger during the rape and he will also verbally abuse his victim.

After the rape, this rapist may sometimes be concerned for the victim and try to compensate for his deeds. He is a good candidate for therapy and rehabilitation.

Sadistic rapist

This rapist enjoys violence and eroticises his aggression. The violence becomes an aim in itself. Sex must be accompanied by aggression for him to become sexually aroused and gratified. Brutal and sadistic violence is employed during the rape and the torture may be extended. He may also use weapons and instruments.

The rapes are ritualistic and bizarre. He plans the rapes and fantasises about them. He might steal a small item as a souvenir of the rape. Many of these rapists experience sexual dysfunctions concerning erections. The rapist does not experience anger during the rape. His attacks are directed towards female genitals, breasts and buttocks.

His personality may present with many psychopathic tendencies like manipulation, impulsiveness, unstable personal relationships, lack of empathy and non-sexual criminal offences. Cruel behaviour will have manifested during his childhood.

The Ripper Rapists Frans du Toit and Theuns Kruger, who raped and brutally assaulted Alison, were anger-motivated, sadistic rapists.

Impulsive rapist

This rapist differs from the other types in the sense that there is no anger or power motivation. He takes advantage of a situation which might offer the opportunity for rape. He is a natural psychopath.

The impulsive rapist will, for example, rape a woman because she happened to be in a house he was breaking into. He planned the burglary, but not the rape. He has no empathy for the victim, but he did not have the specific intention of hurting her. He is an amoral delinquent. He has no respect for the rights of other people, especially women, and believes a man has the right to force a woman to have sex with him. Rape is usually part of a repertoire of other crimes such as burglary, robbery, car theft, etc.

Serial rapists

Ex-FBI agent Roy Hazelwood and Janet Warren in *The Serial Rapist* (1995) summarise findings of research conducted on a group of forty-one serial rapists as follows:

- 54 per cent had generally stable employment
- 71 per cent had been married at least once
- 52 per cent scored above average on intelligence tests
- 54 per cent were raised in average or above-average socio-economic environments
- 76 per cent had been sexually abused as children
- 36 per cent collected pornography

Most of these men had been psychologically and sexually abused by a parent or caretaker. Very few of them were physically abused.

The amended proposed Sexual Offences Act of South Africa provides that it is illegal to expose children under eighteen to any form of sex, including pornography, and also to displaying sexual acts in their presence. This means it is unlawful for adults to have sex in the company of children. There is a definite relation between the sexual exposure a child receives and his developing into a rapist as an adult. The FBI found the following results concerning childhood sexual trauma and later abhorrent sexual behaviour in serial rapists:

Table 8: Serial rapists' sexual history and current sexual behaviours

CHILDHOOD/ADOLESCENT SEXUAL TRAUMA	
Witnessing sexual violence of others	25%
Witnessing disturbing sexual activity on part of parents	44%
Witnessing disturbing sexual activity on part of other family members/friends	25%
Physical injury to sexual organs/venereal disease	14%
Multiple sexual assault	31%
Sex stress situations, eg punitive parental behaviour towards masturbation	46%
ADULT SEXUAL BEHAVIOR	
Marked inhibition or aversion to sexual activity	10%
Compulsive masturbation	54%
Exhibitionism	29%
Voyeurism	68%
Fetishism	41%
Cross-dressing	23%
Obscene phone calls	38%
Prostitution/pimping	15%
Sexual bondage	26%
Collects detective magazines	28%
Collects pornography	33%

Source: FBI

The FBI's research indicated that most rapists selected their victims because of their availability and gender. One would imagine that rape victims are those women who find themselves alone in dangerous places, yet in about 53 per cent of the cases the women were raped in their own homes. Serial rapists therefore tend to target single women in their own homes. Since 68 per cent of the rapists practised voyeurism, one can surmise that they kept the women under surveillance for a time and then gained illegal entry into their homes.

Women must learn to be vigilant of strangers loitering around their homes and take measures to safeguard their homes. Living in a 'secure' complex is no reason not to lock doors and secure windows, for the rapist may be a neighbour or even a security guard. In 2003, Luyanda Mboniswa, a security guard at the exclusive, high-security Dolphin Beach Complex in Blaauwbergstrand, was found guilty of the murder of the former first lady of South Africa, Mrs Marike de Klerk. There was not enough evidence to prove rape.

Rape is a symptom of a psychological dysfunction. It serves the goal of gratifying an impulse, is a defence against anxiety and expresses an unresolved conflict. If rape is the sexual expression of power and anger, then the motive is revenge and compensation rather than sexual.

The question arises why sex is used as a medium to express power and anger. The answer may be found in exposure to sexual activities during childhood. Research shows that one out of three sexual offenders was exposed to a sexual activity of some sort at a very early age.

Child molesters were violently forced to submit to a sexual act by someone outside the family, while the serial rapist experienced sexual pressure from someone within the family. (Thus one was forced, while the other was emotionally blackmailed.) The psychological impact of the violence on the child molester as a child, is fear – fear of grown-ups. The psychological impact the pressure has on the serial rapist as a child is anger. The serial rapist will have been put under sexual and/or emotional pressure by a female family member, and he therefore avenges his anger on females.

It has been found that the child molester will repeat the same act that he was subjected to on his child victim, and the children will be about the same age that he was when he was molested. Norman Avzal Simons, is an example, although he turned to murder in addition to rape.

The sexual pressure of blackmail includes a situation where a child is seduced by an adult – usually his mother – as well as situations where boys are, for example, punished for masturbation. Witnessing adults having sex at a young age also causes psychological damage to the child. The child interprets the sexual deed as one of aggression. He experiences that his mother is being attacked and he hears noises which he associates with pain. Women who seduce their sons and fathers who ignore this are bringing up potential serial rapists.

Some serial rapists were subjected to sexual injury when they were children.

Stranger rape

A stranger rapist is a man who rapes a woman who is unknown to him. He may become a serial rapist if he rapes more than one victim.

While I was being trained as a profiler in Dundee, Scotland, by ex-FBI profilers, I was fortunate enough to learn about stranger rape from Anne Davies of the Metropolitan Police in London. She had compiled a database on stranger rapists and her research revealed the following:

- 85 per cent of stranger rapists have a criminal record
- If there was violence involved in the rape, it is probable that the perpetrator has also used violence in other crimes
- Stranger rapists drink before they rape and therefore it is advisable to make enquiries at bars close to the scene of the crime

- Stranger rapists have two methods of approaching a victim:
  - break into her residence
  - pick her up at a bar, bus stop, shopping centre, etc.
- A stranger rapist who steals the identity document of the victim does so to threaten her and discourage her from reporting the rape. He knows who she is and where she lives
- The most beneficial factors for a rape victim in British courts are the following:
  - sexual inexperience
  - a respectable lifestyle
  - a stranger to the offender
  - did not willingly go with the offender
  - resisted and possibly incurred injury
  - reported the rape immediately

In instances where two of the above factors were present, 33 per cent offenders were found guilty; where three factors were present, 72 per cent were found guilty; and if all six were present, 100 per cent of offenders were found guilty. If none of the above characteristics were present, the offender was found not guilty

- Most victims of stranger rape do not put up a fight because they fear being injured or killed
- Characteristics of the organised rapist are:
  - skilled in the control of the victim
  - take care not to be disturbed – they will, for example, disable the lights and establish who else is on the premises
  - protect their identities (face, fingerprints, semen and tell lies)
  - try to prevent the victim from reporting the incident
  - provide a safe escape route – tie the victim up, tell her to count to 20, leave a window open, etc

- – buffer zone – will not rape within a certain radius of his own home
- It is important to establish the following aspects regarding disrobing:
  - – how far did the victim undress
  - – how far did the offender undress
  - – who took what clothes off
  - – was any clothing torn or damaged
  - – was any clothing cut
  - – did the rapist watch while the victim undressed in front of him (indicates fantasy)
- The stranger rapist who cuts clothing is very dangerous and can become a killer
- Fantasy plays an important role in stranger rape
- Tearing of clothing with accompanying violence, indicates sadistic fantasies
- A stranger rapist who does not wear underwear, indicates experience. He has raped before
- The more violent rapists will only have anal sex and will have committed violent crimes before
- The stranger rapist who insults the victim or humiliates her, has probably raped before
- The stranger rapist can change his modus operandi according to the status of the victim – he may swear at a drug addict, knock an elderly woman's head against a wall, or declare his love for a woman of high social standing
- The rapist's tone of voice can be divided into five categories:
  - – orders: *'Do this and do that'*
  - – announce: *'I'm going to do this now'*
  - – negotiate: *'If you do this, I'll let you go'*
  - – swearing
  - – complacent: *'I won't hurt you'*
- Establish whether the questions asked by the rapist

had a sexual theme, or if he asked them out of personal inquisitiveness
- Many stranger rapists tell the victims lies about themselves because they think it will deflect the police, but when they do this, they usually provide information familiar to them. A man who says his name is John, probably knows someone called John
- A rapist who tells the victim he can get ten years for the rape, has probably been in prison
- Scenes that are important in a rape case are the following:
  - where the rapist met the victim
  - where the victim was attacked
  - where he released her; for example, did he drop her off somewhere?
  - where he left her vehicle if he used it – it is usually close to where he parked his car, or close to his own home
  - where he uses stolen credit cards
- It was found that 75 per cent of the victims were approached within five miles of the perpetrator's own home, half of them were met within two miles and one third were met within one mile of his home
- Younger rapists rape closer to home
- Reasons for raping further away from their homes, are the following:
  - 20 per cent of the perpetrators had no permanent residence and moved around
  - availability of victims: for example, nightclubs, escort agencies, etc
  - intimate knowledge of another neighbourhood: for example, he may once have lived there
  - professional burglar
  - prowler – he cruises around in his car
- Prowling has a lot to do with fantasy. Wives of rapists

often report that their husbands enjoy driving around at night without any specific purpose

- Signs of fantasy on the scene can be an indication that the stranger rapist is also a serial rapist
- Stranger rapists use rape kits. Sometimes there will be towels to wipe the victims, or there may be different sets of wigs
- Patrick Duffy's (Britain's Railway Ripper) rape kit consisted of a match box containing tissues and the thin string he used to tie his victims up. He forced the tissue into their vaginas and set it alight to destroy traces of semen. Forensic tests established that the string matched string found in his mother's house
- During his early thirties sexual and emotional distance from his wife or partner can become prevalent in a man's marriage. This leads to fantasies and masturbation, accompanied by hostility towards females that can lead to rape
- Collateral evidence cannot prove anything in court, but contributes to circumstantial evidence
- One of the rapists was a necrophiliac. While he was being interrogated and while he sat handcuffed to a policeman in court, he masturbated. The mere discussion of his acts aroused him
- When piquerism (compulsive cutting or stabbing of the body) is present, the body will be naked when the perpetrator commits the act, because he needs to see what he is doing

In her article 'Rapists' behaviour: A three aspect model as a basis for analysis and the identification of serial crime' (*Forensic Science International*, 1992), Anne Davies also identified three aspects of behaviour which a serial rapist will reveal during the rape:

- modus operandi

- sexual and personal gratification
- attitude and intimacy

Davies analysed these three behaviour patterns to determine whether different rapes can be linked to a series. Information about the rapist's behaviour is mainly determined by interviewing the victims and questions should be directed according to the behaviour patterns.

Modus operandi

Aspects of behaviour pertaining to modus operandi are the following:

- Choice of time and location: The day, date, time and location of the crimes should be noted since a pattern may evolve. The place where the rapist met the victim, as well as the place where he raped and left her, is important.
- Method of approach: Self-confidence or blitz attack. Should the rapist have used a con-story to gain the confidence of the victim, it is important that the full story be written down as he told it. The longer the story, the more he reveals about himself and certain aspects can be compared with subsequent rapes.

The method of approach is important and can provide more information about the perpetrator. For example, a rapist who breaks into a house and familiarises himself with the environment and then waits for the victim probably has a history of housebreaking. One serial rapist attacked widows visiting a cemetery during the day. It was later established that he was a patient in a nearby psychiatric institution and had to return to the hospital in the evenings. He said that visitors to the cemetery were mainly solitary females and, moreover, it was a peaceful haven to escape to.

- Method of control: Weapon or bondage. To control the victim, rapists usually make verbal threats and use a knife. It is important to establish whether the rapist had the weapon with him or found it at the scene. Many men who break into premises with the intention of raping go first to the kitchen to look for a knife. If the rapist had bound the victim it is important to establish whether he brought the rope with him, or used something from the scene like a telephone cord or clothing.

- Steps taken to ensure personal protection: The rapist will use various methods to conceal his identity, which will differ in level of sophistication and which will reveal his criminal experience. The rapist's biggest fear is that the victim will make a noise or that he will be disturbed. He will ask about other people in the house and will disconnect the telephone. Those who are aware of the presence of flat- or housemates will often say that their partner is holding the other person hostage, or raping her as well. To conceal his face the rapist may wear a mask, tell the victim not to look at him, blindfold her, disable the light bulbs or even turn off the electricity. The existence of DNA has become common knowledge and rapists are careful not to leave semen on the scene. They may use condoms, remove clothing or bedding and burn it, or force the victim to bath after the rape. Many rapists talk to the victims and give false names or false addresses, or pretend not to know the area. Repetition of lies may establish linkages with other rapes.

- Reference to police or legal procedures: Many serial rapists threaten to kill the victim if she reports the incident, while others accept that she certainly *will* report it. The sophisticated rapist takes precautions for his escape route. Davies found that reference to the police or judicial system during the rape was rare. The serial rapist may, however, pretend to be a policeman when he approaches the victim.

- Theft of objects: It is important to determine the value of objects taken from the victim to establish whether the motive was burglary or rape.

Sexual and personal gratification

The aspects of behaviour that should be analysed are:

- Sexual problems: The most common sexual problem rapists experience during rape is getting an erection. The second most common problem is premature ejaculation. It often happens that the victim is unaware that the rapist has ejaculated.
- Sexual deeds – performed, attempted, asked for or named: These include any one or more of the following: kissing, fondling, fingers in vagina or anus, penetration of vagina or anus, oral sex, licking, sucking, masturbating, etc. One offender was linked to several rapes because he insisted that the victims kissed him. Hazelwood found that sadists had a preference for anal sex. Such a rapist can become increasingly violent and dangerous. In contrast, cunnilingus indicates a rapist who has a need for intimacy. This often happens only once in a series, especially if the victim has a higher status than the rapist or if he finds her more attractive than other victims. Oral sex on the rapist is common.
- Sexual verbal themes: Verbal themes can either be what the rapist says, or what he wants the victim to say to arouse him. He may verbalise through a remark, insult, order or a question. One of the most common themes is to ask the victim if she is enjoying the sex. A popular theme of pornography is the scenario of an unwilling victim being raped and being turned on by it. The rapist justifies the rape by telling himself that the

victim enjoyed the sex while she, on the contrary, was in fear of her life.

- Habits associated with sexual or personal gratification: These include any rituals, sources of pleasure, or any indications of an abnormality, such as the tearing or cutting of clothing in a specific manner. One rapist cut the stockings of his victims and then sucked their toes while he masturbated. He may inspect her vagina to see if she is clean, force her to wipe herself after the rape and not remove the tissues, or cover photographs of her loved ones before he rapes her.
- Indications of paraphilias: Investigating officers in rape cases should have a good knowledge of fetishism and pick up signs of this when the victim makes her statement. Items of fetishism may be found in the perpetrator's residence. A specific fetish can also provide information on the perpetrator's personality, and be used to supplement an interrogation strategy.
- Gratifying violence: This is the situation when the rapist enjoys inflicting violence, even if the victim offers no resistance. One rapist bound his victims. His wife said he bound her as well, but lost interest when she showed no resistance. He was aroused only when she showed resistance.
- Verbal cruelty: The rapist may tell the victim he has a venereal disease, or that her breasts are too small and he is therefore going to cut them off, or debate aloud whether or not he should kill her after the rape. One victim told the rapist he was already guilty of rape, whereupon he held a knife to her throat and said: *Let's make it murder too.*

Attitude and intimacy

The following behavioural aspects determine attitude and

intimacy:

- Violence in reaction to resistance: Most rapists use minimal violence to control the victim, usually a slap or a blow with the fist.
- Abuse and profanity: Insults are usually used only when the victim offers resistance. One rapist was linked because he always referred to his victims as *You old cow*.
- Use of language to exercise control: Vocabulary and syntax may indicate linkage between cases. The degree to which the rapist will threaten the victim is largely based on her resistance. One rapist threatened two victims that he would kill them if they alerted the police, to another he remarked that she would probably alert the police, and to another he didn't even mention the police but tried to make a date with her. The first two victims offered a lot of resistance and the last one none.
- Concerned reassurances, which may be divided into four categories:
  - lies: *I'm only going to rob you*
  - implied threat: *Do what I say and I won't hurt you*
  - inappropriate: *I'm only going to rape you*
  - direct concern: *Don't worry. You'll be OK*
- Inquisitiveness: The rapist will show the same sort of inquisitiveness towards the victim that any person will show towards another when they meet for the first time. He will also ask general questions about her name, address, work, habits, boyfriends, etc. Usually rapists do not ask more than three general questions. A larger degree of inquisitiveness may therefore be used to link cases.
- Self-revelation: A rapist will often lie about himself to mislead the victim and the police, but the lie is usually close to the truth: for example, he will use the name

of a friend or family member. The degree of truth of self-revelation can be determined if it is analysed in the context in which it was made, or measured by his body language.

- Compliments: The rapist may use compliments when first approaching the victim, or when she does something he likes.
- Concerned behaviour: Concern is shown, for example, when a rapist warns the victim to keep her windows closed in future, or does not take anything that may have sentimental value for her, or offers her money to get home.
- Apologies: Rapists make excuses to justify their behaviour to themselves.
- Affection expressed or required: A rapist who shows or demands affection is conducting himself totally inappropriately, if the fact that the victim is in fear of her life is taken into consideration. Inappropriateness indicates his loneliness.
- Extending the relationship: Many rapists experience the rape as a continuation of normal sex. One rapist violently attacked his victim, raped her in several manners and then offered to return that Sunday night to cook her dinner. He was upset when she declined the offer.

When the above information is being sought, the investigating officer needs to establish what the victim's attitude was: for example, the measure and method of her resistance, her verbal behaviour, etc because the rapist's behaviour will be influenced by the behaviour of the victim. He may react differently to different victims. Although modus operandi can change, sexual preferences usually remain stable.

The attitude and intimacy shown by the offender

depends a great deal on the victim's resistance, but can provide valuable information: for example, how quickly he gets angry, how he manipulates others, what his self-image and emotional condition are.

INTERVIEWING RAPE VICTIMS

During my training in Dundee, ex-FBI profiler Roy Hazelwood provided valuable information regarding the interviewing of rape survivors. This can be found his article 'Introduction to the serial rapist: Research by the FBI' (*FBI Law Enforcement Bulletin*, 1987). If a victim is correctly interviewed it will provide a valuable source of information to the profiler. Usually all that is expected of the victim by the investigating officer is a description of the circumstances of the rape and a description of the offender. However, many rapists use some kind of disguise, which makes description of his physical appearance difficult. Important aspects, such as the verbal, physical and sexual behaviour of the rapist, are often ignored by the investigating officer.

Although the victim will be traumatised, a sympathetic, professional investigating officer should structure the interview in a way that focuses on the following three aspects: physical, sexual and verbal behaviour of the suspect. If all three aspects are covered, the profiler will have enough information to create an accurate profile.

Physical behaviour

Method of approach

There are three methods of approaching a victim, namely:
- Confidence trick: The rapist who uses this method approaches the victim openly with some kind of con-

story. He may ask her to help him with something, and is usually friendly and charming. He tries to win her confidence, but his behaviour will quickly change once she is in his control. This type of approach is that of a man who exhibits a high level of self-confidence in the company of women, which will be manifested in his daily dealings with them.

- Blitz: This rapist also approaches the victim directly, but quickly overpowers her by physical force. He may approach her from the front or from behind. He does not allow her any opportunity to resist verbally or physically, and will bind, blindfold or gag her. He may also use some chemical substance or gas to disable her. This rapist's social interaction with women is that of a man who is hostile towards them: he has little self-confidence in their company, is selfish and will probably have had only short-term relationships with women. He is usually young and has not developed any social skills.

- Surprise: This rapist will wait for the victim, either along a deserted road, in her car or in her home. He will threaten her or use a weapon. This type of approach may indicate two things:
  - The victim has been pre-chosen and the rapist has been watching her
  - He does not have enough courage to con her or overpower her during an attack

Controlling the victim

When the rapist has gained initial control over the victim, he has to ensure he retains it. The method he uses will be based on two factors:

- The measure of passiveness the victim displays
- His motive for the rape

There are four methods of extended control:

- Mere presence: The emotional condition and fear of the victim may be such that the mere presence of the rapist is intimidating enough for him to be able to control her. To a person who has never experienced a situation like this, this kind of behaviour is difficult to understand, and the investigating officer should be careful not to blame the victim for not resisting or trying to flee.
- Verbal threats: Many rapists threaten the victim with physical force if she offers resistance. It is important that the interviewer write down the threats word for word and establish whether or not the rapist acted on them.
- Use or display of a weapon: If a rapist threatens the victim with a weapon, it is important to establish when he displayed it for the first time, and if he really had a weapon. Secondly, it needs to be determined whether it was a weapon of choice – one that he brought with him, like a gun, knife, screwdriver, etc; or a weapon of opportunity – a pair of scissors or an object he found in the victim's home. Thirdly, it is important to find out if he ever relinquished control of the weapon by putting it down, putting it away or giving it to the victim. Fourthly, it should be established if he caused any harm with the weapon.
- Physical violence: The amount of violence used plays a vital role in determining the motive of the rapist. It must be determined how much violence was used, when it was used and what the rapist's behaviour was before and after the violence. Since the victim may be very subjective in describing the type of violence, the following guidelines may be used to measure it:
  - Minimal violence: When the rapist used little or no violence; for example, a few slaps on the face or

a few pushes and shoves. The aim is to bring the victim under control and not to punish her. The rapist will usually not use swear words

- Moderate violence: The rapist will continuously slap or hit the victim, even if she offers no resistance. He will use swear words and insults
- Extensive violence: The victim will be beaten all over her body and many marks and bruises will be visible. She will probably have to be hospitalised. The rapist will definitely swear, humiliate her verbally and make derogatory sexual remarks
- Brutal force: The victim will have been sadistically tortured with instruments. Physical and emotional pain have been consciously inflicted. The rapist is very aggressive verbally, insulting and profane. The victim will definitely be hospitalised, may have lost consciousness and may be in danger of losing her life

Rapist's reaction to resistance

The victim has two options when the rapist threatens her:
- Compliance, or
- Resistance

There are three methods of resistance:
- Verbal resistance: shout for help
- Physical resistance: put up a fight
- Passive resistance: when the victim does not offer verbal or physical resistance, but also does not comply with the rapist's demands

The rapist's reaction to the victim's resistance will reveal information about his personality. Every human being reacts differently to stress. For several reasons, the rapist is under stress when he rapes. He may be scared of being caught, scared of being injured, or scared that the victim will recognise him, etc.

Research indicates that there are five reactions the rapist may have to stress:

- Ceasing the demand: If the rapist demands a specific deed or reaction from the victim and she refuses, he leaves it and demands something else or progresses to the next stage of the rape
- Compromise: The rapist will react to the victim's resistance to a specific demand by asking her to suggest an alternative. He may demand anal sex but when she refuses, he will rape her vaginally
- Flight: When the rapist flees after encountering the victim's resistance, it indicates that he never intended to use violence, or that he was unprepared for resistance and the attention it might attract
- Threat: Threats can be physical or verbal. If the victim continues to resist after the rapist has threatened her, it is important to establish whether or not he carried out his threats
- Violence: Some rapists will revert to violence only if the victim offers resistance. The measure of violence should be determined

Sexual behaviour

Sexual dysfunction

Research has indicated that 34 per cent of a group of 170 rapists had sexual dysfunctions. Often the victim will not be asked about the rapist's dysfunctions, but this information is valuable to the profiler. The victim may be shy about answering these questions, or she does not think that they are important, or she does not know anything about dysfunctions. The interviewer should be very sensitive when asking these questions and explain the different dysfunctions to her.

- Erectile insufficiency: This is impotence, when a man cannot obtain or maintain an erection. There are three variations, which will be discussed for interest's sake, because the investigating officer will not be able to determine which kind prevailed until after the suspect has been apprehended:
  - Primary erectile insufficiency: This is a man who could never maintain an erection sufficient for penetration
  - Secondary erectile insufficiency: This is a man who cannot maintain an erection in a particular situation or for a certain period of time
  - Conditional erection: This man will only have an erection under certain circumstances; for example, when he has to force the victim to have oral sex or any other sexual act with him. Other activities may include insistence that the victim wears certain clothes, says certain words, etc
- Premature ejaculation: This is when ejaculation occurs immediately before or after penetration.
- Delayed ejaculation: This rapist struggles to ejaculate or cannot ejaculate at all. The prevention of ejaculation cannot be ascribed to the man's control. Fifteen per cent of rapists have this problem. This may explain why no semen is found after the rape, although no condom was used
- Conditional ejaculation: This man can only ejaculate if certain sexual acts or words are complied with

Type and order of sexual deeds

The type, sequential order and preferences of the rapist's sexual deeds reveal something of his personality. A rapist who first demands anal sex, then forces the victim to have oral sex with him and then rapes her vaginally, is more sadistic than the one who first has oral sex followed by vaginal sex and then anal sex.

Investigating officers should not concentrate only on questions about the sexual act itself, but also ask questions about kissing, cuddling, use of other objects, hands and fingers, fetishism, voyeurism or exhibitionism.

Rapists will often repeat certain acts or sequences of acts. This type of modus operandi may have linkage value. By determining the sequence of sexual acts it can be established whether the rapist was acting out a fantasy, experimenting or committing the acts to punish or humiliate the victim. When a rapist cuddles or has oral sex with the victim, he is usually entertaining a fantasy, imagining himself to be her lover.

Verbal behaviour

The rapist's verbal behaviour

The specific language and words the rapist used explains much about his motive. The investigating officer should not only record word for word what the rapist said, but also enquire about the pitch and attitude the rapist revealed.

Research identified twelve themes in the conversations of rapists:
- Threats
- Orders
- Obscene names
- Self-confident remarks
- Personal questions about the victim
- Personal remarks about himself
- Racist comments
- Enquiries about the victim's preferences
- 'Soft' greeting
- Sexual put-offs

- Possessiveness of women
- Taking the 'property' – referring to the victim – of another man

Accuracy is very important. For example, a rapist who says: *I'm going to hurt you if you don't do what I say*, has threatened the victim, while one who says: *Do what I say and then I won't hurt you*, has tried to reassure the victim and gain her cooperation without using violence.

A rapist who says: *I want to make love to you*, uses an affectionate phrase to indicate that he does not want to hurt her, while one who says: *I want to fuck you*, is more aggressive and hostile towards women in general.

Any compliments to the victim, courtesy, excuses or concern about her welfare or discussions of her personal life, whether it be fictitious or real, are indications of the low self-esteem of the rapist. On the other hand, humiliating, insulting, threatening or derogatory remarks are indications of a rapist who uses sex to punish his victims.

The victim may be asked to describe every remark the rapist made, for example:

- *You have beautiful breasts* – compliment
- *Am I hurting you?* – depending on the pitch and attitude, it will show either concern or hostility

Verbal behaviour of the victim

Many rapists demand that victims say certain words to them during the attack. The profiler can establish what is sexually arousing to the rapist, thereby determining his motive.

A rapist who demands that the victim should say: *You are much better than my boyfriend*, shows a need for affection and ego-stimulation. One who demands that the victim begs or screams has sadistic tendencies. A rapist who demands that the victim should refer to herself in derogatory terms has a hostile attitude towards women in general.

Sudden changes in the rapist's behaviour

These behavioural changes may be either physical, verbal or sexual. The victim should be asked if there were any sudden changes in these three categories of behaviour, which contrast with previous behaviour.

Should there have been a change, the victim should be asked to indicate what happened immediately before the change. A sudden change can indicate a weakness or fear on the part of the rapist and it is important to determine what precipitated it.

Contributing factors could include a dysfunction, external interruptions, resistance, lack of fear from the victim, the victim laughing at or provoking the rapist, or even completion of the sexual act. This information can be successfully incorporated into an interrogation strategy and will greatly assist the profiler.

To determine the rapist's experience of the rape, the victim should be asked what precautions the rapist took to conceal his identity, to remove evidence, and to escape.

Missing items

Some rapists steal items from victims. If the items are of little value, further enquiries are not usually made. But to the profiler it is not only important what was stolen, but why it was stolen.

Sometimes the victim will not immediately realise that something has been stolen, for example a photograph or a pair of panties. The investigating officer should ask the victim to check her belongings systematically and inform him as soon as possible if anything is missing, even if it is of little value.

Missing items can be classified into three categories:

- Evidential: A rapist may take an object because it could tie him to the crime; for example, something with his fingerprints or semen on it. This indicates experience gained from a previous arrest
- Valuable: A rapist who steals a valuable item probably has financial problems, is unemployed or earns a living by burglary. The item stolen may give an indication of his age or status
- Personal: Personal items usually include pictures of the victim, underwear, her identity document, etc

Return to the victim

Many rapists make contact with the victim after the rape. Some do it to intimidate her, while others apologise or ask her on a date. He may want to see the victim personally, phone her or write to her. It is important that this information (verbatim conversations, copies of letters, etc) be provided to the profiler.

When the investigating officer interviews the victim, he or she should put aside personal prejudices towards the victim and the rapist. He or she should be able to stand in the shoes of both victim and rapist, and ask questions accordingly.

RAPE INVESTIGATION IN SOUTH AFRICA

Rape investigations in South Africa can be conducted by detectives at station level, or by detectives attached to Domestic Violence, Sexual Offences and Child Protection Units. The latter will mostly have been trained to manage the victims sensitively. A victim will be provided with a rape kit, consisting of clean underwear etc. Although it is understandable that a victim would want to bath and change clothing immediately after being raped, it is essential that she/he does not. The victim should take a clean set of clothing with her and the investigating officer will accompany her to a district surgeon, where a medical examination will be conducted, DNA smears taken and a J88 form be completed. The detectives will also put the victim in touch with a rape counselling service, if the victim so wishes. I would recommend that the victim attend counselling. The investigating officer will lay claim to the victim's clothes as well as to bed sheets, etc in order to search for evidence. The sooner the rape is reported, the better the chance of apprehending the suspect and the better for the victim's testimony in court.

Lauren Netto submitted a valuable thesis for her Master's degree in psychology at Rhodes University entitled *The Development of a Pro-Forma Document for use in Police Rape Investigations in South Africa* (2000). She devised a pro-forma for interviewing rape survivors based upon the following aspects:

- Victim-offender interaction
- Verbal interaction
- Modus operandi
- Signature behaviour
- Relationship to victim
- Crime scene information
- Perpetrator information
- Victim information
- Practical procedures
- Context of the crime
- Description of the event
- Witnesses
- Psychological support
- Forensics

I strongly recommend that detectives investigating rape cases get hold of this document, which is obtainable from the Department of Psychology at Rhodes University, since Ms Netto includes suggestions on the approach of the police officer to whom the crime was reported and the approach of the investigating officer.

CASE STUDY: MABOPANE STATION RAPIST

Background information

The case of Dan Mathebula, the Mabopane Station Rapist, is a far cry from that of the Station Strangler. In the Station Strangler case, where young boys were murdered, the entire community of Mitchell's Plain was aware that a serial killer was active in the area and any man seen walking with a boy was regarded as suspicious and pursued by an angry mob. In Mabopane, where young girls were raped, it seemed no one was aware that a serial rapist was operating in the vicinity of the railway station. Detectives did not visit schools to warn young girls of the modus operandi of the serial rapist; no one confronted men walking hand-in-hand with young girls in the vicinity of the station; there were no newspaper reports and no posters on the streets warning the community. No plain clothes detectives were posted at the railway station. No operations room was set up by the police, nor was an investigation team established. No wonder Dan Mathebula had the confidence to continue his rapes after his escape from custody. Why was his cell door not checked for malfunctioning in the first place, and why was a warrant for his arrest only issued a year later? It was members of the public who finally caught Dan Mathebula, ironically for an attempted rape.

This case study illustrates linkage blindness in a serial rape case. For three years Dan Mathebula got away with raping young girls using exactly the same modus operandi in a relatively small area. Cases 1, 4, 5, 8, 15 and 16 were committed in the vicinity of the Mabopane railway station. The Central City shopping centre at Mabopane featured in cases 2, 3, 7, 14 and 15.

Constable Catherine Makhubela from Rietgat took statements in cases 1 and 4. Sergeant Shadrack Mhekang of the Child Protection Unit took a statement in case 4 and was the investigating officer of the escape charge. Inspector Bongani Gama of the Child Protection Unit took statements in cases 4, 8 and 15. Sergeant Magdalena Matsimela of Rietgat took statements in cases 5 and 8. Sergeant Matthews Ramoshaba of the Child Protection Unit took statements in cases 5 and 6. Sergeant Sophana Leboalo from the Child Protection Unit took statements in cases 6, 9 and 11.

All the statements reported exactly the same modus operandi. Many of the detectives wrote in their reports that since the victims could not identify the suspect, or provide an identikit, they were unable to investigate the case. Is this gross negligence on the part of the detectives or can it be attributed to a lack of training? Clearly none of them had been trained to recognise and investigate a (quite obvious) serial rapist. Luckily, Captain Frans Visagie of the Child Protection Unit, whom I had trained in this type of investigation, realised that a serial rapist was at large, collected all the dockets he could trace and brought them to the Investigative Psychology Unit for profiling. As commander of the unit, I assigned the case to Inspector Elmarie Myburgh for profiling. Two months after the profile was completed Dan Mathebula was arrested by the public.

The profile

Inspector Myburgh did not receive the dockets of cases 4 and 16. For the sake of completeness, her profile has been supplemented with material that was not available at the time she drew up the profile.

Key to cases and CAS numbers

CASE NUMBER	CAS NUMBER	DATE OF INCIDENT
1	Rietgat 183/5/96	1996/05/12
2	Rietgat 346/8/96	1996/08/24
3	Loate 54/9/96	1996/09/05
4	Rietgat 116/10/96	1996/10/06
5	Rietgat 40/11/96	1996/11/02
6	Loate 229/11/96	1996/11/23
7	Rietgat 338/3/97	1997/03/18
8	Rietgat 216/4/97	1997/03/22
9	Rietgat 223/5/97	1997/05/18
10	Rietgat 198/8/97	1997/08/13
11	Silverton 478/8/97	1997/08/26
12	Rietgat 111/10/97	1997/10/08
13	Mabopane 367/12/97	1997/12/27
14	Rietgat 110/1/98	1998/01/08

Note: The column listing the names of the victims has been deleted. Since they were all minors they may not be identified.

The profile

Reconstruction of crime

The victims were black girls between the ages of 9 and 14 years. They were all on their way somewhere, and most of them were accompanied by a friend or sister. The suspect approached them with a ruse that he was a police officer investigating a theft. The children were suspected of committing the theft and have to accompany him to the complainant. He forced them to take a 'short cut' through the veld, where he ordered them to remove their underwear and proceeded to rape one of the girls. The other child had to watch the rape. He robbed them of their money and disappeared. Should they be inclined not to cooperate, he threatened to stab them with a knife or shoot them.

Victim risk
High risk. The victims are young and cannot defend themselves.

Offender risk
High risk. The incidents took place during the day in the vicinity of Central City or Mabopane railway station, where anyone could have seen the offender with the victims. Although he took them into the bush where it was quiet, he spent enough time with them for them to be able to identify him later.

Escalation
The rapes took place at monthly intervals, with some lapses of three months between rapes.

Time for crime
The offender spent time with the victims. He met them and persuaded them to accompany him. After they had walked for a while and he had entered into a conversation with them, he took them into the bush where he raped them. In some cases the victims were forced to commit certain acts to arouse him, but the rape itself lasted only a few minutes.

Location
In most cases the offender met the victims close to the Mabopane railway station and lured them into the nearby bush where he raped them.

Clothing

In most cases the offender commanded the victims to remove their underwear. If they refused, he undressed them. In some cases he only opened the zip of his trousers, but in others he removed his trousers. In one case he pulled his trousers down to his knees.

Victim profiles

Rietgat 183/5/96

Age:	12 years
Date of incident:	Sunday, 1996/05/12, at about 14h00
Crime scene:	Bush next to block BB Soshanguve, on the way to Mabopane railway station
Weapon:	Threatened with firearm
Clothing:	Suspect removed victim's pants and underwear. He only opened his zip
Rape:	Only raped one of the victims

Reconstruction: The victim and a friend were on their way to Mabopane railway station to buy a train ticket for her mother. They were approached by a man posing as a police officer. He informed them that a woman at the BTH gate was looking for two girls who stole her money. They matched the description of the girls and he asked them to accompany him to meet the woman. The girls believed him. On the way he took out a firearm and forced the girls into the bush. He took the victim's cash. He took off the victim's pants and underwear, but only unzipped his trousers. He raped the girl and disappeared. The victim's friend was not harmed.

The victim returned home, informed her mother of the incident and unfortunately washed herself. The mother reasoned that since it was late and she had no money, she could not accompany her daughter to the police station immediately. Her grandmother took her to the Rietgat police station on the Monday. Their statements were taken by Constable Catherine Makhubela at Rietgat. The case was referred to Sergeant Mthombeni of the Child Protection Unit. He wrote in his report that the victim was unable to identify the rapist. He had patrolled the area and alerted his informers. *All means have been done to trace the suspect, but all in vain*, wrote Sergeant Mthombeni. The girl reported to the local district surgeon on 14 May and it was confirmed that she had been raped.

Rietgat 346/8/96

Age:	11 years
Date of incident:	Saturday, 1996/08/24, at about 11h30
Crime scene:	Bushes along Soshanguve railway
Weapon:	Threatened with firearm
Clothing:	Suspect forced victim to remove her underwear
	He unzipped his trousers
Rape:	Only one of the girls was raped

Reconstruction: The victim's mother sent her and a friend to Central City (near the railway station) to buy groceries. They were approached by the suspect, who used the same ruse: they had stolen money from a woman and should accompany him to block BB, Soshanguve. He took both children by the hand and led them into the bush where he made them sit down. He promised to free the first girl who was able to urinate. The victim urinated. He forced her to stroke his penis and ejaculated into her mouth. He took the victim into the veld and told her to wait. He returned with a cardboard box and instructed her to lie down. He threatened to kill her if she did not cooperate. The friend had to watch him raping the victim. After the rape the victim was told to get dressed quickly. The suspect gave them directions for the way home and watched them as they walked away.

An hour later, the victim arrived home and told her mother what had happened to her. At about ten o'clock that night Inspector Freddie Mogetsi of the Child Protection Unit took her and her mother's statement at Rietgat police station. Both girls said they would be able to identify the suspect, but that they had never seen him before. Inspector Mogetsi wrote in his report: *The suspect cannot be traced. Enquiries were made several times about him but to no avail.*

Loate 54/9/96

Age:	12 years
Date of incident:	Sunday, 1996/09/05, at about 14h00
Crime scene:	Construction in progress, block N, Mabopane
Clothing:	Victim forced to remove her under-wear
	Suspect removed his trousers
Weapon:	He threatened to shoot her
Rape:	Only one girl

Reconstruction: The victim's mother sent her to the shops after school. The suspect approached her with the same ruse: a woman had been robbed and since she was a suspect, she should accompany him. He threatened to shoot her if she screamed. He took her to the building under construction and ordered her to remove her underwear. He removed his trousers and raped her. After the rape he stole her cash (R21).

The girl ran off but told an adult she met on the way

about the rape. The adult took her home and reported the incident to her mother, who took her to the Loate police station where Sergeant Merafe took statements from both the victim and her mother. The case was referred to Sergeant Papole of the Child Protection Unit who, a week later, took the statement of the adult woman who had found the girl. The docket contains no reports from these officers regarding any investigation into the rape. A district surgeon's report confirmed the rape.

Case 4
This docket was not available to Inspector Myburgh at the time of drawing up the profile. For the sake of completion, the details are given below.

At about 9 am on Sunday, 29 September 1996 a 13-year-old girl was waiting for the bus after buying paraffin for her family at Mabopane railway station. A man standing on the platform approached her. He informed her that a woman had been robbed of R200 by a young girl fitting her description. She accompanied him willingly. He led her across the railway line to an unfinished building under construction. He instructed her to wait. A few minutes later he returned, ordered her to undress and then raped her. The girl ran home and told her mother, who took her to the police station. Constable Catherine Makhubela at Rietgat police station took the victim's statement. The case was referred to Sergeant Shadrack Mhekang of the Child Protection Unit, who wrote in his report that he had investigated the case for a long time and that the commander should close the docket as unsolved.

Rietgat 116/10/96

Age:	12 years
Date of incident:	Sunday, 1996/10/06, at about 17h00

Crime scene:	Bush near Mabopane railway station
Weapon:	Knife
Clothing:	Victim was forced to remove her clothing and lie on her trousers
Weapon:	Threatened with a knife
Rape:	Only one girl

Reconstruction: The victim's mother sent her and her younger sister to the station to buy a train ticket. The suspect approached them at the station and repeated the ruse about a woman who had been robbed. He identified himself as a police officer and instructed them to accompany him, as they were suspected of the theft. He told them not to be frightened because he was a police officer. He led them into the bush and told them that he had killed a girl there the previous day, because she wouldn't listen to him. The victim's sister screamed, but he instructed them to remain calm because he was a stranger. He threatened them with a knife. He instructed the victim to undress so that he could search her for the stolen money. He robbed her of the R52 her mother had given her for the train ticket. He instructed her to lie down on her pants. When she screamed he threatened her with the knife. After the rape, he told her to get dressed and gave her directions to the railway line. The victim asked for her money back, but he refused.

The girls encountered two adult women on their way home, who advised them to report the rape to the police. When they arrived home they found their father asleep. At about nine o'clock that night they found their mother at their grandmother's home and told her what had happened. Since it was late, the mother took her daughter to the clinic the following morning, where the rape was confirmed. They then went to the Rietgat police station.

Sergeant Magdalena Matsimela took the victim's statement and Sergeant Matthews Ramoshaba of the Child Protection Unit took the statement of the sister and the mother. There are no reports of the investigating officers in the dockets.

Rietgat 40/11/96

Age:	13 years
Date of incident:	Saturday, 1996/11/02, at about 12h00
Crime scene:	Veld next to block BB, Soshanguve
Weapon:	Knife
Clothing:	All the girls were forced to remove their underwear
Rape:	Raped two of the girls

Reconstruction: The victim's mother sent her to the shops at block BB, Soshanguve. She met the suspect in the company of two other girls. He informed her that a woman had been robbed of her money by young girls and claimed that she was under suspicion. He led the girls into the veld opposite block BB and robbed the victim of her money. He ordered all the girls to remove their underwear because he wanted sex. When the victim refused, he threatened her with a knife. Then he ordered all the girls to lie on the ground and proceeded to rape one of the other girls while holding the victim's hand. Then he raped the victim. The man got dressed and ordered the children to wait for him, but he did not return.

The girls exchanged addresses and the 13-year-old proceeded to block BB where she informed an adult woman of the rape. The woman took her home to her mother who took her to Rietgat police station where she made a statement. There is no stamp on this statement to identify the police officer who took it. On 19 November 1996 Sergeant Leboalo wrote that she was the investigating officer in the case, but that she could not trace the suspect, nor the medical report pertaining to the victim's injuries. She reported that the original statement was made to Sergeant Mary Mahlangu, but that she had died on 16 November 1996. Her statement was verified by Sergeant Matthews Ramoshaba of the same unit.

Loate 229/11/96

Age:	12 years
Date of incident:	Saturday, 1996/11/23 at about 15h00
Crime scene:	Near a shopping centre at Winterveld/Mabopane
Weapon:	Knife
Clothing:	Victim was forced to remove all her clothing
	Suspect removed his trousers
Rape:	Only one girl

Reconstruction: The victim and three friends were on their way to the Mabopane shopping centre. The suspect approached them, identifying himself as Dan Mathebula, a police officer. He confronted them as suspects in an incident where R250 had been stolen from a woman. He led them into the bush and demanded money from them, threatening them with a knife. When one of the girls refused to hand her money over, he instructed all of them to lie down in a row. He removed all the victim's clothing and removed his trousers, telling her to insert his penis into her vagina. When she refused he did it himself. After the rape he instructed her to get dressed quickly while he went to check whether anyone was approaching.

When he did not return, the girls ran off. They spotted policemen at a roadblock and reported the rape to them. The girls saw the suspect buying vegetables at the station and the policemen arrested him. Sergeant Lucas Legapo took their statements at Loate police station. Dan Dodo Mathebula was kept in custody at Loate.

It was seven days after this, on 30 November 1996, that Mathebula escaped from the holding cells. Sergeant Hendrick Setoy took Sergeant Legapo's statement in which he said that he had been in the charge office at seven o'clock that night. At half past seven he visited the cells and confirmed that the awaiting trial prisoners had been fed. All the prisoners were present and had no complaints. At about eight o'clock Sergeant Setoy went to inspect the cells and returned to inform Sergeant Legapo that a prisoner had escaped. Sergeant Legapo and the commanding officer, Inspector Mosiane, went to the cells and confirmed the escape.

In turn, Sergeant Lucas Legapo took a statement from Sergeant Hendrick Setoy that he had visited the cells between ten to and ten past eight that night to check on the prisoners. One of the prisoners informed him that Dan Mathebula had escaped. He called Sergeant Legapo and they searched the cells. Dan Mathebula's cell door was open. Sergeant Setoy stated that it seemed as if the prisoner had managed to open the cell door himself. The lock appeared to be defective. He reported the case to Inspector Mosiane, who opened a docket.

Sergeant Shadrack Mhekang of the Child Protection Unit was appointed investigating officer in charge of the escape case. He reported that the suspect's residential address was searched, but the suspect was not there. The Mabopane railway station was also searched, but to no avail. He stated that the case was *investigated for a long time but without success*. A warrant of arrest was issued for Dan Mathebula on the escape charge on 22 October 1997 – almost a year after he escaped.

Four months after his escape another rape was reported.

Rietgat 338/3/97

Age:	14 years
Date of incident:	Tuesday, 1997/03/18, at about 18h30
Crime scene:	Bush near Soshanguve railway station
Weapon:	Knife
Clothing:	Both children had to remove their clothing
Rape:	Only one girl

Reconstruction: The victim's mother sent her to block GG, Soshanguve. Near the clinic the suspect accosted her, showing her his police identification card. He informed her that a girl matching her description had stolen money from a woman at the railway station. She went with him and on the way they met another young girl in her school uniform. The suspect repeated the story to this girl. He asked them their names and took them to the station. He instructed them to wait while he checked if there were other people in the area. When he returned he instructed the children to remove their clothing. He told the victim to lie on top of the other girl and open her legs. He raped the victim while the other girl watched. When the victim cried, he threatened her with a knife. He then told them to go home.

The 14-year-old took the other girl to her home, where she told her mother what had happened. Their statements were taken by Constable Magdalena Matsimela at Rietgat police station. Rape was confirmed by the district surgeon's report the following day. The case was referred to Inspector Bongani Gama of the Child Protection Unit. He noted in his report that the victim did not know the suspect, but said that she would be able to identify him.

Rietgat 216/4/97

Age:	Unknown
Date of incident:	Saturday, 1997/03/22, at about 12h30
Crime scene:	Near the railway station, Soshanguve
Weapon:	Iron bar
Clothing:	The victim had to remove her skirt and underwear
	Suspect only opened his zip
Rape:	Only one girl

Reconstruction: While on her way to the Soshanguve railway station, the victim was approached by the suspect who asked for directions. He identified himself as a police officer. While she was buying tickets, he walked over and took her hand. He told her that she was suspected of stealing money and that she should go with him. On the way they encountered another girl whom he told to accompany them. Further on they encountered a boy and a girl. The man called the children to come with him, but they ran away. He chased and caught them and forced them to go with him. He took all the children to a tree about 500 metres from the Soshanguve railway line where he hit the victim on her back with an iron bar and took her money. Another man sitting under the tree instructed the boy and girl to have sex with each other. The suspect led the first two girls away and ordered them to undress. He raped the victim while warning her to keep quiet. He then left.

The victim asked the others for their addresses and then went home. When her older sister arrived home, she told her what had happened. The next day they went to the Loate police station and reported the rape. The 12-year-old's statement was taken by Inspector Letsono of the Child Protection Unit at Soshanguve. Her sister's statement was taken by Sergeant Molete Mokone. The case was referred to Inspector Sophana Leboalo of the Child Protection Unit who reported that the suspect could not be traced and that the victim could not complete an identikit, and so she was unable to conduct an investigation.

Inspector B P Pholoana of the Child Protection Unit made a statement on 2 April 1997 that this case was referred to Rietgat police station by Soshanguve police station. He and Sergeant Segopolo visited the scene of the crime with the victim and he had come to the conclusion that the area fell within the jurisdiction of Rietgat police station.

Rietgat 223/5/97

Age:	13 years
Date of incident:	Sunday, 1997/05/18, at about 09h30
Crime scene:	Bush in Soshanguve
Weapon:	Knife
Clothing:	The suspect removed the victim's underwear
	The suspect removed his trousers and underpants
Rape:	Raped the girl

Reconstruction: The victim was on her way to Soshanguve when the suspect confronted her and accused her of being a thief. She denied this but he insisted on taking her to the complainant for identification. As they walked through the bush he took out a knife and threatened to kill her if she screamed. Then he removed her underwear and raped her standing up. The victim cried and he warned her to keep quiet. He told her the way home and took a different route himself.

When the girl got home she told her relatives about the rape. Her statement was taken by Sergeant Mosemeki Ringani of the Child Protection Unit. He also took the child in his car and drove to the area of the rape in an effort to spot the rapist, but without success.

Rietgat 198/8/97

Age:	14 years
Date of incident:	Wednesday, 1997/08/13, at about 09h30
Crime scene:	Veld at block AA, Soshanguve
Clothing:	Suspect removed the victim's clothing
	He pulled his trousers down to his knees
Weapon:	Suspect threatened to shoot the victim
Rape:	Suspect raped the victim twice

Reconstruction: The victim was on her way to school when the suspect approached her and asked if she was a scholar. He accused her of stealing another child's money and instructed her to accompany him to Vulibondo School. When the victim complained that she would be late for school, he threatened to shoot her for shouting at him. They walked through the veld and after a while he told her they should rest. He said that they had to come to an agreement and she should give him money. When she answered that she had no money, he told her to choose between life and death. He ordered her to undress, but she refused. He forced her to lie on his jersey and raped her while she screamed with pain. After the rape he handed her her underwear and they continued to walk through the veld. He told her that he was not yet satisfied and raped her again. Then he left.

The girl ran to the road and flagged down a police van which took her to the Rietgat police station where Sergeant Clive Maleman took her statement. The case was referred to Sergeant Sophana Leboalo of the Child Protection Unit. She reported that unregistered informers were tasked, that the child could not compile an identikit and therefore the suspect could not be arrested.

Silverton 478/8/97

Age:	15 years
Date of incident:	Tuesday, 1997/08/26, at about 18h00
Crime scene:	Veld near Koedoespoort railway station
Weapon:	Knife
Clothing:	Suspect removed victim's under-wear
Assault:	Suspect knocked victim to the ground, and threatened to kill her with the knife
Rape:	Suspect raped the victim

Reconstruction: The victim was on her way home from the Koedoespoort railway station. The suspect accosted her from behind, knocked her to the ground and threatened her with a knife. He threatened to kill her if she did not cooperate. When she screamed he began throttling her. He forced her to hold his penis and then he raped her.

She reported the incident to Silverton police station, but it is unclear who took her statement.

Rietgat 111/10/97

Age:	9 years

Date of incident:	Thursday, 1997/10/08, at about 14h30
Crime scene:	Bush near Boekenhout
Attack:	Suspect threw victim to the ground
Clothing:	Suspect removed victim's underwear
Rape:	Suspect raped victim
Wounds:	Victim was hospitalised for a long time after the incident

Reconstruction: The victim was on her way to her grand-mother's home after school. The suspect approached her and pulled her into the bush. He removed her underwear and threw her to the ground. After the rape he allowed her to dress herself and then he carried her to the railway station. The victim knew the suspect as 'Patrick'.

Unfortunately it is not known who took her statement at Rietgat police station.

Mabopane 367/12/97

Age:	12 years
Date of incident:	Saturday, 1997/12/27, at about 13h00
Crime scene:	Bush near Mabopane railway line
Clothing:	Victim removed all her clothing Suspect opened his zip
Assault:	Suspect slapped victim
Rape:	Attempted

Reconstruction: The victim and a friend were on their way to the Mabopane shops when an unknown man on a bicycle stopped them and enquired about two other girls. He asked them to help him find them. When the victim refused, he told them that he was a police officer and that they should obey him. He forced them into the bush and robbed the victim of her money. He ordered her to remove her clothing and when she refused he slapped her. Both children were forced to lie on the ground, with the victim on top of her friend. He lay next to the victim and simulated rape but did not penetrate her. She noticed semen on her legs. He then left on his bicycle.

The girl reported the incident to her grandmother who told her not to wash and took her to the hospital. Her statement was taken by Sergeant Sydney Moeti at Mabopane police station.

Rietgat 110/1/98

Age:	14 years
Date of incident:	Thursday, 1998/01/08, at about 15h00
Crime scene:	Near Mabopane railway line, Soshanguve
Clothing:	Victim removed her pants Friend removed her dress
Weapon:	Knife
Rape:	Only one girl

Reconstruction: On their way to Central City the victim and her friend were approached by the suspect who accused them of theft. He asked them to accompany him to sort the matter out. He assured them that he was a good person who would not harm them. He led them into the bush near Mabopane railway station, slapping the friend when she lagged behind. He instructed the girls to remove their clothing. He told the victim to urinate, but she could not. He threatened them with a knife and then raped the victim. After the rape he instructed them to wait for him, but he did not return.

The girls fled. The victim only reported the incident to her mother the following day. Her statement was taken by

Inspector Bongani Gama of the Child Protection Unit at Rietgat.

It was at this time that the profile was compiled. The profiler, Inspector Elmarie Myburgh, was not given the docket for case number 16, but the details of this are given below for the sake of completion.

Case 16

At about 4.15 on the afternoon of 1 March 1998, a 14-year-old girl was on her way to the Mabopane railway station when a man introducing himself as a police officer told her that she was suspected of stealing R400 from a woman. He asked her to accompany him to sort the matter out and assured her that she need not be frightened. The suspect led the girl into a building under construction near the station. Once inside he began insulting her and threatening to kill her. He ordered her to undress and then attempted to rape her, but did not succeed in penetrating her. He got dressed and took her money. He told her to wait for him, threatening to kill her if she left the building.

When she saw he had gone she ran away. She met four adults on the road and told them what had happened to her. They flagged down a taxi and went looking for the suspect, whom the girl soon spotted among the crowd. The adults gave chase and caught the suspect and took him to Loate police station. Dan Dodo Mathebula was back in custody at the same police station from which he had escaped months before.

Offender profile

Type and style

The offender is a preference molester because he prefers

children as victims. He is also a power rapist and manifests a combination of power reassurance and power assertiveness because:

- He rapes to assert his manliness
- He shows a weapon to the victims to control them
- His motive is sexual
- He uses foreplay in some cases
- The rape does not last long
- He shows concern for the victims after the rapes by giving them directions to get home or telling them how to get safely back to the railway line
- The rapes have a pattern
- The rapes are committed in the same location
- He uses violence and aggression in some cases to achieve his goal
- He uses a ruse to persuade the victims

Primary intent

Rape and robbery.

Socio-economic status

The offender fits into the environment where he meets his victims. Therefore it can be assumed that he is of the same middle-class socio-economic status as the victims.

Level of education

Although the offender probably did not pass high school, he is intelligent and 'streetwise'. Because of the ruse he uses and specific choice of words, it is assumed that he knows legal procedures and the rights of suspects when they are arrested.

Vehicle

The suspect walks freely in the area where he comes

into contact with his potential victims. The victims are children, most of whom had been sent on errands by their parents and will take appropriate routes.

Appearance

The offender fits in with the environment. According to the victims and witnesses he does not stand out either because of a neat or a slovenly appearance.

Criminal record

The fact that the offender has a criminal record is the reason for him knowing legal procedures.

Emotional temperament

The offender is initially friendly, because he misleads the victims with a ruse that persuades them to accompany him. He sets them at ease in order to win their trust. He abuses their fear and respect for the police by informing them that he is a police officer. He tries to set their minds at ease in some cases by telling them that they should accompany him to clear up a misunderstanding. In other cases he remains patient until they reach the bush, although some victims were assaulted to force them to accompany him to the bush. They are slapped on the face and one was hit on the back with an iron bar. It can be assumed that the offender has a high level of aggression and low impulse control. The fact that he selects children as victims indicates that he lacks self-confidence in the presence of adults. It is far easier to manipulate children. The exhibitionism that manifests by having witnesses to the rapes indicates an inferiority complex.

Attitude towards women and sex

The offender lacks self-confidence in the company of

adult women and therefore rapes children. He can easily persuade them to accompany him, because they are naïve and believe his ruse. Children are also easier to control since they respect adults (especially police officers) and will not oppose him. He further demonstrates his dominance to himself by taking two children simultaneously. He believes he has the right to sex and wants to confirm his dominance by raping in front of a witness, which proves his strength and manliness. He manifests exhibitionism.

He also manifests a sexual paraphilia, namely a fetish about watching the children urinate.

Childhood years

The offender probably grew up in a home where he did not have a good relationship with his parents. The discipline was probably too strict and he was dominated, especially by his mother. He was probably physically abused and now rapes children to prove his dominance and to make others feel the way he felt as a child.

Motive and fantasies

His primary motive is to relieve his sexual urges. His secondary motive is to prove power and dominance to himself by raping. He accomplishes this by misleading the children and the fact that he can persuade children to accompany him. Making the children witness the rapes is a further proof of his manliness and gratifies his need for exhibitionism.

His fantasy is not sophisticated. When he realised his ruse to persuade the children to accompany him proved successful, he kept strictly to it. He repeated every step in the process to the last detail, because it is part of his fantasy.

Mental health

The offender is not psychotic or mentally ill. He does not suffer from a mental disorder such as multiple personality disorder, but acts normally and leads a normal life.

Outcome

Dan Mathebula made his formal confession to Magistrate L Pretorius at Soshanguve Magistrate's Court on 14 April 1998. In a relaxed mood he said the following:

> (Translated) I verify there are nine cases of rape against me. I only have knowledge of three of these nine cases. I raped these persons, but I cannot remember their names. The rapes took place on three different days. I did it at an open veld next to the clinic. The first woman I found at the railway station. I had food with me. I told her at the station I am a police officer. I said a woman had lost her money and she wants to see you, come with me. At the above-mentioned veld I had physical communion with her. All three women gave consent. I followed this modus operandi with each one. PS: Not one of them ate the food with me.

Dan Mathebula was identified by several of the witnesses and his DNA matched that obtained from the victims. He was 31 years old at the time of arrest, unemployed, residing at Block G, Soshanguve, and had a grade 10 education. He had no previous convictions. On 20 November 2000, he was found guilty by Mr Justice W R C Prinsloo of nine rapes, five robberies and one kidnapping, and escaping from custody. He was given nine life sentences.

Child Molesters

DEFINITIONS

The word paedophile is a psychological term referring to a sexual disorder in which children are the preferred sexual objects. Not all paedophiles will necessarily transgress the law. A paedophile may act out his or her sexual fantasies with other consenting adults who are of small build, with flat breasts and no body hair and who mimic childlike behaviour. Paedophiles who have sex with children are child molesters.

Not all child molesters are paedophiles. A person who normally prefers sex with adults may have sex with a child for reasons of curiosity or opportunism or to hurt the parent of the child. Persons who do not have a preference for children as sexual objects, but who use them in child pornography, are also child molesters.

TYPOLOGY OF CHILD MOLESTERS

Kenneth Lanning, an FBI agent employed at the National Center for Missing and Exploited Children in the USA, compiled two extensive reports: *Child Molesters: A Behavioral Analysis* (1987) and *Child Sex Rings: A Behavioral Analysis* (1989). I did not work on many cases of child molestation during my career in the SAPS, as such cases are usually referred to the Child Protection

Unit, but now and again when a case crossed my path, I found Lanning's reports to be extremely useful.

Lanning differentiates between two major types of child molester, each with subcategories.

The situational child molester

This type of child molester does not have a true preference for children as sexual objects, but may have sex with a child, depending upon the situation. This may happen once or often, and he or she will usually have sex with fewer different child victims. They may also have sex with the elderly or with the ill and the mentally retarded.

The four subtypes of situational child molesters are:

Regressed child molesters

This type has low self-esteem and underdeveloped coping skills. They use children because an adequate partner of their own peer group is not available. They often molest their own children because of availability and probable marital problems. They may collect pornography.

Morally indiscriminate child molesters

This type molests children as part of their general pattern of abusing others: they abuse their partners, colleagues, friends and family members. They will lie, steal and cheat if they can get away with it. They are typical psychopaths (antisocial personality disorder) who take advantage of the child's natural helplessness and vulnerability, and they may coerce or manipulate their victims. They may abuse their own children. They will be interested in pornography, detective magazines and perhaps sado-masochistic literature.

Sexually indiscriminate child molesters

This type experiments with sex. In the same way as they might experiment with homosexuals, they will experiment with children purely for the sake of experience.

They may abuse their own children and are likely to involve their children in sex games with other adults. They may collect pornography and erotica.

Inadequate child molesters

This type suffers from psychoses, personality disorders, retardation or senility. They are society's outcasts who do not have the self-confidence to approach other adults for sex. Typically, this person may be a shy teenager, or a young man still living with his parents. They are motivated by uncertainty and curiosity and their inhibited frustrations explode into child molestation, which may lead to torture and murder. Their victims may also include the elderly and other vulnerable people. They might collect pornography.

Preferential child molesters

In contrast to the situational child molester, the preferential child molester prefers children as sexual objects. He will have many more victims than the situational child molester and has a need to have frequent and repetitive sex with children.

The three subtypes of preferential child molesters are the following:

Seducers

This type will seduce the selected child victim with attention, presents and affection, in the way that adults court each other. The child's inhibitions are broken over time until he or she is prepared to exchange sexual favours for gifts or attention. This type of offender often participates in child sex rings, and usually selects children who have been abused or neglected and are hungry for attention.

The seducers encounter problems when the children outgrow their usefulness. They will threaten or use violence to prevent the child from disclosing their secrets.

Introverts

This type does not have the social skills to court their preferred child victims and will molest very young children or strangers. They will hang around playgrounds and have short quick sexual relations with their victims. They may expose themselves or make obscene phone calls to children. They may marry an adult woman just to have access to her children and may also molest their own children from a very young age.

Sadists

This type is sexually aroused by torturing their preferred child victims. They will abduct children and may murder them.

CHARACTERISTICS OF CHILD MOLESTERS

Lanning and his colleagues identified four main characteristics to identify child molesters. He warns that these signs should be read cumulatively.

Long-term and persistent pattern of behaviour

- Many paedophiles will have a history of sexual abuse in their own backgrounds. However, I have found that boys who have been sexually abused by a female

family member will rape women as an adult because of aggressive feelings towards women, while a boy who has been sexually abused by a stranger, is more likely to grow up to become a paedophile
- They had limited social contact as teenagers, especially sexual contact with their own peer group. Their preference for children will have begun during their own teenage years
- The male paedophile is likely to have been dismissed from military training, or not selected at all
- They tend to relocate fairly frequently, especially when rumours begin to circulate or when they have been identified
- They may have a record of prior arrests, perhaps not for sexual offences but for fraud, impersonating a police officer or violating child labour laws
- There are multiple victims involved
- They plan their crimes carefully and will often take great risks in attempting to secure victims

Children as the preferred sexual objects

- Offenders are most likely male, older than twenty-five years and single. They will not have had long-lasting relationships with other adults, unless these adults were also involved in child sex rings
- They prefer to live alone or with their parents. Lanning warns that this should not be taken as a single indicator, but in conjunction with other signs
- If they are married, the wife may be either very domineering or very weak in character. She will not have a strong libido. Some wives are aware that their husbands are paedophiles but prefer to ignore the fact, because it relieves them of the burden of having sexual relations with him
- Paedophiles have an excessive interest in children.

All their friends are children; they hang around playgrounds, video game parlours, sports fields, etc
- Most paedophiles have specific preference for age and gender. How old the child looks is more important than the chronological age. There is less of a gender preference when the children are very young; for example, babies
- They refer to children in superlative idealistic terms, such as 'pure', 'innocent', 'clean', 'angels', etc or as objects, for example: 'the kid has a low mileage'

Well-developed techniques in obtaining victims
- Paedophiles have an amazing skill for homing in on vulnerable children – the ones from broken homes, for example, who are hungry for attention
- They identify with children and can 'speak their language'. They are also skilful listeners
- They frequent places where children go and may even marry just to gain access to children. They treat neighbourhood children to field trips and seek employment or extramural activities involving children. Such activities would most likely exclude other adults. Paedophiles will volunteer to babysit, to allow parents quality time on their own. Norman Avzal Simons was a primary school teacher but he would often round up the neighbourhood children and take them to the beach or treat them to ice-cream
- They use sophisticated techniques such as manipulation, peer pressure, courting, gifts and child psychology to seduce children. Many progress to showing children pornographic videos. In South Africa it is illegal to expose children to pornography of any description. Even when children watch soft porn at home on late-night television while their parents are out or sleeping, the parents may be held liable

- Their hobbies are appealing to children. They collect dolls, build miniature aeroplanes, play with remote control boats in park ponds, fly kites, etc. A paedophile interested in teenagers will seduce them with cigarettes, alcohol, drugs and pornography

Sexual fantasies focusing on children

- They decorate their homes in the way a child would decorate his or her room
- They love photographing children and will have many seemingly innocent albums containing photographs of children. These albums have erotic value to paedophiles
- They will collect child pornography or erotica, like swimwear, underwear, nappies, hair brushes, etc which they use as stimulation during masturbation

Lanning and his colleagues at the FBI also provide valuable information on child pornography. Paedophiles who can afford it will make their own pornographic videos; those who live with others will hide their collections, and those who cannot afford it will draw their own pictures. Some may be closet collectors who keep their collections secret, while others may be involved in commercialising their collections. Not all collectors may be actively involved in child molestation, but it is still against the law to watch, produce, keep or trade child pornography.

Commercial child pornography (children are abducted or coerced into participating) is produced mainly for sale; home-made pornography is usually private property but can also be sold or swapped, and simulated child pornography involves adults dressed up as children.

Children stay forever young when captured in a photograph or a video. Some children have committed crimes in attempts to retrieve these items when they are older, and paedophiles often use them to blackmail older children into acquiring younger victims for them.

Lanning and his colleagues describe the different types of child erotica:

Published material relating to children

This includes books, magazine articles or videos dealing with topics such as child development, sexual disorders, sex education, incest, child prostitution, personal ads, children's clothing catalogues, adoption agencies, etc. Even flyers advertising a sale at a children's department store or gifts for Christmas have been used as erotica. When paedophiles advertise these items they use terms such as 'family fun' and 'youth training'.

Unpublished material relating to children

This may include letters, drawings, telephone and address books, diaries, newsletters, albums, etc.

Souvenirs and trophies

Any item belonging to a child, including clothing, jewellery, toys, etc may be kept as a souvenir or trophy; for example, photographs, movie ticket stubs, dried flowers, etc. Many parents keep mementos of their children, but the paedophile keeps mementos of other people's children.

Miscellaneous items

Computer games, sex aids, toys, costumes, child decorations, alcohol and drugs, condoms, etc fall into this category.

Collectors are compulsive about their collections, regardless of whether they are butterflies, stamps, miniature figurines, etc. Paedophiles are as well. They treasure them, label and catalogue them and preserve them at all costs. Some will display their collections if they feel safe enough but others hide them away. Like all collectors, they invest time and money in their collections and like to discuss, boast about and swap items.

The collections serve the purpose of providing sexual gratification and arousal. Paedophiles also use their collections to lower a potential victim's inhibitions and resistance, persuading the child that it will be fun to pose and flattering them on their looks. They also employ educational books on sex in this manner.

Some material might seem innocent at first, for example an album of photographs of young girls in ballet tutus. On closer inspection a trained eye will recognise that the girls' poses represent sexual arousal for the paedophile; for example a dancer performing the splits. Sometimes sexually explicit captions are written beneath the photographs. Careful analysis of a scrapbook of girls modelling dresses may reveal that all the dresses happen to be black and lacy. It should be noted that many parents take innocent photographs of their children naked; for example, in the bath or taking an outside shower after a swim in the sea. The age and comfort level of the child and the number of pictures should be taken into consideration.

In *Child Sex Rings* (1989) Lanning defines a *sex ring* as the activity of an offender who has sex with other children before terminating sexual relationships with earlier victims. A child sex ring therefore does not necessarily involve two or more adults, but rather the number of children. There will be multiple victims and there may be multiple offenders. When multiple offenders are involved, it is more likely to be called a *syndicate*. Most child sex rings involve male offenders and male victims. A sex ring is dynamic: at any given time victims are being recruited, seduced, molested and discarded. Victims are sworn to secrecy, put under peer pressure, vie for special attention and recruit other victims. The offender may seduce them into having sex with each other.

Child sex rings or syndicates may occur within religious sects. Women are also involved in these activities and while they may not derive sexual pleasure from them, they enjoy the domination and enslavement of children, often referring to it as 'spiritual enlightenment'.

When paedophiles or child molesters are confronted or identified, they will most likely deny or try to justify their actions. Lanning and his colleagues noted the following typical responses:

- They feign shock and are indignant and uncooperative
- They minimise the seriousness, quantity and quality of the offence, arguing that it only happened once, under the influence of alcohol. The victims may also minimise the crime because of the embarrassment it causes them
- They justify their actions by arguing that they care for neglected children, provide the sexual education that their parents neglected or, worse, they blame the victim for seducing them
- They fabricate excuses; for example, a doctor may plead that he was conducting research, or a teacher may argue that his or her good intentions were maliciously misinterpreted
- They feign mental illness
- They refer to themselves as pillars of society who succumbed in a moment of weakness and try to elicit sympathy
- They attack, harass, threaten and try to bribe detectives, parents and victims, and sully the reputations of the victims and their families
- They feign amnesia and will try to make a deal with the prosecutor in order to avoid publicity
- They attempt suicide or use the threat of suicide as blackmail

Kirby, in 'A Typical Child Molester' (*Police Review*, May 1994), and McIvor and Duthie in 'MMPI Profiles of Incest Offenders' (*Criminal Justice and Behaviour*, December 1986), provide a typical profile of child molesters:

- Previous convictions would more likely be for fraud or theft than sexual offences
- 60 per cent of paedophiles prefer victims younger than eleven years, 35 per cent prefer children between twelve and fifteen years, 7 per cent have no preference regarding age, and only 14 per cent were immediate family members of the victims
- Molesters of children younger than eleven years are more prone to depression. Their profiles resemble those of rapists, while those who molest children older than eleven years will have profiles resembling exhibitionists
- The more 'intimate' offenders who treat their victims as individuals and lovers are less likely to harm the children. They have fewer previous convictions and are often married
- Those who molest stranger children on outside premises, such as parks, are likely to use alcohol or other stimulants before the event and probably began molesting children in their teenage years
- Those who molest boys are more likely to be single and to change residences often

The above statistics are American. In 1996, Superintendent Anneke Pienaar, National Head of the Child and Family Violence Unit of the South African Police Service, and her colleague E Schurink conducted research on more than 4600 cases of crimes against children. (These cases represent about 25 per cent of all crimes reported each year to the Child and Family Violence Unit.) Their findings were published under the title *Analysis of the patterns of crimes against children* (Human Sciences Research Council, 1996).

The following is a summary of Pienaar and Schurink's findings:

Was the offender known to the victim?
- 84 per cent of offenders were known to the victim
- 35 per cent of offences were committed in the child's own home
- 21 per cent of offenders were close family members of the victim
- 17 per cent of fathers or stepfathers were offenders
- 10 per cent of other family members were offenders
- 9 per cent of offenders were friends of the family
- 6 per cent of offenders were next-door neighbours

When did it happen?
- about 50 per cent of the offences happened during the weekend
- 33 per cent of incidents happened during the afternoon (12h00 to 18h00) and evening (18h00 to 24h00)
- more than 10 per cent of the incidents were repeated over a period of time
- in 96 per cent of the cases there was only one victim involved
- in 93 per cent of the cases there was only one molester

Where did it happen?
- 35 per cent of incidents happened in the victim's home
- 24 per cent of incidents happened in the offender's home

Were there any eyewitnesses?
- 48 per cent of incidents happened while other people were present in cases of incest, 81 per cent of the

victims were alone
- in 25 per cent of cases other children, such as friends or siblings, were witnesses

How were the victims approached?
- 21 per cent of offenders persuaded the victims to comply in a friendly manner
- 11 per cent threatened the victims
- in 35 per cent of the cases physical violence was used
- 49 per cent of the victims did not offer resistance

Were the victims injured?
- 58 per cent of the victims had no physical injuries
- 28 per cent had light injuries
- 51 per cent of those injured had genital injuries
- 14 per cent had injuries to their backs, heads, necks or faces

Behaviour after the crime
- 67 per cent of molesters left the victims at the scene
- 16 per cent of molesters took the children home or to places of safety
- 59 per cent of cases were reported to the police within 24 hours
- 13 per cent of cases were reported to the police within 24 days

What are the profiles of the victims?
- 75 per cent of the victims were female
- the older the child, the higher the risk of molestation (until age of fifteen)
- 30 per cent of victims were between the ages of thirteen and fifteen years
- 20 per cent of victims were between the ages of ten and twelve years

What are the profiles of the offenders?

- Coloured offenders committed more assaults (45 per cent) and sodomy (56 per cent)
- Black offenders were more involved in rape (63 per cent) and kidnapping (65 per cent), abduction (60 per cent) and neglect (55 per cent)
- White offenders committed indecent assault (46 per cent) and other sexual offences (47 per cent)
- In 19 per cent of the cases the offenders were younger than nineteen years
- 54 per cent of the offenders had never married, 24 per cent were married and 7 per cent were divorced or widowed
- 40 per cent of the offenders were unemployed
- in 41 per cent of the cases the offenders' educational qualifications were higher than grade 8
- 22 per cent of the offenders were under the influence of alcohol or drugs when the crimes were committed

Does the offender have previous convictions?

- 63 per cent of the offenders had previous convictions of which only 10 per cent were for sexual offences
- 63 per cent of the offenders with previous convictions were not sentenced

People often ask me whether children will lie about being abused. Lanning points out that children will not lie about sexual abuse, if one considers a lie to be a deliberate, malicious intent to deceive. However, children may say what they believed happened to them, they fantasise, have misperceptions of events, try to please adults and respond to leading questions.

There are several ways in which children may acquire sexual knowledge without being physically exposed to it.

- Personal knowledge. Children may witness their

parents in sexual acts, view pornography, have had sex education, or witness sexual abuse of other children
- Other children. Children exchange sex stories and are naturally curious about the subject. Most of them do not discuss these stories with their parents
- Media. There are countless books, videos, magazines, television programmes, songs and toys available on the subject
- Leading questions and suggestions: Often in child custody cases one parent may suggest sexual acts have taken place, or ask questions in such a manner that the child will respond to please that parent
- Misperception and confusion. Children may misinterpret an innocent event; for example, one child said that coins had been inserted in her anus, while they were in fact suppositories
- Education and awareness programmes. Well-intended sex education and AIDS education programmes, as well as religious programmes, may provide children with information about sex

It is imperative that one first sensitively establishes possible sources of sexual knowledge before jumping to conclusions; however, any suspicion of child molestation should be acted upon immediately. All South African citizens are required by law to inform authorities immediately of suspected child abuse.

CASE STUDY: JOE LORENCO

Background information

(The names of the complainants* in this case have been changed.)

In October 2002 the gymnastics community of South

Africa and the general public were shocked to learn about the arrest of Joe Lorenco, Springbok gymnastics trainer, for alleged sexual abuse of children. The arrest was broadcast by Carte Blanche, an investigative programme, on national television. What makes this case study notable is that the charges were laid by six adult men.

Joe Lorenco was born in Portugal where he lived with his mother and sisters. His father had deserted the family and they were very poor. When he was 12 years old, Joe was sent to live with extended family members in Johannesburg, South Africa. During the afternoons, after school, he worked in the family butchery, but all his free time was consumed by gymnastics. In 1978, at the age of 17, when he was in grade 12, Joe became his school's gymnastics coach. Joe claimed that he had no social life and, although his family cared for him, he felt unloved and isolated.

After he completed grade 12, Joe's extended family returned to Portugal. Joe, who had not seen his mother and sisters since he was a boy, had no desire to return. He decided to carve a future for himself in gymnastics in South Africa. He trained as a coach in accordance with the requirements of the South African Gymnastics Federation. From 1985 to 1994 he was the coach for the Springbok gymnastics team.

In the early 1990s Lorenco initiated a business called Monkeynastix, training pre-school children in gymnastics. This venture was successful and Lorenco and his partners soon began franchising the concept. He got married but the marriage lasted only three years; his wife allegedly caught him in bed with another man. However he claimed this was not the reason for the divorce. A son was born of this marriage, but his ex-wife did not allow the son to sleep over at Lorenco's home.

Lorenco produced many young Springboks during his

career, but at what cost?

For twenty years a group of men kept quiet about the sexual abuse they had suffered at the hands of Joe Lorenco. For twenty years this secret wrecked their adult lives until one of them could no longer stand it and came forward. He approached a fellow ex-gymnast and told him about the abuse. The sluice gates were opened. Other men came forward and, for the first time, confessed that they too had been victims of Joe Lorenco. Their statements did not make pleasant reading.

In his statement Grant* said that he had joined Lorenco's classes at the age of 11 years. Lorenco was twelve years his senior and he was a strict coach ... *who would break us down mentally in the gym, before building us up again in his bedroom.* The boys were required to practise four hours a day, six days a week. Their parents trusted Lorenco completely, allowing him to take the children out of town and even on overseas trips to compete. He was a hero in the minds of children and parents alike. No one questioned him or his methods. The children would do anything to stay in his good books and received the green and gold colours as their reward.

Lorenco often made jokes about sex during training and used explicit terminology: *You owe me a blow job*, he would tell the children during training. When he dropped the children home after training, his combi became a crime scene. His current 'favourite' was the last child to be dropped off. He would park the combi along a dark deserted road and discuss sex with the boy. He made ridiculous statements, like he needed to inspect the child's penis and the colour of his semen to monitor his physical development. In the combi, Lorenco touched the child's genitals and encouraged the child to touch his. This soon progressed to mutual masturbation and in time to oral sex.

The boys were about 11 to 12 years old. When they stayed over at his apartment he showed them pornographic videos. He organised the sleeping arrangements so that the current favourite shared his room. He would discuss the pornographic video with the child and then encourage the child to masturbate. Over time, this progressed to mutual masturbation and oral sex and in one case to anal penetration.

Lorenco abused his position as coach and hero role model. He manipulated the children to such an extent that they vied for his attention, each one trying to be the best in his books. Not one told the others that this included sexual favours as well. Springbok colours were on the line for them. Nor did any of them tell their parents.

Grant was abused from the age of 12 to 17 years, resulting in tremendous psychological damage. At one time Lorenco told Grant that he should accept that he was gay. Confused about his sexual identity, Grant had a homosexual relationship. He was relieved when it did not work out for it proved to him that he was not gay. However, he had difficulty in maintaining relationships with women and was devastated when he was rejected. He dropped out of university in his first year.

He suffered from depression and anxiety attacks and had a major problem with trust. At the age of 21 he considered suicide and out of desperation he told Jean,* an erstwhile fellow gymnast, about the cause of his suffering. Jean confessed to Grant that he had been abused as well and for the first time Jean told his parents what had happened to him. Grant confessed to Jean's parents as well, which gave him the courage to tell his own parents. Both sets of parents were devastated and advised the men to lay criminal charges. Grant felt too embarrassed, and even guilty; emotionally drained as he was, he did not see his way clear to confronting Lorenco publicly. At the age of 25 he was still tormented by the issue and again contemplated suicide. When he was 26, he entered therapy and continued this for six years. Grant realised that laying charges against Lorenco would help in his own healing and he was concerned that Lorenco might have been continuing to abuse children. By then he was mentally strong enough to lay charges.

Grant confronted Lorenco and taped their conversation. Lorenco claimed he was not a paedophile, yet a few minutes later he said: *Do not ask me, I cannot explain why I wanted to have sex with you*. He gave as an excuse that he loved that particular group of boys dearly, having missed out on love all his life. Grant challenged him, saying that his love for Lorenco had been hero-worship and not sexual in nature. He asked Lorenco if he could fathom the damage he had caused. Lorenco answered: *I did something wrong ... but if I am going to be – carry on being – crucified for it, I cannot*. At first Lorenco claimed that he did not have sexual relations with any other child, but as the conversation progressed he admitted that he had, but that 99 per cent of the time it was with Grant. Even years later, Lorenco was still in the habit of making the victim feel that he was the 'chosen one'. Later in the conversation, he again explained that he loved the group and that he did not think the sex part was the worst of it.

Throughout the conversation it was quite clear that Lorenco did not understand the trauma that Grant and the others had suffered in their adult lives. He even alleged that one of the boys had been exposed to only one incident and that no physical contact was involved; he clearly had no insight into the major damage that this single incident caused. He claimed he never meant to harm the boys and was acting out of love. This is a typical answer from a paedophile, yet Lorenco claimed time and again that although he acknowledged that he was at present a homosexual, he was not attracted to young boys. He even made the comment that he would be upset if anyone did the same thing to his 15-year-old son.

State Prosecutor Advocate Beverly Edwards took the case on and with the help of Grant and Jean, rallied more victims. One came forward after the Carte Blanche programme exposing Lorenco. Advocate Edwards invited me to talk to the victims and prepare my testimony for court. The devastating effect of Joe Lorenco's abuse on their adult lives became apparent to me during the interviews. Two of the men had committed suicide; four of them still refused to talk about it as adults. Some became alcoholics and gamblers and resorted to stealing money to cover their debts. Others indulged in self-destructive behaviour and moved to other towns. Many considered suicide and all said that they struggled to maintain normal sexual relationships with women. Some thought that sex was 'dirty'. Eventually six of them agreed to lay charges against Joe Lorenco.

The profile

The word *paedophile* is a psychological term referring to a sexual disorder where children are the preferred sexual partners. Not all paedophiles necessarily transgress the law. A paedophile may act out his or her sexual fantasies with an adult of childlike proportions and physique. A paedophile who has sex with minor children is a child molester.

After interviewing the complainants I came to the conclusion that the accused manifested characteristics of a preferential child molester: seducer type (see page 297).

Preferential child molesters prefer children to adults as sexual partners. The word 'prefer' indicates that children are the partners of choice, but this does not exclude sex with adults. Child molesters may have sex with adults to cover up for their paedophilic activities.

- Seducers charm and seduce their victims as any adult would a potential partner with attention, affection and presents (rewards). *The accused used a punishment and reward system on the children. He was very affectionate towards them.*
- The process takes time until the child's inhibitions are lowered and he/she is willing to exchange sexual favours for attention, affection and rewards. *It is clear from the victims' interviews and statements that the accused seduced them over a period of time.*
- Seducers prey on children who are neglected or abused at home. *The victims claimed that they did not have good relations with their parents, came from conservative families and could not discuss things with their parents. Some of them were from poor families. According to (social worker) Ms Burden's report, they appear to have been emotionally neglected.*
- This type of child molester usually has a problem getting rid of the children when they get older. They may use violence or threats to ensure the child does not reveal their secret. *The accused had beaten and humiliated the victims, they would therefore understandably fear a violent retaliation from him.*

Preferential child molesters are identified by the following characteristics:

Long-term pattern

- Sexual abuse in the abuser's own background. *The accused claimed not to have been sexually molested, but rather emotionally neglected.*
- Isolated as a teenager. *The accused claimed he was*

315

socially isolated as a teenager.

- Continuous moving of residence. *The accused often moved residence.*
- Previous arrests – for example, fraud. *Not available.*
- Multiple victims. *Multiple victims have come forward.*
- Planned high-risk attempts to acquire victims. *Abusing the victims in the gym, his combi and his residence, as well as in hotels, did not seem a high risk to the accused; however, one of the other children could have walked in at any time. He also risked his business, reputation and financial status, should he be exposed.*

Children as preferred victims

- The child molester is 25 years or older and single – no long-term relationships with adults. *The accused was 25 years old and divorced. His marriage lasted three years.*
- Lives alone or with parents. *The accused sometimes lived alone and sometimes with another man.*
- Should they be married they have a 'special' relationship with the spouse, who is either over-dominant or passive. *The accused's ex-spouse would not allow their son to sleep over at his home.*
- Extensive interest in children – too good to be true. *The parents of the victims hero-worshipped the accused because of the 'good' he was doing for their children and his absolute devotion to them.*
- Circle of friends are all young – they frequent places where children go. *The accused's adult male friends were all younger than him. He frequented the gyms where the children practised.*
- Age and sex preference of victims. *The accused had a preference for boys between 12 and 17 – ie teenagers.*

- Refer to children as 'clean, innocent, naïve, cute, lovable, etc' or as objects. *The accused claimed he 'loved' the children and was 'in love with them'.*

Well-developed techniques

- Identify vulnerable children. *The children were vulnerable not only because of their family circumstances but also because they were dependent upon the accused for their gymnastic success.*
- Identify with children – use their terminology and listen to them. *The accused became the confidant of the children in place of their parents. He fulfilled their desire to talk about gymnastics.*
- Access to children – extramural activities involving children. *The accused was a gymnastics coach and had access to them four hours a day, six days a week and 24-hour access on trips.*
- Activities with children exclude other adults. *At his home and during the trips no other adults were present.*
- Seduce children with attention, affection and presents. *Already stated that this was the accused's modus operandi.*
- Manipulate children – use peer group pressure, competitiveness and favouritism, as well as humiliation, lower children's inhibitions by inviting them to sleep over, show them pornography and undress in front of them. *According to the victims, the accused did all of these.*
- Hobbies that will attract the attention of children. *Gymnastics.*
- Show explicit sexual material to children. *The accused showed them pornographic videos.*

Sexual fantasies are centred around children

- Décor in their homes is child-orientated. *Nothing is known of the accused's décor, but it is supposed there would be material relevant to child gymnastics.*
- Take photos of children that might seem innocent to other adults, such as children in costumes, practising sport, etc, but which is child erotica to them. *One victim said the accused always chose tight-fitting costumes for them, which he designed himself. He had photographs of them.*
- Collect child erotica and child pornography. *Accused had adult pornography, later of a homosexual kind.*

After identification

- Denial, shows offence and refuses to cooperate. *The accused denied the charges at first and was offended by them.*
- Minimising – minimising the quality and quantity of the abuse, the harmfulness thereof. *The accused minimised the trauma the men suffered as adults, as well as the trauma they suffered as children. (Taped conversation)*
- Justification – saying they cared more for the children than their parents did, did not know the child's exact age, or blame the children for seducing them, had a duty to teach the children about sex because their parents failed to, alcoholism, drug abuse etc. *The accused said he loved the children, referred Grant to a card that Grant had sent him (being seduced by the victim), thought it his duty to teach them about sex.*
- Fabrication – a doctor claimed he had child sex pornography for research purposes. *The accused fabricated by saying he needed to inspect their private parts and the colour of their semen to monitor their physical development.*

- Mental illness – they claim mental illness as an excuse. *During the conversation with Grant the accused said he had cancer in order to elicit sympathy.*
- Sympathy – they claim remorse. *The accused said he was sorry and paid an amount towards Grant's therapy – in order to keep him quiet.*
- Attack – they attack, humiliate and denounce the victims after disclosure.
- Guilty but not guilty – they plead guilty in order to avoid trials and exposure.
- After conviction they contact the investigating officer with information about other paedophiles.
- Suicide.

These characteristics were derived by following the FBI's research on child molesters.

The trial was set for April 2002. Advocate Edwards drew up a list of sexual incidents over the (almost) ten-year period, which included the following:
- Showing pornographic videos and discussing sex
- Touching the victim's private parts
- Masturbating the victim
- Forcing the victim to masturbate the accused
- Having oral sex with the victim
- Forcing the victim to have sex with the accused
- Arranging to sleep in the same room and continue oral sex and mutual masturbation as well as anal sex
- Exposing private parts to the victim
- Masturbating before the victim

Joe Lorenco, 44 years old at the time, '*emphatically denied the complainants' allegations*', attributing them to professional jealousy and financial difficulties. Denial in the face of evidence is a characteristic of child molesters.

He said all of them except Grant became Springbok gymnasts or tumblers. He had established Monkeynastix in the early 1990s and claimed to know that Grant's business venture as a gymnastics coach had suffered financially because of his (Lorenco's) success. Jean was a member of the SA Gymnastics Federation and asked Lorenco to use his influence among the Monkeynastix franchises to encourage each student to become a member of the Federation, which would generate income. Lorenco refused to cooperate, which could have resulted in Jean's animosity. He maintained that after his exposure on Carte Blanche, one of the complainants must have contacted Danbet – a competitor – who sent an email to all Monkeynastix franchises inviting them to subscribe to Danbet rather than to Monkeynastix, because of the bad publicity the exposure had generated. In other words, Lorenco alleged that the complainants were bent on destroying his business with their trumped-up charges because they were jealous of his success. He also found it strange that it had taken twenty years for the men to lay charges and questioned why they had not complained when they were children. He alleged that the gyms were always full of people who could testify that nothing untoward had happened, as could people who had lived with him, but that unfortunately some of these people were now dead. Attacking the reputations of the victims is typical behaviour of child molesters after they have been exposed.

Advocate Edwards called social worker Ms Ilse Burden, who testified about why children will not talk about sexual abuse. She quoted research findings that 50 per cent of abused children will not tell anyone about it at the time.

Regarding the complainants, Grant came from a conservative family where contact with his father was limited, because of his father's extended hours of work.

Lorenco became a surrogate father figure and hero, who had to be obeyed and pleased at all times. His parents also worshipped Lorenco because of the success he was achieving for their son, and they trusted him. Once when Grant walked away from gymnastic practice in Krugersdorp to their home in Roodepoort, his mother slapped him for not showing respect for Mr Lorenco. Grant experienced his brother as the 'blue-eyed boy' because of his academic achievements; he could find acceptance in his parents' eyes only by excelling in gymnastics. Grant spent most of his time outside school in the company of Joe Lorenco. Competition amongst the children was tough. Under these circumstances it is understandable that Grant would not discuss the abuse with his parents.

Jean experienced his father as a strict disciplinarian. He would never have dared to approach his father about the subject of sex. His mother did not discuss sex with him either. Jean was not an academic achiever, but when he became successful at gymnastics, his father's attitude towards him changed. He also realised that his parents had made financial sacrifices for his gymnastics. He did not want to disappoint them and was scared that Lorenco would tell them he was not training hard enough. Lorenco's attitude towards Jean was ambivalent. Sometimes he would hit him with a stick and humiliate him in front of the others and at other times he would praise him. He brooked no opposition and a poster in the gym which read 'Rule 1: The coach is always right. Rule 2: If the coach is wrong, refer to Rule 1' reminded him of his position. Physical contact between Jean and Lorenco increased over time. Jean said he could not tell his parents, for they had never provided sexual counselling for him and he suspected that his father would not believe him, but would chastise him. He also feared Lorenco's wrath.

Ricky* stated that his father resented the time he spent

on gymnastics, and that it caused stress in their home. His father referred to Lorenco as a homosexual and did not like him. He feared that if he told his father about the abuse, it would have been the end of his gymnastics career. His father also felt that his mother neglected their other children because of the time she spent on Ricky's gymnastics. The family was conservative regarding sexual matters, which were never discussed. Ricky gained social status on account of his gymnastic achievements. As with Jean, he was beaten and humiliated by Lorenco in the gym. He had to find a way to please Lorenco in order to gain his approval. The intensity of the physical contact between them increased over time. Ricky feared telling anyone about the abuse, as he did not want to be called a homosexual. He experienced the abuse as his due because he had done something wrong in class.

None of these boys experienced the emotional safety zone at home that would have enabled them to tell their parents about the abuse. A sexual abuse accommodation syndrome existed between Lorenco and these three boys. Although the boys experienced the abuse as extremely negative, they accommodated it. This syndrome encompasses five categories:

- Secrecy
- Helplessness
- Entrapment and accommodation
- Delayed and unconvincing disclosure
- Retracting

Each one of these children had valid reasons for not disclosing the abuse when it happened. They all came from families where discipline was strict. As a result the children experienced helplessness both at home and outside the home. The authority of adults was not to be questioned. The boys all had dreams of becoming

Springbok gymnasts, their only option for gaining recognition. Their success depended on Lorenco. Lorenco used a 'grooming' process by gradually exposing the children to more intimate sexual contact. Ms Burden did not find it strange that the children never revealed their dark secret.

During the trial the court fell silent when Advocate Edwards produced an enlarged photograph of the complainants posing in their gymnastic costumes. The vulnerability of the children spoke volumes.

In his heads of argument Lorenco's advocate drew attention to the close connection between Grant, Jean and Ricky to Danbet, and considered the possibility of a conspiracy and fabrication of evidence. When Advocate Edwards cross-examined Lorenco on why the complainants would expose themselves to the negative publicity of the court case if they were not telling the truth, Lorenco replied that the complainants were the abusers, not the abused. Blaming the victims is typical behaviour of child molesters.

Lorenco's advocate made the following statement in the heads of argument: *If the accused was such a manipulative monster, as made out by the state witnesses it is strange that his popularity grew during the very period of the alleged abuse. The growth of the gym and his popularity does not tie in with the alleged abuse, sexually suggestive, and harsh training methods, described by the first group of witnesses ... The accused's own concessions in that regard about the times he used a stick and the reference to 'pielstyf' was placed in context, and I submit that no fault can be found with that explanation.* A tendency to minimise events is typical of child molesters.

Despite Ms Burden's explanation of why further victims would not be inclined to come forward, he said that he also found it strange that only one person, Lenny,* had come forward after the Carte Blanche exposure, arguing that if

Lorenco *was* a paedophile, more boys would have come forward. The fact that no more came forward was not to say that there were no more victims.

He alleged that some of the so-called victims declined to testify because they themselves were lawyers and knew they had no case.

Lastly, the advocate stated: *If the Court finds in favour of the State then I advance that the defence of 'permission' or 'consent' is good. On the facts it is clear that all participation in the watching of porn, the sex talk and any sexual contact was done with consent.* Children cannot legally give consent.

On 28 November 2002 Joe Lorenco was found guilty by Magistrate Alberts of indecently assaulting Grant and sentenced to five years' imprisonment, suspended for five years, and he had to pay Grant an amount of R61 500, towards therapy in monthly instalments. He was found guilty of indecent assault on Jean, and sentenced to five years' imprisonment, suspended for five years and had to pay Jean an amount of R74 000 for therapy in monthly instalments. At the time it was the largest amount awarded in such a case.

Joe Lorenco defaulted on his payments and was re-arrested.

I have the greatest respect for these six men who had the courage to come forward and bring a child molester to justice. They told me that in the interests of preventing other children from suffering, they would endure the media exposure and the mental stress of the trial. It was a privilege to have met them and I honour them in this book. Their trauma lasted for twenty years, and I hope that one day they will recover fully. I also hope they set an example to others as role models for courage, for pursuing justice and for protecting the innocent.

Stalking

DEFINITION

Stalking is psychological terrorism. Its components are the surveillance and harassment of the victim, threatening physical injury to the victim or his or her property, and it can even escalate to the murder of the victim. Inflicting terror upon the victim can be intentional or unintentional, but the fact remains that the victim of the stalker is unsafe wherever he or she goes.

In 2004 the South African Law Reform Commission began investigating stalking with the possibility of introducing specific legislation to cover it. Stalking is recognised in the Domestic Violence Act (1999), but only if there is or was a relationship between the stalker and the victim. To me, it is absolutely imperative that South Africa should institute legislation to address stalking based on the current law in California in the USA. Stalkers target anyone, not only celebrities. Colleagues, company directors, politicians and private persons all fall prey to the stalker and there is at present very little legal protection for victims. Most stalkers are anonymous, which makes their apprehension difficult, although not impossible. If an anonymous stalker were finally to be identified and apprehended, with the law as it stands in South Africa at present, he or she would probably receive a fine, perhaps serve a minimum prison sentence, or get away with it. Given the damage a stalker inflicts on the victim, he or she should face a severe prison sentence.

PSYCHOLOGICAL DAMAGE TO THE VICTIM

It is impossible for anyone to comprehend how a normal person's life can be turned into a living hell by a stalker, unless he or she have themselves been victims. Without proper psychological management the victim will become the psychological captive of the stalker. Just as the stalker continuously thinks about the victim, the victim is continuously aware of the stalker, and has to deal with a burden of unnecessary emotions, ranging from irritation and anger to absolute fear. The victim is not free to think his or her own thoughts or to feel his or her own emotions. The awareness of the stalker is pervasive, always lurking in the background.

Apart from the psychological consequences of being stalked, the victims' physical environment becomes a prison. They are reluctant to leave the safety of their home, commuting only to work and back. Friends and neighbours have to do their shopping; they do not want to socialise outside their home or seek outside entertainment and they become socially isolated. They may even lose their job if the stalker turns up at their place of work and causes a disturbance.

Communication and contact between victims and the outside world becomes limited. They are too scared to answer the telephone. Telephone calls at work have to be screened and answering machines connected to home telephones. Friends start avoiding the victim for fear of becoming victims themselves.

Victims may be forced to spend money on extra security systems, employ bodyguards, or even relocate and, in extreme circumstances, change their identities. The families of victims live in fear of their own lives, as well as that of their harassed relative. Their lives become complicated patterns of coded telephone rings and door knocks.

It is impossible to imagine how a stalker can disrupt the different aspects of the life of an innocent person and her family.

TYPOLOGY OF STALKERS

The following typology has been accepted by experts in the field worldwide:

Celebrity stalkers/erotomanic stalkers

The majority of stalkers of this type are mentally ill. They suffer from a delusional disorder with the predominant belief that a person, usually of a higher status (such as a celebrity or public figure), is in love with them. A small number are just disillusioned fans. They are self-absorbed loners, characterised by feelings of inferiority.

The erotomanic stalker has the delusion that he is loved by the victim and believes that he has an idealised romantic love relationship with the victim in which they share spiritual union, rather than a purely sexual relationship. The stalker generally does not understand the harm he is inflicting and is convinced that the victim enjoys the attention.

Celebrities often send autographed photos of themselves to fans. The stalker will interpret this fairly usual public relations exercise as a personal invitation. Research has indicated that a personal confrontation, whether friendly or not, between the stalker and the celebrity is ineffective in changing the stalker's behaviour; indeed, such a confrontation may only reinforce his behaviour since he has now gained the personal attention of the celebrity.

Successful counteraction will involve the celebrity enforcing complete separation from the stalker. All personal contact should be severed and the matter referred to a professional who can manage the case.

This type of stalker tends to engage in the following activities: phoning, sending letters, pestering family or friends of the victim, spreading rumours, surveillance, sending gifts, breaking and entering, showing up at the workplace. Damage to property, causing the victim physical harm or killing the victim is unlikely, but has happened in extreme cases.

Stalking of this nature tends to continue for years. It is seldom that an erotomanic stalker will follow through on a threat, although precautions should always be taken.

Love obsessional stalker

This type of stalker differs from the erotomanic stalker in that the erotomanic delusion is only one of several delusions and other psychiatric symptoms. Psychiatric diagnoses which are applicable to this group are bipolar affective disorder, schizoaffective disorder or schizo-phrenia, and borderline personality disorder might also apply. This type might include stalkers who are ob-sessional in their 'love' for their victims, but do not believe that the victims reciprocate the love. The obsessional 'love' is therefore not necessarily a delusional disorder, but an extreme emotion directed at the victim.

This type of stalker will perceive obstacles to their adoration of the victim as tests of love which they have to overcome to win or be worthy of the victim's love. They are unlikely to engage in physically harmful acts, but this has been found in isolated cases. The duration of the obsession can last up to twelve years but the duration of actual contact with the victim, which might include anything from telephoning to letter writing, is brief.

Dependent, rejection-sensitive stalker/simple obsessional stalker

This type of stalker is usually the jilted lover of the

victim. He will gather information about the victim and pester friends, family or neighbours to reveal the victim's whereabouts and facts about the victim's lifestyle. He will usually send love letters and gifts to the victim, having established the victim's preferences for certain items; for example, favourite flowers, perfume, etc. He will also often call or visit the victim and look for excuses to make contact.

This type of stalker has also been known to break into the victim's house just to read her mail, listen to her answering machine or to watch her sleeping.

Such stalking is psychological torture for the victim and it can also escalate to include damage to property, attacks on pets, threats to family members and friends and even the murder of the victim. The stalker's usual perception is: 'If I can't have her, no one else will.'

Stalkers of this type will have experienced losses during their childhood years; for example, losing a parent through death or divorce, rejection by parents, abuse and neglect. They have suffered intolerable hurt as children and fear subsequent rejection by adult partners. They are unable to grieve naturally or accept the ending of a relationship. They are ultimately dependent on their partner, but at the same time hate the partner for their dependency. Some of them may suffer from mental illnesses and personality disorders. Many of the men in this category will hide their feelings of dependency behind a macho image and are generally abusive towards women.

I was the first South African to attend the Advanced Threat Assessment and Management course presented by Gavin de Becker in Los Angeles in 1999. This course specialises in stalking, analysing threatening letters and workplace violence. Gavin de Becker became one of the most important educational mentors in my life, although my encounter with him was brief. His training proved invaluable and I would like to share some of his pointers. In his highly recommended book *The Gift of Fear: survival signs that protect us from violence* (1997), De Becker provides the following indicators of 'intimate enemies', where the ex-lover or spouse is the stalker:

The person

- accelerates the pace of the relationship by premature commitment, living together or pressure to get married
- mostly resolves conflict by intimidation and violence
- is verbally abusive
- uses threats and intimidations as instruments of control and abuse
- breaks or strikes at things in anger – symbolic violence like tearing up photographs is relevant
- has battered a partner in previous relationships
- has an alcohol or drug abuse problem and cites these as excuses for behaviour
- has a history of police encounters – even if they are not related to interpersonal violence
- uses money to control the activities and purchases of the partner
- is obsessively jealous and often projects this jealousy
- refuses to accept rejection and is oversensitive to criticism
- expects the relationship to last forever
- minimises incidents of abuse
- enlists friends, family and colleagues of the partner to keep in contact with the partner or as sources of information
- has inappropriately followed or kept the partner under surveillance
- resists change and is inflexible
- identifies with other violent people
- has moods swings

- blames others
- has an interest in or access to weapons and instruments of power, or weapons are a substantial part of his/her persona
- if male, uses male privilege and is generally derogatory towards women
- has experienced or witnessed violence as a child
- the partner of such a person fears that he or she will harm or kill him or her

Should you recognise a combination of these elements at the beginning of a relationship, my advice is to terminate the relationship as soon as possible. To remain will turn your life into a living hell.

Simple obsessional stalkers may also include those who target persons with whom there was no romantic involvement, but some prior relationship such as a customer, neighbour, acquaintance or a professional relationship.

The duration of the stalking in these cases tends to last less than a year. This type is also more likely to make person-to-person contact with victims and issue more threats than the other types of stalker. They are also more likely to follow through on their threats.

Immature romantic stalker

This kind of stalker is a teenager who develops a crush either on a person known to him or a stranger. They seldom resort to making threats or injuring the victim and usually grow out of it.

The adolescent will write anonymous love letters, phone the victim and put the phone down, leave messages on an answering machine, watch the victim from a distance, leave notes or flowers on the victim's car, etc.

Unfortunately this kind of behaviour can escalate into a more serious type of stalking.

THE DIETZ 10 INDICATORS OF STALKING

Professor Park Dietz of the University of California and president of the Threat Assessment Group, Inc, has identified the following ten indicators of persons who attacked public figures in the USA:

* A mental disorder
* An exaggerated idea of self
* Inappropriate contact with a public figure
* Random travelling or targeted travelling
* Identification with a stalker or assassin
* Ability to circumvent ordinary security
* Kept a diary or journal
* Repeated approaches to a public figure
* Obtained a weapon or fascination with weapons
* Researched the target or victim

MENTAL DISEASES WHICH MIGHT LEAD TO STALKING

As I said in the introduction to this book, psychological training is invaluable to a profiler and knowledge about the following disorders assisted me in predicting the behaviour of stalkers I was called upon to investigate. Many people make the mistake of expecting rational behaviour from a stalker. Stalkers, however, are irrational and one needs an understanding of their mental dynamics in order to stay one step ahead of them.

Paranoid delusional disorder

A person with this disorder has non-bizarre delusions involving situations which might occur in real life, such as being followed, having a disease or being deceived, but in reality there is no substance to these delusions. Apart from the delusion, the person's behaviour is not otherwise odd or bizarre.

Kaplan and Sadock (*Synopsis of Psychiatry*, 1991) define a delusion as a false belief based upon incorrect inference about an external reality, not consistent with the person's intelligence and cultural background, that cannot be corrected by reasoning.

The following are specific types of paranoid delusions:

- Erotomanic type: the person is convinced that another person, usually of a higher status, is in love with him or her
- Grandiose type: The person has a self-perception of inflated self-value, special powers or knowledge or identifies or has a special relationship with a deity or famous person
- Jealous type: The person believes his or her sexual partner is unfaithful without any substantiation
- Persecutory type: The person believes he or she, or someone close to them, is being malevolently treated. They repeatedly take their complaints to legal or law enforcement authorities

The development of a paranoid delusional disorder starts during the childhood years when the child grows up in the following environment:

- A high value is placed on achievements and pride, but an unhealthy pride
- Discipline is aimed at humiliating the child rather than rectifying the behaviour
- Good behaviour is not praised but rather devalued
- Parents project their own shortcomings on to others
- The child has no privacy from prying parents
- There is a lack of basic trust between parent and child
- There is no intimate relationship between parent and child, resulting in 'remote controlled' children

Schizophrenia: paranoid type

A person suffering from this disorder will have one or more systemised delusions with frequent auditory hallucinations related to a single theme. There is no incoherence, loosening of associations, flat or grossly inappropriate affect, grossly disorganised behaviour or catatonic behaviour. (A hallucination is a sensation or perception which occurs in the absence of any external stimulus. The person sees, hears, smells or feels something which is not there.)

Such persons have no sense of interpersonal boundaries and tend to 'fuse' with the victim, taking on the victim's personality. They may also be convinced that the victim has a bad double who should be exterminated.

Paranoid personality disorder

Individuals with this disorder have a long-standing suspicion and mistrust of people in general, refuse to take responsibility for their own emotions and are often hostile, irritable and angry. They function adequately in their daily lives, but all of their interpersonal relationships are characterised by friction and conflict. Their suspiciousness is not only directed towards their romantic partners, but also towards their families, friends and colleagues.

Borderline personality disorder

A person with this disorder cannot tolerate the dichotomy of opposites in a relationship. They will either over-idealise or completely disparage others. At one moment they may absolutely adore a person, only to hate them the next.

Borderlines have difficulty in differentiating between reality and fantasy. They therefore often perceive a celebrity in the role that the celebrity takes in his or her professional life; for example, in a movie, or on television, and cannot conceptualise that the celebrity has a private life and personality completely different from his or her professional role.

Stalkers suffering from borderline personality disorder are impulsive, emotionally unstable and experience mood shifts and depression. The mildest criticism or perceived insult evokes feelings of rejection, abandonment and shame. This results in them venting their anger on the victim by ruining the victim's career, reputation, family life, friendships, or even by killing them.

This type of stalker often commits suicide.

VICTIM EMPOWERMENT

It is essential that victims of stalkers understand and educate themselves on the phenomenon of stalking in order to empower themselves to manage the situation. De Becker suggests that an understanding of intuition, fear, danger and threats are the elements necessary for managing stalking.

Understanding intuition

Violence is a threat that permeates every aspect of life in South Africa. Danger seems to lurk at every corner and no one feels safe any more, not in their homes, not in public and not at the workplace. Fear has become an epidemic disease that has affected every citizen in this country. People react differently to fear; some ignore it, some rationalise it, others allow it to take on paranoid proportions. However, just like any other problem, fear can be managed. The better one understands it and the more information one gains about it, the better one will manage it. Yet, although many people live in fear of something bad happening to them, just as many people escape dangerous situations 'miraculously'.

How often do we reflect back on a dangerous incident which we escaped and say: *I don't know what motivated me, but I just knew I had to do this or that?* How often do we acknowledge in retrospect that we saw danger coming, but ignored it? What is the mechanism that warned us? It is the same mechanism that told us what to do to escape.

There is nothing miraculous about it: it is called *intuition*. It has also been called a gut-feeling or a sixth sense, but whatever it is called, all humans are equipped with it. Regarding this sense as an irrational power, an alien ability, an old wives' tale or witchcraft, is to ignore the most powerful natural ally within us. Intuition is based upon perception. Our senses alert us to danger. We can see, hear, smell, feel or taste it and in a split second we may either react instinctively, as lower animals do, or rationally choose to ignore it. According to De Becker, the cognitive process which sends the signal from the senses to the brain is faster than our normal cognitive process of step-by-step analysis. Our intuition will tell us how to react to danger, unless we override it by rationalising or ignoring the danger. De Becker discusses how judgement can deter intuition. We differ from animals in that we have been equipped with judgement. Using our judgement, we like to explain things logically and find the explanation which suits us best. In the process we disregard our intuition and waste valuable time which might save our lives.

As De Becker says, what animal on earth would, when it intuitively feels the presence of danger, think: *Oh, that's probably nothing*, turn around and go back to sleep, just because it would be very uncomfortable to leave the warmth of its bed? Or what animal would, when it intuitively feels that it is being stalked by a predator, decide to ignore it and go merrily on its way? Why then do humans do it?

Understanding fear

De Becker explains fear as a reaction to an anticipated threat. In this context, the word 'anticipated' should be understood as 'that which is not happening now'. There is time to evaluate the situation to determine a reaction. If the situation is severe, our intuition will take over and protect us, if we trust it and do not succumb to panic. It will tell us to run, lie still, play dead, scream, attack, etc. De Becker says that trusting our intuition is the opposite of living in fear. Fear is a brief signal. Panic is the enemy of fear for it debilitates our natural reaction to our intuition. *Real fear is energizing, not paralysing*, says De Becker.

If the situation is not too dire we may indulge in the luxury of taking time to analyse it and decide on the best option to either avoid or influence an outcome. For example, your intuition will wake you and alert you to a noise downstairs in the middle of the night. If you trust your intuition you will realise that the noise could indicate a potentially dangerous situation and you will not go back to sleep hoping it was just the cat. Now you realise there is an intruder in the house and fear sets in. But you realise that panic will be debilitating to your ability to take sensible action. The intruder is not yet threatening your life and you have time to make a decision. The desired outcome would, first of all, be for the intruder to leave without hurting anyone. There is not enough time to do extensive planning on how to attain this outcome. You have to make a split-second decision. You may decide to confront the intruder, which may result in injury or even loss of life, or you may decide to hide to avoid being hurt, bearing in mind that the cost is that you will be robbed; or you can activate an alarm, which will probably cause the intruder to flee without taking anything or hurting anybody.

On the other hand, if you receive a letter from someone threatening to sue you because your dog bit him, you have enough time to analyse the situation and prepare for it. You can evaluate the pros and cons of going to court, or the pros and cons of negotiating the issue, thereby avoiding going to court. The principle is: intuition will warn and protect you instantly, fear will energise you to make an effective decision, but panic and worry will debilitate your senses.

De Becker explains the difference between fear and worry. *Worry* is something we manufacture, a defence mechanism we employ in order to avoid change. By worrying, we avoid admitting powerlessness. Worry wastes time and mental energy and the cost of worrying is greater than the cost of changing. Fear is instinctive, but worry is something we create ourselves and we need to explore why. Why do we prefer to worry – a useless mental exercise – rather than take action?

Understanding danger

The average South African citizen perceives life to be dangerous. However, danger is not a permanent state of being, nor is it a permanent characteristic of a person – danger is situational. For instance, the notorious serial killer Moses Sithole who was found guilty of killing thirty-eight women in Gauteng is labelled a 'dangerous' man. The Moses Sithole who roamed the streets of Johannesburg looking for easy prey, or enticing an unsuspecting female to accompany him to his remote killing field outside the Boksburg prison, was indeed a very 'dangerous' man. But the Moses Sithole who is incarcerated in the C-Max facility of Pretoria Central prison is not 'dangerous'.

However, the absence of the label 'dangerous' does not guarantee that a person is *not* dangerous. A stalker who writes love letters to a celebrity, never mentioning violence and never once making threats to harm the celebrity, cannot be labelled 'not dangerous'. To decide whether or not he is 'dangerous', one needs to determine whether he has the means to come into one-on-one contact with the celebrity. If he is paralysed and bedridden, he is not 'dangerous' and poses no threat. But if he is capable of travelling to where the celebrity lives one needs to assess how vulnerable the celebrity is. Previous incidents of violent behaviour may be an indication of future violence, but this is not to say that a lack of previous violent incidents means that a person will not become violent. Given the circumstances – a situation – a non-violent person might become violent. De Becker warns us not to confuse *potential* to do harm with *intention* to do harm.

According to De Becker, for a situation to be dangerous there must be sinister intent or disregard for another's safety; there must be a means to deliver harm; there must be a victim who is accessible and vulnerable and, lastly, there must be a set of circumstances that provides advantage to the attacker. Most of these elements can be determined. For this assessment one needs an expert in human behaviour, and one who has had experience with dangerous situations and 'dangerous' men. Gavin de Becker runs a company which specialises in this sort of risk assessment, provides bodyguards and manages stalking cases for celebrities in the United States. There are some private investigation companies in South Africa who offer similar services. I consult for some of them.

Understanding threats

Threats take many forms. They can be verbal, written, delivered by a third party or just implied by behaviour. Threats may be anonymous or the person making the threat may link his or her name to the threat, or use a pseudonym. It is important, therefore, to establish what a threat is and what it is not.

De Becker defines a *threat* as a statement of intention to do harm. A person who makes a threat is in fact admitting to failure to influence events in any other way. By definition, a threat is something that, at least for the moment, is not happening, and the person making the threat has, for the moment, decided against acting on it. More often than not, a threat is indicative of desperation and not intention, but it is always wise to take a threat seriously. After making a threat, a person can only advance or retreat.

De Becker explains the different categories of threats:

- *Direct threats* carry a straightforward intention to commit harm with no conditions; for example, 'I am going to kill you.' There are no conditions, no alternatives and no way out

- *Veiled threats* are indirect, vague or subtle, suggesting potential harm, but also do not contain any conditions to avert the harm. For example, 'Something bad is going to happen to you one day and you should not wonder why'

- *Intimidations* are conditional threats containing potential harm unless certain conditions are met. The words: 'if', 'or else', 'until', 'unless', etc feature in the intimidation. Intimidations are less likely to be carried out than threats. Perpetrators who make conditional threats usually set personal attention as a condition. Intimidation is therefore a high-stake manipulation

De Becker explains that the currency of threats is fear. The threatener gains advantage by intimidating and causing fear and anxiety in the person whom he is threatening. If the other party shows no fear, the threat loses currency and the threatener has to retreat. Unfortunately this might also be the point where the threatener carries out the threat to save face. It is therefore important to allow the threatener to save face. By restoring the threatener's dignity the situation might be resolved.

One of the worst ways to manage a threat is to counter-threaten, especially if there is little likelihood that the counter-threat will be acted on. The threatened party should therefore not warn the threatener of any steps he plans to take – for example, an interdict – but simply serve the interdict and make sure it is acted upon.

To establish the identity of the person issuing an anonymous threat one needs to ask who would be best served by the conditions of the threat, or the result if the threat is carried out.

De Becker explains that extortion is also a form of intimidation and there is usually a self-explanatory currency involved. Extortions are rarely anonymous; they will be anonymous only if the extortionist fears that the victim might expose him or her. The victim's reaction to the extortion will set the price of the currency. Pleading, shock and compliance will raise the extortionist's appraisal of the price tag. It is recommended that the victim asks the extortionist to state explicitly what he or she wants in order to assess whether the motivation is greed, revenge or mental illness. Extortionists motivated by malice are more likely to carry out the threat than those motivated simply by greed.

Threatening and inappropriate letters

The greatest fear of the recipient of a threatening or inappropriate letter is whether the author of the letter has the means to carry out the threat and whether the person is in a position to make contact with the recipient.

I am always surprised when people who have received more than one threatening letter continue to open them and show them to others, thereby contaminating possible fingerprints and other clues. Both the letter as well as the envelope should be kept and the fewer people who touch them, the better. Rather place both letter and envelope in a larger envelope for safe keeping.

INTERVENTION STRATEGIES

Williams and his colleagues in their article 'Stalking: successful intervention strategies' (*The Police Chief*, 1996) define intervention as any of several measures initiated to modify, control or eliminate inappropriate behaviour of a victim or suspect. Intervention is therefore directed at the victim as well as the stalker.

Each case merits its own intervention strategy. For example, in some cases there is no suspect intervention at all. Becoming the victim of a stalker's unwanted attention is extremely unfair. Often the victim has done nothing to elicit the stalker's attention and it is enraging that a stranger may have so much influence over an innocent person's life. Yet, no matter how unfair, irritating or enraging, the problem remains and one's feelings about it will not make it go away. In fact, in some cases, it may never end. It is therefore essential that it is managed and I strongly recommend that the victim engages a reputable company to assist him or her in doing this. Tackling it alone is a daunting task and to hope it will go away is wishful thinking. Remember, stalkers do not respond to rational argument.

The police can only intervene once a crime has been committed. Unfortunately many police officers regard stalkers as nuisance offenders, which is in a way understandable given the more serious crimes they have to deal with. Yet it is a reality that a stalker who initially sent only letters may progress to breaking and entering, destroying property or eventually killing the victim. Sending letters (especially if they contain no threat), making silent telephone calls, lurking about someone's house, etc does not warrant serious attention from the police and nor will these offenders face a serious jail sentence if they are eventually charged. Yet stalking remains psychological terrorism and should be recognised as unlawful behaviour. As long as it is not, one needs to revert to experts, who should cover the following aspects in their management plan:

Victim intervention

Victim intervention encompasses an educational, behavioural and therapeutic approach.

Victim education

Once a person becomes aware of the fact that she is being stalked it is best to gain extensive knowledge about the issue before taking action. Rather rely upon experts to provide this knowledge than the 'good advice' of family, friends and colleagues, which may have disastrous results. It is, for instance, not always a good idea to confront the suspect or to get an interdict as this may only worsen the situation. Confrontation or serving a protection order represents contact with the stalker, and he thrives on contact. It has been shown that the best way to get rid of a stalker is to avoid contact completely, although this may take a long time. Remember, one is not dealing with a rational person.

If the victim understands the phenomenon of stalking her immediate emotions (anger, irritability and fear) can be addressed, after which a rational decision regarding the management of the issue may be taken.

The police are not always in a position to react immediately, and the stalker may even as yet be unidentified. Just reporting the case to the police gives the victim a false sense of security. The police cannot provide round the clock protection. Yet I would none the less recommend that the incident be reported to the police, for this will constitute an official record, which is important if the matter ever goes to court. A professional consultant will offer the victim the best advice, including when to contact the police, who to contact, and what can be expected of the police.

The professional consultant can also advise the victim on special safety precautions as well as on measures that might be expensive but ineffective. For example, surveillance of the perpetrator would be expensive but ineffective, since it will only monitor the suspect's movements. It will not provide insight into what the stalker does or fantasises about in the privacy of his own home, nor does it give any insight into the suspect's motives or mental disorders. A professional consultant should endeavour to identify the suspect and do a thorough background check, including criminal history, access to weapons, stressors and inhibitors to violence as well as mental status. With this kind of information on the suspect, the case can be managed. The same amount of money spent on surveillance of the suspect can rather be spent on enhancing the victim's security systems. It might not be fair, but the victim's safety is more important than the philosophical question of fairness in life.

Behavioural modification

The victim will need to improve security measures and to change her lifestyle in order to circumvent the stalker's making contact. Additional security measures can be expensive, and although again this is not fair, it is necessary for the protection of the victim. Basic security such as an alarm system, a guard dog, security gates, burglar bars and spotlights should be considered. These security measures will not only protect the victim from the stalker, but also from other intruders. The victim should also consider installing an answering machine. Times of calls and messages will then be recorded and can be kept for possible court procedures.

The victim can protect herself by supplying a postal address instead of a home address when filling in forms. Home ownership may be transferred to a trust and not registered in the victim's name. In severe cases the victim might need to relocate.

In less severe cases the victim should use alternative driving routes and avoid dark and dangerous places. If it is apparent that the stalker is aware of the victim's routine, she should modify her social life; for example, change the gym or local pub or church she favours and shop at a different centre. Victims should alert friends and family not to give out information about them unnecessarily. In one case a stalker rummaged through the garbage of the victim's parents and found the envelopes of letters from the victim to her parents. In this way he managed to trace her to the town to which she had relocated.

It is important that the victim informs her employers about the stalker in order for them to implement a work-place violence policy. Should the employer not have a workplace violence policy designed to protect employees from dangerous situations at work, the victim can insist that such a policy be developed, and can at least alert the security staff at the building and her co-workers. Telephone calls at work should be screened by an answering machine. The victim should realise that as long as she is working in the same location, this is the one place where the stalker may be sure to strike. The victim may request a temporary transfer to another branch or take a vacation to create the impression that she is no longer on the premises.

Therapeutic intervention

By appointing a professional to manage the stalking the victim is transferring the daily pressure of dealing with unwanted mail and telephone messages to an objective professional. The professional will advise the victim on precautions to take and periodically update her on progress, but at least the psychological burden of being conscious of the stalker at all times will be relieved and the victim can get on with her life. Although she still has to take responsibility for her safety, at least there will be peace of mind in knowing that a professional is also involved.

The professional case manager will arrange for the victim to have personal contact with a police officer who can be called in an emergency. She need not therefore contact the charge office and speak to strangers who have no knowledge of her predicament.

Taking self-defence classes might enhance the victim's self-confidence and she may feel empowered to become more assertive. By taking steps to control her own destiny the victim will feel more competent to handle the situation – in fact, feel less like a victim. She needs to make a paradigm shift from thinking about herself as helpless to that of an adult who is able to acknowledge that although it is unfair and unfortunate that she has been selected by the stalker, the problem needs to be managed in a calculated and professional manner. Being angry and taking foolhardy and impulsive actions against the stalker is just as ineffective as allowing fear to paralyse one into becoming a recluse.

The victim might consider psychological counselling to address the range of emotions which are typical in these cases. Victims tend to feel helpless, angry, scared, irritated, frustrated and incompetent. These emotions may fluctuate daily, reducing victims to emotional wrecks if they are not managed and addressed.

The victim needs to recognise risk in order to reduce it. One of the greatest causes of anxiety in a case of stalking is that the victim might not know the stalker and might not recognise a situation where the stalker makes contact.

De Becker identified the following elements in a perpetrator's behaviour to which the victim should be alert:

- Forced teaming: 'We'. Forced teaming is the term for a situation in which a stranger uses the word 'we', or any other word implying a team, to create a false sense of intimacy between himself and the victim. For example, a woman might be carrying grocery bags home and a man offers to help her, saying: 'My wife also tries to carry too many bags; here, let me help you.' Or a woman wearing high heels may be walking down a slope and a man takes her arm with the words: 'We wouldn't want you to hurt yourself, would we?' Forced teaming is not an act of kindness, it is intentional and directed and it is one of the most sophisticated forms of manipulation. The victim should remember that the man is a stranger and there is no relationship – no 'we' – between them. She should refuse the offer: 'I did not ask for your help and I do not want it.' The cost is only appearing rude, the possible risk involved is worse than that. Any decent man will understand a woman's disinclination to accept help from strangers. A woman's greatest fear is being killed by a man; a man's greatest fear is being ridiculed by a woman. Her life is at stake, not his.

- Charm and 'niceness'. To charm is to compel, to control, by allure or attraction. The majority of serial killers are very charming men who used their charm to lure victims to their deaths. A smile may mask other emotions, such as intense hatred of women. The predator will use his charm, along with other elements, to manipulate the woman to do what he wants.

- Too many details. When a perpetrator strikes up a

conversation with an intended victim, he is likely to use too many details in his story. The reason for this is that he needs additional details to make his story sound convincing, since it does not sound credible enough to him. The man who said: 'My wife also tries to carry too many bags,' need not have volunteered this kind of private information to a stranger. Too many details are designed to distract the victim's attention from the obvious.

- Typecasting: Typecasting occurs when the perpetrator criticises the victim's behaviour to prove that her opinion of him is inaccurate. For example: 'Don't be too proud to accept help', or 'Are you too good to accept my help', or 'I did not mean to offend you, I just want to help you'. The victim may feel the need to defend herself or to make retribution for her rudeness. To fall into this trap can have disastrous consequences. The best defence is silence.

- Loan sharking. This perpetrator places the victim in his debt by assisting her and making it difficult for her to refuse. For example a traffic officer decides not to issue a speeding fine to an attractive woman and she is very grateful. Later he traces her address and turns up at her house, inviting himself in for coffee. The woman feels compelled to invite him in, since he has done her a favour. Another example is that of a man who changes a flat tyre for a woman in a parking lot and then invites her for coffee. The examples are infinite and the risk is the same. The victim should remind herself that she did not ask for help.

- Unsolicited promise. According to De Becker, the unsolicited promise is one of the most reliable signals of danger, since it is nearly always of questionable motive. A promise is used to convince someone of an intention, but it is not a guarantee. It offers no compensation if the one promising fails to deliver. The victim needs to remind herself of why the perpetrator needs to try and convince her of something. 'I promise I will only follow you home to make sure you are safe', or 'I promise I will leave after we have had coffee', or 'I promise I only want to come in to talk to you' – none of these remarks offers a guarantee.

- Discounting the word 'NO'. A universal signal of danger to a woman is a man's discounting a woman's 'no'. 'No' *cannot* be negotiated. Negotiations are about possibilities. If a woman wants help, she should choose whom she asks. An example: A woman once found herself in the company of a large crowd around a table in a plaza. A man sitting opposite her singled her out by offering her some of his food. He did not ask if she wanted any, but simply presented her with a piece of meat stuck on a fork. She refused politely, adding that she was a vegetarian. He promptly ate the meat himself and then loaded the fork with a vegetable and stuck that in her face, regardless of the fact that her own plate was full of vegetables. She refused again. He tried to make conversation with her, but she avoided eye contact and turned her attention to the people seated beside her. The man got up, walked around the table and offered to fill up her wine glass. He did not offer to fill up anyone else's glass. She declined. 'Have some anyway,' he said as he filled up her glass. She promptly lifted the glass and poured the contents on the ground. 'I said no,' she said. 'Which part of that did you not understand?' After that he left her alone. I was that woman. If a man cannot accept a woman's 'no', whether it is about a glass of wine or any other seemingly trivial matter, in my opinion that man has the profile of a potential rapist. I would rather be labelled rude or something even nastier than risk having to ward off his unwanted attentions later in the parking lot. Why would he believe my 'no' later, if I had capitulated earlier?

PROFILING STALKERS

The profiler should endeavour to categorise the stalker in one of the typologies, bearing in mind the possibility of one of the relevant mental disorders. The main purpose of profiling a stalker is to identify him, to predict his level of dangerousness, and to predict future behaviour. A secondary aim will be to advise the victim on how to deal with the situation.

I have profiled many stalkers and I have selected for discussion three case studies of people from different walks of life who became the victims of stalkers who sent them threatening letters. I hope these case studies will illustrate how common the practice is and reinforce the need for specific legislation to deal with stalking. The fourth case study relates to a typical celebrity stalker.

CASE STUDY: EX-SPOUSE

Background information

The names of the parties are not disclosed and many private details have been excluded because of the confidentiality agreement I sign with clients.

In this case a man was being pestered by his ex-wife and contacted a private investigation company to assist him. They in turn consulted me. I was presented with copies of e-mails exchanged by the parties. The contents of the e-mails consisted mostly of the ex-wife complaining about bills not being paid, visitation rights, and so on, which are common issues after divorce. This case was an example of correspondence between two people who did not have an amicable divorce. Although it does not completely fit the description of stalking, it does constitute harassment.

My education (psychologist), specialised training (from Gavin de Becker) and my own experience as a child of divorced parents (my parents provided me with an example of the right way a divorce should be handled) qualified me to profile the ex-wife and make recommendations to the client on how to manage the problem. I submitted the following report.

Profile of the subject

After an in-depth analysis of several e-mails exchanged between the two parties, it was clear to me that the ex-wife is still emotionally dependent upon the client, despite their divorce. She has a psychological need to know that he is available to her on a 24-hour basis. By continuously obstructing his attempts to have access to his children, she is in effect upholding a relationship with him. Her harassment and obstruction spring from a deep need for attention. She cannot fulfil herself and feels abandoned. She needs the client for security, which is a very basic human need, especially to a woman. This is also the profile of paranoia: a person feels unworthy and to compensate for the feeling of inadequacy, she will attribute special qualities to herself. 'I am special, therefore I deserve attention' is the compensatory thought pattern. The need for attention will be gratified even by negative attention – the principle being *any* attention is still attention and fills the void created by unworthiness.

The ex-wife is immature. Her frustration at not being able to help herself is taken out on the client. She shows lack of insight into her own problems. She has an external locus of control and blames the client for her circumstances and inferiority complex. In some of her e-mails she verbalises her failures in the marriage, yet her actions lack conviction of her taking responsibility for them.

If the client is unavailable to attend to her needs – which she disguises as the need to have bills paid immediately – she feels insecure and abandoned. Whenever she feels thus rejected she retaliates by subpoenaing him. He is being punished for not gratifying her immature, immediate need for attention. Punishing another adult for one's own inadequacies is a sign of immaturity and her abuse of the legal system demonstrates her pettiness.

Her lack of insight is clearly demonstrated by the fact that she wants him to pay bills immediately – *her* deadlines – but refuses to read his e-mails or respond to them immediately – *his* deadlines. Her immaturity is further demonstrated by the fact that she has petty excuses for not allowing him to speak to the children every night, etc.

By obstructing and delaying, she is upholding continuous communication and a relationship. Clearly she is not accepting the fact that they are divorced. Her request to be put back on to his medical aid also demonstrates that she needs him as her lifeline.

As the ex-wife has no insight into her own condition, any attempt by the client to appeal to her sense of moral justice – for the sake of the children – will fall on deaf ears. On the contrary, it will seem to her as if he needs her permission/approval for his actions. He is effectively relinquishing this power to her and she will only abuse it. Appeals to her will be interpreted as a sign of weakness on his part. For example, requests that she not teach the children to call someone else 'dad' will not succeed. She knows this irritates him and will therefore persist in it. He needs to take this up with the children themselves. Even a stepfather cannot claim the title 'dad' if the true father is alive and actively participating in the children's lives.

It is clear that the ex-wife is using the children as a means to gratify her own personal need for his attention. Since they are divorced, it is no longer the client's responsibility to gratify any of her emotional needs.

I suggest that the client keep all e-mails strictly factual and impersonal and deliver them on a point by point basis, as he has done on some occasions. He should refrain from the salutation 'Hi First Name' as this is too personal. He should deliver e-mails in the format of legal correspondence, setting clear deadlines and he should react if the deadlines are not adhered to. He should ask the ex-wife to answer point by point and should not fall into the trap of responding to emotional provocation. By following this advice, the client will avoid feeding her need. The more he feeds her need, the longer she will persist and, because she has no insight, she will never stop.

The ex-wife is sure to retaliate to this new style of communication and the client should brace himself for a vengeful and spiteful retaliation. Unfortunately this will probably mean that the client will have to take legal action – which will cost money – but since money is important to her, this is the only way she will learn. It is however recommended that he take legal steps whenever she misses deadlines.

It is unreasonable of the ex-wife to expect the client to pay bills immediately as suppliers usually give clients ninety days to pay bills. Payment of bills is a matter strictly between the client and the supplier and he is under no obligation even to inform her when they are paid. A factual point by point account when bills are paid would be courteous and will serve his case in court proceedings. It will eliminate 'nag mail' and make his life easier. This can be regarded as management of the ex-wife's emotional condition, without falling for it.

It is unreasonable of the ex-wife to set a deadline of

seven days for her responses to his emails. Since they both agreed to this method of communication, she has absolutely no excuse for not replying within 24 hours, especially since she insists on his being immediately available when she needs him. Again, only *her* deadlines are important and this is a further indication of her lack of insight.

As to the children: it is advised that the client keeps a record of all these communications. Children grow up. As adults they will hold their mother responsible for bad-mouthing their father and eventually this will reflect negatively on her and not on him. The client should therefore refrain from calling her 'delusional', etc. He is not a psychologist. The client could serve an interdict to restrain her from discussing finances with the children.

The client has clearly demonstrated his maturity, his financial generosity by paying for the ex-wife to accompany the children on outings, his willingness to support his children financially, his active involvement in their lives, and an obvious concern for their well-being. The client is the only one who used terms of endearment when referring to the children. In contrast, the ex-wife sometimes seems to regard them as merchandise to be delivered.

From my reading of the e-mails I can find no reason to believe that the ex-wife is an unfit mother; however, her immaturity, lack of insight and tendency to bad-mouth the father are not exemplary parenting qualities and are detrimental to the children. Further investigation into her private life could deliver proof of unfit parenting.

Outcome

The client was provided with a profile of his ex-wife, based on a psychological analysis of her behaviour. Since she is the mother of his children, she will always be a part of his life. However, he was put in a better position to manage her, and to avoid stepping into emotional traps that would drain his energy. The client cannot change his ex-wife. He can only change how he responds to her. She can only change if she seeks psychological help and realises that the void she is experiencing cannot be filled by her ex-husband. Her key to happiness lies within herself.

CASE STUDY: COMPANY CHIEF EXECUTIVE OFFICER

Background information

In the following case, I was called in by a private investigation company to analyse threatening letters and transcripts of threatening phone calls directed at a chief executive officer (CEO) of a company and his wife. I analysed each letter individually and provided a profile of the author of that particular letter and then presented a general profile. Again, I have changed some facts and not disclosed identities, because of my confidentiality agreement with the client.

Analysis of letters

Letter 1

- Contents: This letter is accusatory, full of grudges and promises to ruin the company in order to put the CEO out of business. There is loyalty towards the company, but not to the CEO.
- Profile of the author: The subject will be a former employee who has inside knowledge of the company, as is evident in references to employee training. The subject also has knowledge of employees' salaries and refers to bribing employees. He or she would like the reader to believe that he or she has won the trust of the employees. This would more easily be

done by someone who was well acquainted with the employees and would fit the profile of an ex-employee, at managerial level.

The subject is intelligent, educated, has a good command of the English language and has business sense, as is evident by references to foreign currency and offshore accounts. The subject would like the reader to believe that he or she has substantial funds available, not only to bribe employees, but also to take over the company.

The subject is likely to be a white person. Reference is made to non-white staff. A black person would use the word *black* and not *non-white*. *Non-white* infers that *white* is superior to *black*. Therefore although the subject would like the reader to believe that he or she is concerned about people of different races and religions, the subject is in fact being racist by using the word *non-white*. There is a sense of a patronising manner.

The subject is likely to be a female. The words '*old boy*' are in inverted commas. Inverted commas are used when one means the opposite of what is being said. In this case the inversion does not pertain to *old* for it has already been established that the person has inside knowledge of the company and has some loyalty towards the company (but not to the CEO). Therefore the inversion can only pertain to the word *boy*. This means the author is female.

Although the subject refers to the fact that she has manpower available to help her, she uses the first person singular ('I'), thereby indicating that she alone is in charge of the takeover and vendetta.

- Threat: The CEO is identified as the antagonist. He is identified by name and surname. No title or 'dear' is used in the exordium. This means that the CEO has become a concept to the subject. Although the subject must know the CEO quite well, he or she has stripped him of his personality. He has become the concept against which the grudge is borne. There is a formality here. The exordium was not 'Dear First Name'. He has become an institution to the subject – he is larger than life.

The threat is to put the CEO out of business. There is no threat of personal violence or physical harm. The envelopes are addressed to the business address and not to his home address, which would have made the threat more personal.

The subject would like the reader to believe that she has the means – money, people and power – to carry out the threat.

- Envelope: The date of postage and region of post office were on the envelope.

Letter 2

- Contents: The general tone of this letter is an attempt to convince the CEO that he cannot trust his staff.

  The exordium this time is *'Dear First and Last Name'*. The word *dear* is perhaps intended as sarcasm. First and last names used together still indicate that the CEO is considered to be an institution in the mind of the subject.

  In this letter, the subject did not use the first person singular ('I') but the first person plural ('we'). She would like the reader to believe that she has formed alliances and has now more of a power base than before. When a subject believes that power is increased by numbers, it indicates that she does not really believe that she has sufficient power on her own. It is a sign of weakness and a sign that subconsciously she does not have confidence in her own abilities.

The subject would like the CEO to believe that she has formed a consortium with other ex-employees. She uses the word *seem* which means that she has not succeeded in tracing all the former employees.

The postscript has the sole purpose of trying to create paranoia within the CEO. The subject wants to indicate that her takeover and bribery have paid off. There is a hint that someone in the company is feeding her information or that she has access to computer data.

- Profile of the author: The fact that the subject used '*we*' instead of '*I*' indicates that she has no confidence in her own personal power base.

The nuance of this letter is one-upmanship. The subject wants to show the CEO that she has out-manoeuvred him. She regards him as a worthy adversary, whom she has managed to beat. This, as well as the lack of a personal power base, indicates an underlying inferiority complex.

The subject is inviting the CEO to a metaphorical game of chess. She wants him to acknowledge her as a worthy opponent. Subconsciously, the CEO represents someone the subject looks up to. This is a distortion of the father figure. Subconsciously, the subject needs the CEO's approval.

- Threat: The threat of putting the CEO out of business still prevails. Added to this is a veiled threat directed towards the CEO's family. This increases the level of danger of the threat. It has become personal and extended. No direct threat of violence has been made, but there is a veiled implication.

- Envelope: The letter was mailed at least a week after it was composed. The subject refers to a future date in the letter, and the date of postage indicates that the letter was mailed a week after that date. It was mailed from another town.

Letter 3 (postcard)

- Contents: The contents of the letter are spiteful. The aim of this communication was to prove to the CEO that the subject is at a well-known resort in the company of other ex-employees, as she had promised in the last letter. The subject would like to convince the CEO that she has the financial means to treat ex-employees to a trip to this resort, but there is no proof that the postcard was sent from the resort. It is a very transparent manoeuvre.

  There is no exordium on the postcard. It is probable that the subject got someone else to write a seemingly innocent message and did not want this person to know to whom the postcard was addressed. This is probably why the CEO's name and address were not written on the postcard itself, as would have been usual, but rather mailed within an envelope.

- Profile of the author: The handwriting will differ from the suspect's handwriting, because it will have been written on her behalf.
- Threat: The subject is trying to prove that she has the means – financial and manipulative – to carry out the threat.
- Envelope: The letter was posted on a certain date, but not from the resort. If the subject was really at the resort, why did she not post it there?

There is a disparity between the dates of this communication and the previous one. The second letter was written before a certain date mentioned in the letter and posted a week later from another town. The postcard was supposedly written at the resort on the date mentioned in the previous letter yet posted days later, and not at the resort. Had the letters been posted in the order in which they were written, the second letter should have been dated before the postcard, and the postcard should have been dated later. This sloppiness on the part of the subject indicates a strong possibility that she made up the resort idea and that it did not happen in reality.

Letter 4

- Contents: The exordium is informal, as opposed to previous exordia. The subject will only use this informality if she feels that she and the CEO are now equals. She has beaten/gained some victory over her adversary.

  The contents of this letter are intended to have the CEO believe that she has the means to cause him considerable business harm. The subject probably has an old client list and has devised the strategy of sending them messages that the company is closing down. It might still be possible that the subject has access to the company's offices or that someone inside is providing her with information.

- Profile of the author: Again the use of '*we*'. The subject has risen in her own self-esteem, probably because she has devised the 'brilliant' strategy of sending clients the message that the company is closing down. In fact, this strategy is amateurish. It is also amateurish to warn an adversary of an intended strategy.

- Threat: Again, the subject wants the reader to believe that she has the means to cause harm.

  This was the last letter. To summarise, the subject has so far only attempted to convince the reader of her ability to take over the company. There is no actual proof that she has done anything yet. So far, the threats are only in her mind.

  There is a possibility that she has contacted ex-employees, may have access to the building or insider help and might have a client list/computer data.

- Envelope: The letter was posted from another town.

Note

The subject used different fonts in each letter. This is usually done by anonymous letter writers to try and confuse the recipient about the identity of the author. People who do this want the recipient to think that different people authored the letters. But in this case it is quite clear that the letters were all authored by the same person. There is no attempt to conceal this fact; only the name of the author has not been revealed. There is thus no purpose in using different fonts. The only conclusion one can reach is that the subject is enjoying a little game, playing it out with imaginary paraphernalia to accompany the charade. People who fail in their lives usually have rich imaginations in which they play the role of hero to perfection.

The letters are neat and there are no spelling mistakes. The grammar is sophisticated. Stamps are placed squarely – an indication of perfectionism.

Telephone calls

- Phone call to CEO's wife: The subject wanted it known that she had the means to make contact with the CEO's family.
- Phone call to CEO on his birthday: This indicated that the CEO was still important enough to the subject for her to remember his birthday. She is preoccupied with him and has the need to make contact with him. This fits into the Oedipal father figure scenario.

Profile of the author

The author is most probably a white woman and an ex-employee of the company, who held a managerial position.

She is intelligent, has business sense and likes to play mind games. It seems that she suffers from an inferiority complex, and she compensates for this by becoming a hero in her imagination. When a person experiences some sort of failure in life, they need to compensate for this elsewhere, usually in their imagination. The author has probably suffered some loss, or has reached a point in her life where she has to balance her achievements and failures and, at this time, the balance is negative. People at this stage of their lives are facing a midlife crisis, which would put the suspect in her early fifties. Since her career is so important that it has driven her to the desperate measure of writing threatening letters and a preoccupation with an imaginary hostile takeover, she has probably failed in her marriage. She does not have the support of a husband or children. People who fail often cannot take responsibility for their lives and therefore they blame others. The author blames the CEO for her current failure in life. He has become responsible for her lack of success. This elevates him to more than just a human being and makes him an institution. The author needs to take revenge. In the perfect scenario she imagines that once the CEO has been eliminated, she will take over the company and everything will be fine from there on. This is the mindset of the author.

The CEO has been identified as the authoritative figure. If she can outmanoeuvre him, she has won and her self-confidence will be restored. By putting him in the authoritative position, the author is subconsciously acting out an Oedipal scenario. She needs the approval of the father figure – might even have been in love with the father figure – but has been rejected. The phone call to his wife is a clear indication that the author had some romantic Oedipal inclinations towards the CEO, which also supports the theory of a failed marriage. This rejection hurt her deeply and she is desperate. Threats are desperate moves by people who have no other way of influencing situations.

In keeping with the Oedipal theme, the subject sees the father figure as powerful. She wants to identify with him and prove she is worthy of his attention. The attempted alienation of current employees falls into the category of sibling rivalry. She is making the other siblings gang up against the father figure in order to dethrone him. This is also acting out what Freud called the Totem Theory. To be worthy of the father figure and in order to dethrone him, the subject needs to prove that she has the means and power to carry out her threats. It is quite obvious from the contents of the letters that the author needs to convince the CEO that she has the means to carry out the threats.

The question remains as to whether or not she will carry them out. So far she has taken little action, possibly only chatting to previous employees and spreading rumours. The miminal action she has taken makes her feel competent. There is no proof that she has actually acted to cause serious harm. Currently the battle is more in her mind than in reality, but this does not eliminate her potential to do harm.

The handwriting indicates that the author might be suffering from an obsessive personality disorder. People suffering from personality disorders generally have interpersonal problems in their home and work environments. They do not seek therapeutic help, as they can see nothing wrong with themselves. The obsessive-compulsive personality disorder is characterised by emotional constriction, orderliness, perseverance, stubbornness, and indecisiveness. The essential feature of this disorder is a pervasive pattern of perfectionism and inflexibility. These people alienate others, are unable to compromise and insist that others submit to their needs. However they are eager to please those they see as more powerful than themselves. Again, this fits in with the Oedipal scenario. Anything that threatens to upset the routine of their lives or their perceived stability can precipitate stress.

Is the author dangerous? The general trend of the letters does not imply physical harm; however, the veiled threat to the family and call to the wife is cause for concern. It should be established whether she has the means and opportunity to cause harm. Whether she has the intention of being violent is not clear at this stage.

Investigative recommendations

Identify author

The author can be identified by several means:

- Fingerprinting. It is recommended that the CEO receives all mail and that he opens the letters wearing gloves, taking care not to damage any fingerprints. The letter should be replaced in the envelope after he has read it. The private investigation company has the capacity to lift fingerprints.
- Movements: Petrol slips. The private investigation company can determine whether the suspect undertook trips to the particular town on the days the letters were posted. Her cellphone record may also prove her presence in that town, the resort, etc. Petrol card slips are also useful in this instance. Obviously legal routes to obtain this evidence must be followed.
- Interviewing previous employees. The private investigation company has the ability to establish discreetly whether ex-employees have been in touch with the suspect.
- Observation of current employees. The private investigation company can tap company phones or trace cellphone calls to establish if the suspect has contact

with any current employee.

- Computer. The private investigation company also has the means to establish if the suspect has electronic access to the company's computer systems.
- Security. A closed-circuit television can be installed inside the company premises to establish whether anyone has illegal access to the premises. It is preferable that this be done rather than changing the locks, for when someone is actually videotaped, it is direct evidence.
- Identi-call and tape recorder at home phone. It is recommended that the CEO install an identi-call system and tape recorder on his home phone. Should the suspect phone his home, her voice will be recorded and this is evidence.
- Cellphone records. The cellphone records of the CEO and his wife will probably show calls received from the suspect.

Strategy

Once the suspect is positively identified as the author of the threatening letters, she should be confronted with the consequences thereof, preferably by the private investigation company and not by the CEO. She may be charged with:

- Industrial espionage
- Intimidation
- Bribery
- Harassment
- Slander

An interdict can be obtained against her. Once she realises that she could face a prison sentence she will probably back off. If she does not, it is recommended that the CEO proceed with criminal or civil charges.

Outcome

When the profile was presented to the CEO, it confirmed his suspicion that the author was a particular ex-employee – a woman in her fifties, married to an alcoholic husband and childless. She had military training and her previous and subsequent business ventures had failed. She was described as being over-perfectionistic, dominant, preoccupied with detail, and was incapable of making quick decisions.

I summarised her current life stressors. Since she had military training and access to firearms, she could become violent if most of the stressors were activated. She probably blamed the CEO for all the stressors and would direct her aggression towards him.

The CEO decided to monitor the situation, to warn clients and employees of the situation, and in this way try to foil her.

CASE STUDY: ATTEMPTED EXTORTION

Background information

A private investigation company required my assistance in the following case in which a woman had received threatening letters. The author of the letters made it quite clear that he was a former employee of the woman's husband. He alluded by encryption – which was easily decoded – that he had spent several years in prison, probably for fraud, and that he held her husband accountable. He had been converted to religion in prison. Initially his motive was unclear, although it was obvious that he was intent on taking revenge. The subject had managed to trace the woman's whereabouts after he was released from prison. He did not know where her husband was. The husband had in fact passed away. The letters were sent to a PO Box, and not to the woman's residence. Again, for reasons of confidentiality, certain facts and names have been changed.

Analysis of letters

Letter 1

- Technical: The letter is undated. It is typed, indicating that the subject has some level of criminal sophistication, knowing that his handwriting can be traced and analysed. He has access to a computer, which means he either uses one at work or has one at home. He is therefore not a homeless person. The font he uses indicates that he also has some level of computer literacy, although no formal training in typing. I would predict that he is English-speaking. His education would have been government school, not private.
- Contents: The exordium of the letter is formal, *Dear Mrs X*. Although the subject knows Mrs X's first name (as indicated by the way the envelopes were addressed) he does not use it. This indicates that he was once in a subordinate position to Mrs X – since she was the wife of his employer – and at this stage he is still operating from this stance. The respect that the previous relationship demanded from him is still operative at this stage. Personally, the subject is therefore someone who probably has a puritanical regard for his reputation. He will consider himself a gentleman and will mind his manners carefully. What comes to mind is the image of a well-trained lackey or butler, who secretly resents the upper class, but supposes that imitating their manners and showing the correct amount of respect will eventually lead to his being accepted as an equal.

The use of the word *delightful* fits in with his wish to be of the same upper class as Mrs X and emphasises the fact that he is an outsider to this class and resents it. Since it took him a long time to discover Mrs X's whereabouts, it is clear that he lost contact with her movements and could therefore have been out of circulation for a while.

Although Mrs X may not know the subject personally, she will know of him. He introduced himself as a former employee of her husband and therefore gave an indication of his identity. He insinuates that he was sold out.

The subject made a simple spelling mistake, indicating that no matter how correct he is endeavouring to be, his 'slip' is showing.

The subject tells Mrs X exactly what kind of work he did for her husband, thereby giving away elements that may identify him. The way in which he describes his work implies that he was used as an agent or spy. A real agent would never give away this kind of information. Therefore we may assume that the subject has worked in this kind of environment but, although he would like to think of himself as an operative, he never really made it through the ranks. He is a 'wannabe' agent and his eagerness to think of himself as a true agent made him exploitable. If he worked for the CCB, NIA, SASS, security police, or defence intelligence, he was probably an informant handled by an agent.

The subject indicates that he has been in prison for a long time and that he has been converted to Christianity. Convicts are often 'converted' in prison and take on a very religious stance on their release. The subject imagines himself as the 'Avenging Angel'. This is a delusion. A delusion may be defined as a false belief based upon incorrect inference about external reality not consistent with intelligence and cultural background and unable to be corrected by reasoning.

Suffering from a delusion can indicate mental illness, although the subject's reasoning abilities and thought structure are not affected. It rather seems to me that the subject has a need to justify his behaviour. Greed is his true motivation, but greed is what he is accusing Mrs X's husband of, so he cannot admit to himself that he is also motivated by the same factor. He is not quite comfortable with what he is planning to do and found religion a convenient vehicle to justify his behaviour. I would predict that he suffers from an inferiority complex, harbours resentment, cannot take responsibility for his actions, blames Mrs X's husband, and has reached the conclusion that it is 'payback time'.

This is confirmed by the fact that he considers Mrs X's husband as the Judas who sold him out because of greed.

He indicates that he has lost his family, which confirms that he might have been in prison, his wife might have divorced him and he is estranged from his family. It is clear that his 'good reputation' and dignity are very dear to him. He feels that he was a confidant of Mrs X's husband – one of the inner circle – and that he was betrayed by him. He thought he had made it into the inner circle, but evidently he had not and this turned him into a fool.

The subject makes a religious reference to being identified as an avenging angel by God. He does not take responsibility for his behaviour and is conveniently placing the responsibility for what he is planning to do in the hands of the Lord. He is merely the instrument, as he was an instrument of Mrs X's husband – he will always be the lackey. People who do not take responsibility for their actions are cowards. Being in the position of lackey means he does not give orders, merely executes them. It is therefore unlikely that the subject will ever execute an action on his own initiative, but since he has appointed the Lord as his master, he might feel himself compelled to do it.

The subject embraces his own death, since he has nothing to lose. A person who has nothing to lose is dangerous. However, once we can identify inhibitors to violence – something meaningful in a person's life – it is a good strategy to strengthen them. Should there ever be direct contact between Mrs X and the subject, where her life may be in danger, she should strengthen his need for acknowledgement and treat him with respect and understanding. But I doubt very much that he would actually confront her physically.

A broad analysis of the contents of this letter reveals no direct threat, nor does the subject state what he wants. What is clear is his resentment at being betrayed and that he wants some kind of retribution. He has clearly adopted religion as his justification and has again put himself in the position of a lackey who operates on the orders of a master.

There is no indication of any physical danger in this letter. The category of stalking would be grudge-obsessional ex-employee.

Letter 2

- Technical: The technical qualities remain the same as in the first letter.
- Contents: The exordium is more familiar, as if she were an old friend. In the subject's mind, therefore, his relationship with Mrs X has progressed from being the 'boss's wife' to someone on an equal level. This indicates that since the last letter he has spent so much time thinking about her, or has maybe seen her, that he is now quite familiar with her. She is no longer just a figurehead to vent his frustration upon, but has become personalised.

The subject makes a biblical reference to 'an eye for an eye'. The tone of this sentence is that the subject is identifying Mrs X as a sort of fellow victim, whom he does not want to hurt or upset. Words such as *distressed* and *dearly* again indicate a need to be on her level, yet he misspells *to* again; once more, his 'slip' is showing. The subject is exonerating himself, putting himself in the lackey position of instrument to a greater master. There is an element of guilt feelings here, but he is negating them by misplacing his responsibility. *An eye for an eye* indicates revenge. This is the first indication of what he wants. He wants revenge/retribution.

The subject is indicating he knows it is unfair to target Mrs X instead of her husband but since, for some reason or another, he cannot locate her husband, he is left with no option but to target her. The fact that he needs to justify why he is targeting her instead of her husband indicates that the subject clearly knows the difference between right and wrong, but prefers to ignore it to suit his own interests.

By using the word *we* the subject is placing himself and Mrs X in the same camp – victims of her husband. He is sympathising with her. It is very difficult to harm someone one sympathises with. This also accords with the informal way he opens the letter.

The subject is identifying himself as someone who was close enough to Mrs X's husband to know more than just personal details about his business; at some stage he was some kind of confidant. It will not be difficult to identify him.

The subject is not quite sure whether Mrs X had inside information about her husband's business exploits. If he knew for certain, he would not find it necessary to remind her. This may cause an intrinsic predicament for him, for if Mrs X did not know what her husband was up to, it would be very unfair of him to target her.

The subject uses erudite words in order to impress and to hide his inferiority, but again he gives himself away by misspelling simple words. He sees himself as a messenger, which is degrading to his ego. He wanted to believe himself to be 'one of the boys' not a 'messenger'.

Reference to Mr X's exploits during a certain era would date the relationship between subject and Mrs X's husband to the 1980s. This will further help to identify him.

By referring Mrs X to certain persons, such as her father and other particular men, he is indicating that these people should know about him. Note that one of these men has been elevated to *Mr*, which means the subject was in some kind of subordinate position to this person.

The subject again makes a biblical prediction. This is a veiled threat, but it is generalised and does not pose any physical harm towards Mrs X per se. This sentence is also a turning point in the letter. Previously it was clear that the subject identified Mrs X as a fellow victim with whom he had sympathy. Yet, after this sentence he is clearly changing tone and is attempting to intimidate her. We need to establish what changed his mind to put her into the enemy camp. The only factor that I can identify in the letter that has anything to do with Mrs X and might suddenly have changed his mind while writing the letter, is the reference to her father. The fact that Mrs X's father was part of the enemy camp in his mind, clears his doubts as to whether or not Mrs X had intimate knowledge. If you recall, I said earlier that not knowing whether she was 'guilty or not' would create an intrinsic predicament for him. By recalling that her father was involved, the subject made up his mind within seconds that she must have known as well, and this is the reason for the change of tone in the letter. In his mind, she is no longer also a victim, but now firmly belongs in the enemy camp.

The subject is suggesting that he knows everything about Mrs X and will find out more. Quite clearly he is trying to intimidate Mrs X, but he is not succeeding. If he already knows everything, why would it be necessary for him to find out anything else? The subject has called his own bluff, which again confirms my suspicion that he was never a trained agent; if he had been, he would never have made such an obvious mistake as this.

The subject is attempting to project the idea that he is going to put the outcome of this whole operation into Mrs X's hands, giving her a choice. Clearly he is again exonerating himself from blame. If, in his view, Mrs X makes the wrong choice, she will carry the consequences and this will not be his fault. I would like to remind the reader that people who do not take responsibility for their own actions are cowards.

The subject continues to name a number of people who had contact with Mrs X, as well as details about her personal life, her business and her residence, and her children. This is done in order to intimidate; however, anyone in this game will acknowledge that this kind of information is easy to obtain and that it takes no special skill to acquire it. The subject is therefore not such an effective 'spy' as he would like to believe. As a matter of fact, his attempt is amateurish.

Obviously the subject obtained his information by talking to people close to Mrs X. I would suggest that these people, whom he names, have been targeted by him as sources of information.

The subject only mentioned Mrs X's children in order to intimidate her and it is highly unlikely he would ever physically harm them. They are now competent adults and authoritative figures, who are quite capable of taking care of themselves.

A general analysis of the contents of this letter is that there is still no direct physical threat towards Mrs X or her family. The subject has still not indicated exactly what he wants (apart from revenge) but he has implied that Mrs

X would be given some kind of choice when he does state what he wants. He is still venting his resentment and still exonerating himself from blame. The religious justification is still present.

Letter 3

- Technical: The technical analysis remains the same.
- Contents: The subject has reverted back to the more formal greeting. This makes sense, since in the second half of the previous letter he has placed Mrs X in the enemy camp and no longer identifies with her as a fellow victim.

The subject indicates that he does not know whether she received his previous letters. If the subject had such intimate knowledge of Mrs X's personal life as he would like her to believe, he would have known whether or not she received the letters – again, he is calling his own bluff in a very unprofessional manner. The subject craves Mrs X's understanding, perhaps because he wants her to understand him, or perhaps he wants her to understand why something is going to happen to her. In the first case – her understanding him – he is reiterating his inferiority complex, and in the second case – her needing to understand why – he is exposing guilt feelings.

His underlying guilt feelings play up in the second sentence when he again uses the word *we*. Although he would consciously deny it, he cannot rid himself of his intrinsic predicament that Mrs X might be innocent.

This letter is much more religious, which indicates that the subject is having second thoughts and needs to reinforce his distorted justification for why he is taking this action. He uses a biblical reference to something being taken, but does not indicate *what* he will take; he might not even be sure himself what he wants to take. He will leave Mrs X something, but does not indicate what. I would estimate that this would be evidence or proof of her husband's doings. In any case, for Mrs X to receive this something, she must be alive, so there is no death threat in this paragraph, no matter how ominous it may sound.

The subject is confident that the police will not be able to identify him. He does not realise, however, how much information about himself he has already revealed.

He takes against Mrs X when he indirectly accuses her of wanting to take away his memories. He is placing words in her mouth. The subject is referring to the loss of his own family and is not threatening Mrs X's family.

A general analysis of this letter is that there is still no physical threat, and the subject is still not stating exactly what he wants. He is venting his anger and is clearly in need of justifying his actions. As a matter of fact, he is procrastinating. Procrastination is a characteristic of losers, not of doers. I doubt the subject has the courage to actually do anything, but since he has appointed himself the lackey of a greater master, his warped sense of 'honour' might compel him to do it.

Letter 4

- Technical: The original analysis remains the same.
- Contents: The formal exordium remains, since Mrs X has to remain in the enemy camp in order for him to be able to justify his actions. It should be noted that this time there are no ostentatious attempts to impress as in the first letters. Mrs X has been put in the enemy camp and he is attacking her.

He refers to an acquaintance of Mrs X. This acquaintance needs to be identified for he will be able to identify the subject once he recalls the conversation. He substituted a derogatory term for the word 'friend'. The subject does not like this person.

At last, the subject covertly reveals a financial motive.

Since he cannot identify himself as a person who is motivated by greed, he is projecting this thought into Mrs X's mind. He is going to attempt to extort money from Mrs X by threatening to make public supposedly sensitive information about her husband's business dealings.

Since the subject considers himself a man of honour as well as an instrument meting out God's justice, he will never admit that this is his motive. Yet if money was not that important to him, why is he the one who mentions it?

The subject is projecting his own thoughts into the mind of Mrs X. He is having internal conversations with her. This happens to lonely people. They cannot fathom that the object of their obsession does not even think about them, and therefore they imagine role-playing scenarios. It relieves their loneliness.

The subject is reiterating that he would not physically harm Mrs X – they would have to meet for him to do that. He indicates that he has stood right next to her on some occasions, but this might be a reference to the time when he was still working for her husband, before the prison sentence. If he had been close to her since he started writing the letters, I do not think he would have been able to resist mentioning this.

The records that he has kept are probably the evidence or proof with which he is going to blackmail her. This indicates his intention of extortion. His pathology of being preoccupied with his own loss of 'dignity', which only re-emphasises his inferiority complex, comes into play when he mentions the loss of self-respect, the shunning and disgrace. Clearly he wants to avenge upon Mrs X the humiliation that he perceived he suffered from her husband. He threatens her with public disgrace, which to him is worse than losing his family.

Clearly Mrs X is no longer the fellow victim; she has become the antagonist who has to bear the burden of his revenge. The subject provides a deadline by which he will conclude his blackmail. This may indicate that he does not in fact have all the information at hand with which to blackmail Mrs X. The more contact he makes with other people, the greater the chance that he will be identified.

It may seem strange that the subject makes so many blatant mistakes that will make it possible to identify him, but it makes sense if we take his pathology of inferiority complex into consideration. He has a subconscious need to be recognised and is therefore subconsciously telling us exactly who he is.

A general analysis of the contents of this letter is that the subject intends using confidential information to blackmail Mrs X and to extort money. He is not inclined to become physically dangerous as he lacks the courage and it would probably offend his 'code of honour'. Nor would he harm her children. However, should he become desperate, he might attempt something foolish. He is not desperate yet.

- Envelopes: The fourth envelope was mailed one week after the third, indicating an escalation in the subject's obsession. Although the time period escalated, the low level of physical danger did not.

Note that the envelopes were posted to a PO Box and not to Mrs X's residential address. The subject is keeping the correspondence on a business level, not on a personal one. If he really wanted to be threatening he would have mailed the letters to her home or would have had them dropped off by hand.

Profile of the subject

Personal characteristics

The subject suffers from an inferiority complex and resents the fact that he will always be a 'lackey'. He hides this by presenting the persona of a 'God-fearing', respectable man of principle. Since he portrays this respectable, subordinate, well-mannered persona, he might be overlooked as a suspect. This demeanour should be looked for in possible suspects.

Obviously he has, at some stage, been trusted enough to have gained access to privileged information about Mrs X's husband, therefore others might also consider him to be trustworthy and might disregard him as a suspect. The fact that he can convince others to trust him should be looked for in possible suspects.

This man harbours a deep resentment at being betrayed – not so much for going to prison, or for losing his family, but for being excluded from the 'inner circle'. He probably hero-worshipped Mrs X's husband. This is another characteristic which could identify him.

He cannot take responsibility for his actions. Therefore in his conversation one will pick up the theme of blaming others. This is another characteristic that could identify him.

References to God and the Bible will characterise his speech. People like this tend to be very self-righteous.

He might make reference to himself as being some kind of spy, or to government institutions that have something to do with this shadow world. He will use ostentatious language and will avoid swearing. This could also identify him as a possible suspect.

External characteristics

His relationship with Mrs X's husband probably dates back to the 1980s, which should place this man in his late forties to early fifties, given the prison sentence. He will therefore have served in the army, probably achieving no higher rank than sergeant.

He is probably a divorced ex-convict. It should not be difficult to establish whether one of Mrs X's husband's ex-employees was sent to prison.

Since his reputation is so important to him, he will probably dress as well as he can, trying to imitate the upper class.

Level of dangerousness

The subject does not pose a physical danger. However, given that he is probably an ex-convict, with hardly any prospects of employment, has lost his family, has no cash and is facing a midlife crisis, he may become desperate and act foolishly.

He is intrinsically a coward and prefers to execute orders rather than give them. However he has appointed himself the instrument of God and is therefore obliged by 'honour' to do something.

If ever Mrs X should find herself in a position where she is physically confronted by this man and he threatens her, she should do everything in her power to play up to his need to be recognised. She should present herself as a fellow-victim who did not know about her husband's activities, and should be empathetic towards his unfair treatment. She should respect and confirm his dignity. She might even persuade him that he was courageous about taking the fall for her husband and that her husband did not appreciate his value. This will immediately decrease his level of aggression.

Intervention

Identifying the suspect

It should be very easy to identify the suspect. Apart from identifiable personality characteristics and external characteristics discussed in his profile, I would suggest the following strategy:

The subject has identified the kind of employee he was to Mrs X's husband:

- A messenger or chauffeur
- A Mr Fix-it
- A person who would gather information, deliver goods, get into places, take care of loose ends
- He must also have been some sort of confidant to Mrs X's husband in order to know details about his dealings

The subject has named several people in his letters. He has had contact with some of these people recently. All these people should be interviewed:

- Has anyone recently asked them questions about Mrs X, no matter how innocent they may have seemed?
- Do they recognise anyone who would have the personality characteristics and external characteristics mentioned in the profile, even if such a person has not spoken to them recently?
- Acquaintances or other employees or ex-employees of Mrs X's husband who had business dealings with him should be asked whether they can remember an ex-employee who would fit the profile (including his profile as employee, his character profile and external factors and the fact that he went to prison)

Of course Mrs X herself should consider these questions when trying to identify the man. He knows her and she has met him, although she probably would not have taken much notice of him.

It seems that the subject will not have all the information he requires for blackmailing, so previous or current employees of Mrs X's husband's company should be alerted that they might be contacted for this information. Discretion should be applied here, since some people might also have grudges and be willing to assist the subject.

These interviews would generate a list of suspects, which should be followed up and eliminated one by one.

Fingerprinting of the letters has already been done, although I doubt whether he would have left any.

Once he has been identified, the Department of Correctional Services should be able to provide information on the subject's release address. Cell mates may also be probed for his whereabouts.

Expected future behaviour of subject

The subject will continue to send letters in the same vein. He has given an indication of three months' preparation.

There is no need for Mrs X to read the letters since they will only upset her. Investigators need to intercept them and all personnel handling her mail should be alerted to look out for these letters and wear gloves when handling them.

Once the subject sets the extortion attempt into motion, I am confident that the investigators will be able to apprehend him. The subject should thereafter be charged with extortion and prosecuted. Care should be taken that he does not commit suicide while in custody. Confronting the subject without evidence and appealing to his 'good nature' to cease his activities will not succeed. He must be prosecuted.

Once he has been identified, I would suggest that his movements be monitored and that he be arrested when he makes the attempt to extort, rather than confronting him upon identification. Confrontation without evidence might scare him, but it will not stop him. Extracting money from Mrs X is this man's pension fund. He has nothing else left and will not easily let go of the golden goose.

Outcome

The private investigation company managed the stalker successfully. He was identified from the profile and his attempt at extortion failed.

CASE STUDY: CELEBRITY STALKER

Background information

Some years ago, while I was working for a private investigation company, Associated Intelligence Network, an employee of 702 radio station, Allan Ford, called me. At a function the previous evening he had spoken to several South African celebrities, including former Miss South Africas, television, radio and film stars, who had all complained about a stalker. From their accounts it was obvious that it was the same person in each case, as the modus operandi was the same. The stalker would introduce himself as Braam Kruger, a well-known author, chef and restaurateur, and then invite the celebrity to a party. The stalker would introduce a sexual element to the conversation, asking the celebrity if he or she would be prepared to join him in a jacuzzi, orgy, etc. The then acting news editor of Radio 702, Yusuf Ambramjee, confirmed Allan's report and asked for my help. I discussed the case with my boss and AIN decided to take it on, free of charge. An investigator was appointed to assist me and we solicited the assistance of Captain Wimpie Coetzee of the Linden Police Station.

We interviewed Braam and the celebrities and took their statements. It became apparent that the man had been stalking celebrities for almost twenty years, sometimes impersonating Braam, friends of Braam, or another male celebrity. Braam provided us with a detailed list of incidents. He had sent an e-mail to all his friends and colleagues warning them of the impostor.

Captain Coetzee managed to trace the cellphone number from which the most recent calls had been made. He obtained a court order, which enabled the cellphone service provider to supply us with a printout of numbers the stalker had called. We began calling these numbers, asking them if they knew the cellphone owner. One woman told us that the owner was a man renting a flat from her in Hatfield, Pretoria. She gave us his address. The stalker was identified as 49-year-old Mr X, a deputy director in a government department.

Late that night, Captain Coetzee made the arrest, with a full media contingent in pursuit. Mr X was immensely surprised when the police knocked on his door and presented him with a search warrant. He had been getting away with his phone calls for two decades. He was renting the flat privately, which meant there was no way in which it could have been traced to him. He was using a phone card, believing it made it more difficult to trace the caller. At first he denied everything. Captain Coetzee asked me to talk to him. I approached him gently and he confessed.

Mr X admitted that he had met Braam once or twice at art exhibitions. He liked Braam, for he was an extrovert, a larger-than-life personality. His parties were very popular. (Braam could not even remember meeting Mr X.) Mr X apologised for causing the celebrities concern and claimed that he had made the phone calls because he was lonely. In his mind, the victims had become his friends. He never intended them any harm. He explained to me how easy it was to get new numbers from current victims, as they all believed he was Braam. However, he said that he had thrown the cellphone away after Radio 702 contacted him on the phone. It was never retrieved.

Captain Coetzee asked me to make a statement, including a profile of Mr X. I began in the usual way, giving my credentials as an expert witness, proceeded to define stalkers and their typologies and then presented my profile of Mr X, based upon the conversation I had with him and the evidence presented by his victims.

Profile of the stalker

The subject is an extremely lonely person who has developed a rich fantasy life around certain female celebrities. He suffers from an inferiority complex and idealised Mr Kruger's flamboyant personality. That is why he pretended to be Braam Kruger. It is well known that Mr Kruger throws elaborate parties, which are attended by female celebrities.

In his fantasy life, the subject imagined himself being the host at such parties. He would invite his female 'friends', and engage in conversation with them. The more relaxed they became, the more sexual the nature of the conversation became.

The subject does not lose touch with reality, for he is capable of fulfilling his daily duties at work. He reads the newspaper, watches television and is up to date on current affairs. He reads the social pages in order to research which celebrity has attended which function. He keeps a record of their movements and telephone numbers, birthdays, etc. He is intelligent and has a master's degree.

It is probable that the subject would masturbate while talking to the celebrities. The longer the duration of the conversations, the more sexually aroused he became. Pornographic material was found in his flat and proprietors of sex shops in Sunnyside, Pretoria, identified him as a regular customer.

The subject was aware of the wrongfulness of his act, for when the Radio 702 journalists contacted him on his cellphone he immediately got rid of it for fear of being identified. He knew the cellphone would become evidence. He initially denied being the stalker to the police.

As I did not spend much time with him, I did not make a formal diagnosis. However, I would predict that he suffers from an erotomanic or grandiose delusional disorder. The prognosis for both these disorders is weak. The subject will probably again resort to stalking when he is lonely and if he does not receive therapy. (I added an explanation of the diagnosis to the statement.)

Outcome

Mr X was charged with crimen injuria, and appeared at the Randburg court the day after his arrest. He was not asked to plead and the case was postponed. He told reporters that he intended pleading guilty, for he did not believe that what he did was serious. The case was postponed again and again. I attended each time as an expert witness. Mr X was very friendly towards me. None of the celebrities ever attended.

What I found disturbing about this case was that the celebrities had been stalked for years. None of them knew to whom to report the problem. None of them believed the stalker could be traced. We traced him to his address within a few days, which proves that it is possible. Some of the celebrities were more disturbed by the calls than others. Some thought it a joke, while others took safety precautions. Braam was furious that his reputation was being jeopardised by an unknown impostor. The celebrities dubbed him 'The Media Terrorist'. Mr X caused psychological damage in some cases. I doubt whether he would ever have turned violent, but he would have continued for another twenty years. I found it disturbing that he would only face charges of crimen injuria and that if he was convicted the sentence would probably only be a fine.

By chance, I bumped into Mr X one day in a shopping centre. He was a bit shy, but friendly. He told me the prosecution was going to drop the case and asked whether he could consult me as a psychologist for therapy. Since I was one of the people who had identified him and would have testified against him in court, I did not think that this would be a good idea. I referred him to another psychologist. I hope he went. Given the circumstances, he was under no legal obligation to go.

Mr X seemed to have been a timid stalker who did not cause any physical harm. Many people would have been of the opinion that it would be unfair to send him to prison. I have been contacted by several other celebrities who have been the targets of more serious stalking. There is no doubt in my mind that they would have caused harm. I referred these cases to private investigators and the police and some of the stalkers have been apprehended. Some of the victims have relocated, others have employed bodyguards. One was held hostage for hours. The stalkers have been charged with breaking and entering, assault with the intention of committing grievous bodily harm, disturbing the peace, trespassing, etc. None of them have been charged with stalking. In the United States they would have faced long-term imprisonment and compulsory therapeutic intervention, their victims would have had input in their parole hearings and been pre-alerted upon their release from prison. As yet, South African citizens do not have this protection. I hope this situation will be rectified by our judicial system in the near future.

White-Collar Crime

DEFINITION OF PSYCHOPATHS

Violent crime is highly publicised in South Africa, but the proportion of white-collar crime is tenfold that of violent crime. The purpose of this chapter is to alert the reader to the general characteristics of psychopaths, for they are the ones most likely to be perpetrators in white-collar crime. I am not focusing on the aggressive violent psychopath in this chapter, but rather on the manipulative type. I will also discuss how society condones their behaviour and provide guidelines on how to protect oneself against them and implement damage control.

The term psychopath is commonly misused by the layman. The term *antisocial personality disorder* is used by health professionals and is defined by the American Psychiatric Association (accepted by South African health professionals) as follows:

There is a pervasive pattern of disregard for and violation of the rights of others, occurring since age fifteen years, as indicated by three (or more) of the following:

- Failure to conform to social norms with respect to lawful behaviours as indicated by repeatedly performing acts that are grounds for arrest
- Deceitfulness, as indicated by repeated lying, use of aliases, or conning others for personal profit or pleasure
- Impulsivity or failure to plan ahead

387

- Irritability and aggressiveness, as indicated by repeated physical fights or assaults
- Reckless disregard for the safety of self or others
- Consistent irresponsibility, as indicated by repeated failure to sustain consistent work behaviour or honour financial obligations
- Lack of remorse, as indicated by being indifferent to or rationalising having hurt, mistreated or stolen from another

The individual is at least eighteen years old. There is evidence of a conduct disorder before the age of fifteen years. The occurrence of antisocial behaviour is not exclusive to the course of schizophrenia or a manic episode.

CHARACTERISTICS OF PSYCHOPATHS

To assume that one would recognise a psychopath by relying on stereotyping is a fatal mistake. They come in all colours, sizes and shapes and both genders. Characteristics they have in common are the following: charming; self-confident; charismatic; often very handsome or attractive; deceitful; narcissistic and egocentric; they feel no remorse and they are opportunistic.

Psychopaths distort reality to suit themselves. They will lie in one's face, even if they are aware that one knows the truth. In his book *Without Conscience* (1993), Robert Hare relates the story of a prison inmate who saw a therapist in prison. This therapist was also a university professor. When the inmate was paroled, he decided to enrol for a course at a university. While he was queuing to sign up, the professor happened to walk past him. He called the professor over, tapped the person in front of him on the shoulder and told this person that for years he had been the professor's research assistant in psychology.

Psychopaths also rationalise every situation in order to suit themselves. For example, a classic retort I was once given was: *It was only fraud, no one got hurt*. Another violent psychopath who had killed a victim said: *He didn't even suffer, it was so fast*.

Typically, psychopaths paint themselves as the victim and the victim as the culprit, and have a total inability to take responsibility for their actions. A psychopathic husband who beats his wife will tell her: *Look what you made me do*. A psychopath who was sentenced to imprisonment after beating a man almost to death said: *Here I am in jail. He just landed in hospital and he is out already. I could have killed him but I decided to give him a break*. The victim was in intensive care for months, he had extensive medical bills and his family had to endure the uncertainty of whether he would live or die. The psychopath expected people to feel sorry for him because he would be in jail longer than the victim was in hospital and he wanted approval for his compassion in sparing the victim's life.

Psychopaths have erratic work records and frequent changes of address. When one looks at their curriculum vitae, one will often find the following, for example:

1992: PriceWaterhouse

1993: Deloitte

By excluding the actual months they worked for the company, they may be covering up the fact that most of that year was spent in prison or in a rehabilitation centre, or they were unemployed.

Very few employers ask for a list of addresses for the past ten years to determine whether the person has had stability in his or her life. Reasons for moving are never asked. When things get uncomfortable and they realise they might get caught, psychopaths just resign, pack up and leave without having another job or place to stay.

Psychopaths have a complete lack of empathy for other

people's feelings. Hare (1993) cites the case of a woman who was arrested for fraud and was much more concerned about her car being repossessed than the fact that her children would have to be put in foster care.

Psychopaths do not have a conscience and never suffer from feelings of remorse, although they might fake it very well. *Conscience to them is little more than an intellectual awareness of rules other people made up. They know the difference between right and wrong, they just do not care. To them right is when you get away with it and wrong is when you get caught. They never look back with regret nor forward with concern* (Hare 1993).

They are also impulsive. They insist that their needs be gratified immediately. When they receive money, they spend it immediately on luxury items. A rainy day never exists for them and if ever it should arrive, you may be sure they will con someone else out of an umbrella. They do not weigh the pros and cons of their behaviour and it is usually other people who suffer the consequences. They take offence easily and are short-tempered, but they recover just as easily for they do not feel true emotion.

Psychopaths have shallow emotions and are good at imitating the emotion of others. For instance, if a psychopath is telling a story he will take a split second to assess the facial expression of the listener and take his cue from that. If the listener reacts with shock, he will imitate it; if the listener laughs, he will laugh. Sometimes it is a good idea for the listener not to react at all and to wait for the psychopath's reaction. When interviewing psychopaths I would laugh at first and then express shock and watch them change their reaction accordingly.

Since they do not feel real emotions, they also do not show physiological signs of fear. When one is in a tight corner, one might start perspiring or shaking, but psychopaths do not. They remain cool under pressure.

They have a need for excitement. They cannot bear routine and they get bored easily. One might think that because they fear nothing and have no conscience they might make good soldiers, but this is not so, for they are the 'cowboys' who endanger the lives of others. In the business environment, they will take impulsive decisions and endanger the company's future. They are party animals and like to be the centre of attraction. Their behaviour at social gatherings might also damage their company's image.

Psychopaths are egocentric and narcissistic. They often commit plagiarism and take credit for other people's work. They cannot stand criticism and intimidate their critics either by raising their voices, slamming a fist on the table, or more subtly by making a fool of the critic in front of other people. People therefore tend rather to back off than confront them, and so they get away with it.

We can also identify psychopaths just by listening to their speech. They often make contradictory statements. A psychopath may be asked: *Have you ever committed a violent crime?* and he will answer: *No, but I had to kill someone once. I bumped into his car and he got out with a sledgehammer, so I shot him in self-defence.* Another example: *Have you ever used cocaine? No, I snorted it once or twice, but I prefer marijuana.*

Psychopaths use props to enhance an image. They attend workshops, cocktail parties, etc where they 'network' in order to collect business cards. They then use these social contacts as references to further their own interests. The following ruse is a good example: Mr Psychopath wants to sell stolen plumbing equipment. He looks up your number in the telephone directory. You are Plumber A. He then phones Plumber B, your competition, and makes an appointment with the secretary for Monday at 3 o'clock. He tells her that he was referred to them by you. Then he comes to see you with the stolen equipment at 2 o'clock on Monday. You are interested, but since the price is very low, you have your doubts. Mr Psychopath picks up your apprehension and tells you that he has an appointment at 3 o'clock with your competition, Plumber B. He even gives you his telephone number. You phone Plumber B's secretary and she confirms Mr Psychopath's appointment at 3 o'clock. You buy the equipment because you think you are going to lose out on a good deal. Mr Psychopath has succeeded in setting you up by using your own name as an alibi with your competitor, whom he has never met.

Another example: The psychopath strikes up a conversation with you during a break at a symposium or conference. He will either contact you later, asking for a job or a favour and refer to meeting you at the symposium, or he will use your name as a reference to one of your colleagues. For example: *Mr Big and I discussed this issue during the symposium at the Sandton Sun and he said I could phone you if I needed assistance*. People seldom check with Mr Big to find out if he is telling the truth. Just the fact that Mr Psychopath uses Mr Big's name is enough to convince some people.

Psychopaths have no real friends, they only have acquaintances. They are fond of projecting the image of a big spender. They may make an appointment to see you and rent an expensive car just for the duration of the meeting. They invite you for lunch, and you end up paying the bill.

They steal stationery from your secretary's desk when her attention is diverted, or they create their own stationery. In one case, a psychopath stole letterheads from his previous company as well as from other companies he had never worked for and wrote himself glowing letters of reference. Psychopaths use impressive-sounding names for their businesses. For instance, 'The National Academy for Security Officers Training' might just be a rented one-room office in a derelict building.

Psychopaths attend symposiums and similar gatherings to pick up technical jargon and sound as if they really know what they are talking about. They have been known to attend a few university lectures, just to pick up the jargon and to familiarise themselves with the campus and the names of the professors. It is difficult to spot an imposter in a class of two hundred students. South Africa has experienced a few cases of psychopaths posing as doctors and nurses without having had a single day's training in these professions.

They will attend charity functions just to have their pictures taken with true philanthropists. They sign up as voluntary charity workers simply to show others these pictures, or to add the details to their curriculum vitae.

Religion is a ruse often used by psychopaths because they have learned that people are more inclined to trust religious people. Some print verses from the Bible on their business cards, or quote from the Bible when they talk. However, when one listens carefully, it is easy to unmask them. The psychopath will not tell you how great God is, he will rather tell you what a good Christian he is, how charitable he is, etc. The focus is not on God, but on the psychopath himself. He just cannot escape his own egocentricity.

The prognosis of psychopaths after rehabilitation is virtually non-existent. They will go to a therapist seemingly to please their family or to satisfy parole conditions, but they have the sole hidden agenda of picking up the jargon in order to con others and to manipulate the psychologist. In interrogation situations, I have found they will confess only if it is to their own advantage. Even if they are faced with damning evidence, they will persist in their denial or blame someone else. They are recidivists who will always return to crime, because it is too easy and too thrilling to resist.

Only if one can convince a psychopath that it is in his best interest to apply his strengths and skills to serve others, will he become a useful member of society, or make a contribution to a company. However, he needs tight control and supervision, clear, strict rules and must be made aware of the positive and negative consequences of his actions, in no uncertain terms. Since they are so charming and quick-witted, a psychopath on a tight leash might be an asset to close deals, entertain clients or as a salesperson. One of them, for instance, derived great pleasure in providing me with insights to write this chapter.

It always amazes me how society condones the behaviour of psychopaths. Companies tend to be too flexible in the interpretation of their rules or else their watchdogs are asleep. A psychopath will always be on the lookout for the potential to make a profit. If controlling measures are not in place and applied daily, he will abuse the system.

Society also condones their behaviour in its expectation that people of a particular status or profession will be trustworthy. We seldom check the credentials of our medical professionals, lawyers and church ministers. A university degree or even a postgraduate degree is not a certificate of integrity. Psychopaths trick people into trusting them by attributes of position, association and intelligence.

They make a point of targeting easy and naïve victims, often selecting people who are vulnerable, such as pensioners, single women, etc. Most people do not want to admit that they have been taken in by a psychopath. Psychopths' families protect them either out of fear or obligation or the concern that they will experience loss of income if the psychopathic breadwinner is arrested. Many of them are also intimidated.

Psychopaths have an uncanny ability to spot others' weaknesses and to exploit them. A male psychopath will spot the recently divorced and emotionally vulnerable woman in a crowd. He will woo her as the perfect romantic gentleman. It won't be long before he moves into her home, alienates her from her friends, drives her car and steals her money. A female psychopath will spot a rich man's vanity and manipulate him into buying her a home. Since psychopaths get bored so easily, their relationships don't last and then they resort to extortion. They listen to businessmen's needs and provide the 'perfect solution' to any problem.

How does one survive psychopaths? First of all, prevention is better than cure. Learn to identify them and avoid them. Remember, if it *seems* too good to be true, it *is* too good to be true. Always check the credentials of people, regardless of whether they become romantic or business partners, and especially if you are considering employing them. Reasonable people will not object to this. Do not be taken in by the psychopath's props. One should also be aware of one's own weaknesses and vulnerabilities and beware of people who seem to satisfy all one's needs immediately. The answer to all one's problems does not come wrapped in a gorgeous package.

If one becomes aware that one is already in the clutches of a psychopath, it is time for damage control. I would suggest professional help from a therapist to restore one's self-worth. Blaming oneself for falling prey to a psychopath is useless – even experts are fooled by them. Track down other victims and form a support group to facilitate shared legal assistance, if this becomes necessary. Do not get involved in the psychopath's power plays, or else learn to use them to your advantage. In one case I know of a woman was battling to obtain custody of her children when she divorced her wealthy psychopathic husband. Eventually her lawyer suggested that she agree to grant him custody.

Three months after he had won the custody battle, the man ceded custody back to the woman. He did not really want the children, he only wanted to win the court case.

It is imperative when dealing with a psychopath to set clear rules and boundaries and to stick to them. Sometimes the best option might be just to cut one's losses, learn a valuable lesson and move on. However, when it is a case of damage to a company, I always advise clients to prosecute. Firing a psychopath or forcing him or her to resign will only set them loose to cause more damage to society.

PROFILING WHITE-COLLAR CRIME

Profiling a white-collar criminal is relatively simple, since most of them have the characteristics of psychopaths. However, there are cases where people with no psychopathic tendencies have committed white-collar crime as a result of external circumstances. For example, I investigated the case of a female bookkeeper who had worked for a company for eighteen years and had always been trustworthy when suddenly she defrauded the company. When the evidence was presented to her, she refused to admit to it. Even the threat of prison did not sway her. I realised that when a woman prefers prison to her home, she must have an abusive husband. The moment I introduced the subject of her husband, she cracked. It turned out that he had been retrenched and was physically abusing her and her children. She had been forced to steal in order to maintain their lifestyle. The company decided not to prosecute her. She and her children were removed to a place of safety, her husband was charged, and the company offered her another position, where she would not be exposed to the temptation to steal. She had to pay back the money in instalments.

In another case I know of, a woman stole money to pay for her son's rehabilitation for drug addiction. In cases such as these the culprits would be well advised to find other sources of assistance, for the consequences of committing fraud are not worth it and you will certainly get caught.

CASE STUDY: JAMES

Background information

James (not his real name) was employed as a temporary human resources manager at a company for four months. Just before his contract expired, the company's financial department received a call from a supplier of laptop computers (Supplier A), requesting payment of an outstanding invoice. The financial manager was unaware that laptops had been bought from this particular supplier and asked them to fax him a copy of the invoice, which they did. The financial manager noted that James had signed the invoice for two laptops. Two laptops had disappeared from desks in the office during the past four months and some employees had 'mislaid' their pocket computers.

The financial manager bumped into James in the lift and asked him about the two laptops that had been ordered from supplier A. James replied that two secretaries needed laptops to replace the ones that had been stolen and that one of the company's managers had given him permission to order them.

The financial manager spoke to the manager concerned and she confirmed that she had given James permission to buy the two laptops. She said she had signed the invoice authorising payment. The financial manager checked the invoice faxed by Supplier A and found that there was no other signature besides James's. The financial manager checked with the two secretaries who confirmed that they had received new laptops. At first the financial manager thought that the other manager had probably just forgotten to sign the invoice, but the fact that she remembered giving James permission to buy the laptops and the fact that the secretaries had the laptops almost convinced him that everything was in order. James had been very forthcoming when he asked him about the invoice and had not seemed at all nervous.

Fortunately the financial manager was a diligent person and his gut instinct warned him something was wrong. So he checked all the invoices and found one from Supplier B for two laptops which had been signed by James and the manager. This invoice was discovered the day before James was supposed to leave the company. The financial manager discussed the matter with the CEO, who decided he needed time to investigate. He called James in and asked him if he was willing to work for another week. James had not yet found other employment and agreed.

The CEO called in the help of private investigators. All the employees who worked in James's section, as well as the secretaries, were polygraphed. James failed his polygraph.

Interrogation

I did not have time to profile James and went straight into the interrogation phase, armed with my knowledge of psychopaths and the background information.

At first James denied everything, but after he was confronted with Supplier A's invoice he confessed. In a tearful outburst he admitted that apart from ordering the two extra laptops from Supplier A, he had also stolen the two missing laptops, as well as stationery, toner cartridges, boxes of computer disks and the three 'mislaid' pocket computers. He had sold these items to a pawnshop because he needed the money to support his drug habit.

James told the CEO he would be willing to recover the items from the pawnshop and pay back any amount not recovered. He asked whether the company would be willing to pay for his drug rehabilitation. He said that his wife had divorced him and moved to England. She had taken most of their possessions and the divorce had ruined him financially. He had custody of their only child and he was currently living with relatives and trying to get back on his feet. He said he had turned to drugs to console himself after the divorce a year ago. The CEO almost conceded to this request, for it seemed as if James was truly remorseful, and the CEO was concerned about his child's future.

My colleagues, the private investigators, immediately contacted James's previous employers and found out that he had been asked to leave after cash had gone missing. James told his previous employers that he had a drug problem and they sent him to a rehabilitation centre for three months. While he was in rehab, his girlfriend would smuggle drugs in for him, which he sold for a profit to other addicts. When he came out he paid back the cash he had stolen – probably with the money he made from selling drugs. He promised to marry the girlfriend, but broke off the relationship soon after he was released from rehab. This company also found out that James had hired a car on the company's account for his girlfriend to drive from Cape Town to Pretoria, and he also paid this amount back. (This had happened before the cash went missing.) The company did not dismiss James, but asked him to resign voluntarily, which he did. They did not prosecute because they did not want to attract negative publicity, nor did they want to be involved in a legal case of this nature.

The private investigators established that James's wife had divorced him because of his affair and drug habit and had moved to England, but she had been awarded custody of their child. The child was living with her relatives in

South Africa and James had visiting rights. The mother was looking for suitable accommodation and as soon as the new school term began, the child would join his mother in England.

The company paid James's salary to the employment agency that had placed him and the agency then paid James with a cash cheque because he had no bank account. James paid no tax on his salary. He also regularly borrowed money from his mother and did not pay any rent to the relatives with whom he was living.

All this information came to light within two hours, while James was waiting in the boardroom. The CEO changed his mind and asked that the case be handed over to the police. He told James that he could make a phone call, thinking that James might want to speak to his son. James, however, phoned his girlfriend and told her to tell his relatives that they could pick up their car – which he had been using to commute to work and back – at the police station. He did not mention that he had been arrested, or that he was sorry and nor did he send a message to his son. When asked what his eighty-three-year-old mother would think about the situation, James answered: *It will probably kill her.*

James was offended that the CEO refused his offer to retrieve the stolen equipment and to pay back the outstanding balance and would not give him a second chance to rehabilitate himself. He did not even consider the fact that he bought and used drugs during working hours, that he phoned drug dealers from work, and that he visited the pawnshop during working hours. Nor did he consider the bill of the private investigators, which included polygraphing seven other innocent people who must have found it a stressful experience. He was unperturbed by the fact that his relatives would have to find transport to retrieve their vehicle from the police station.

My interrogation of James commenced at about lunch-time. Earlier that same morning he had visited a drug dealer and had exchanged his sister's cellphone for drugs. He planned to draw R100 from her bank account at lunchtime (he had her bankcard with him) to retrieve the cellphone. He was upset when the investigators would not allow him to go to the bank. *(I promise I'll be back within half an hour.)* He said his sister had given him the bankcard to draw money to buy groceries on his way home because he had the car. It would be the investigators' fault that his relatives would not have anything to eat that night and that his sister's cellphone would now be sold.

James was due to leave the company the following day. The company did not have his address and knew only that he lived somewhere in Boksburg. James's colleagues had even planned a small farewell party for him the following day and they had all contributed towards a small present, because he was so popular.

Outcome

James was arrested. The scary fact is that James could be anyone working in your company. Within four months he had stolen four laptops, two pocket computers, stationery, cartridges and disks. He also stole time, and the company had incurred a bill for the private investigators. No price can be placed on the emotional damage he caused his mother, son, relatives and colleagues. Because of the interrogation, which lasted from about one o'clock to six o'clock that evening, the CEO had to put off an important business meeting and the investigators had to make other arrangements to have their children collected from school. James had a BCom degree, several certificates in human resources management and was thirty-two years old. He committed theft and fraud, and is a liar and a drug addict. James is a typical psychopath.

This case study depicts not only typical psychopathic behaviour, but also illustrates how society condones this behaviour. Had the first company taken legal action against James, he might have been apprehended and removed from society sooner. The employment agency did not check his employment record or the reasons for leaving his previous employment. They did not find it suspicious that he did not have a bank account and asked to be paid in cash. Did it never occur to them that he was attempting to evade tax? No one checked his actual physical address. The last company did not check his background before employing him; they took the employment agency's word. He impressed co-workers with his charm and for a second time almost convinced someone to give him another chance, although he had no intention of changing his ways. He got away with it once and he expected to get away with it a second time. Unfortunately as soon is he is released from prison, James will continue his career of fraud and drug addiction.

Fortunately his child is living in England, far away from his father's influence.

Intelligence Profiling

IDENTIFIED SUBJECTS

In this chapter, the purpose of profiling moves from identifying an unknown suspect to predicting and influencing the behaviour of a known person. Clients who require intelligence profiling are government intelligence agencies and corporate clients. To put it bluntly, these clients require strategies from the profiler on how to influence subjects. In my experience, the subjects fall into two categories: they are either known criminals, particularly within organised crime circles, or they are influential business people, agents and politicians, etc.

One of the basic principles of profiling – namely that people are creatures of habit – prevails when one is profiling known subjects. People create habits to make life easy for themselves. In criminology this is called *modus operandi*. The profiler needs to establish the habitual behaviour of the subject, and also needs to establish the factors that cause the subject to deviate from his normal behaviour.

As I have said more than once in this book, the key to unlocking behaviour is *motivation*. What a person does is not important. *Why* he does it, is the most important question. It will indicate his motive. If one understands what motivates a person one can analyse and even manipulate him or her. With accurate profiling one can devise strategies to manipulate circumstances and predict how the person will react to them. If one understands his motive, one will also understand why he would deviate from expected behaviour.

PROFILING KNOWN SUBJECTS

The process of compiling this type of profile is based upon collecting as much information about the subject as possible. Once the information is analysed and deductions are made, it becomes *intelligence*. With intelligence one can manipulate a situation or influence a subject and predict behaviour.

It is therefore imperative that a comprehensive background study on the subject is conducted. Either the profiler or the client may undertake this study. I prefer clients to present me with information and I will tell them if I need more because I seldom have the time for this very necessary work. The client may also employ private investigators to collect the information. I am referring here not just to traceable information (such as address, education and work records), I am talking about generating sources on the behavioural patterns of the subject. To be able to interpret these usefully, the elements of formal education, training and experience are once again essential to the profiler. When profiling subjects within the corporate sphere, education in industrial and organisational psychology is essential. The profiler can make deductions about a person's lifestyle, his manners, his speech and whatever he writes. Anything about the person will tell the competent profiler something. I have identified several sources of information, which I have found useful when profiling a known subject.

Motivation

In 1954 Abraham Maslow designed a hierarchy of motives, based upon the gratification of needs, arranged from lower needs to higher needs. The lower needs are relatively simple and arise from physical conditions that must be satisfied. Higher needs will come into play only when the lower needs have been satisfied.

The needs are the following, ranging from the lowest to the highest:

- Physiological needs (hunger, thirst, sleep, sex, etc)
- Safety needs (security, etc)
- Belongingness needs (family, friends, etc)
- Esteem needs (achievement, ambition, career, others' opinions, ego, etc)
- Self-actualisation (become a person to best capacity, ideology, spiritual, etc)

People's behaviour is motivated according to which level of need is to be satisfied. A starving person does not care what people think of his table manners. A person on the self-actualisation level will always try to do the right thing and to assist others, even if it means sacrificing something of himself.

When profiling a known subject, one of the first steps is to evaluate which basic need is governing him at that particular point in time. This may differ from time to time, depending on circumstances.

Alderfer and McClelland studied Maslow's theory. Alderfer narrowed Maslow's 'needs' down to three groups – namely, the need for existence, the need to relate to others and the need for personal growth. McClelland identified three needs – namely, achievement, power and affiliation. The profiler can determine which of the above needs are most relevant to the subject at a certain point in time. Gratifying or frustrating those needs will have certain influences upon the subject's behaviour (Schein, 1980).

Observable characteristics

I was fortunate to have been able to attend a course on

interviewing and interrogation strategies presented by Nate Gordon, Director of the Academy for Scientific Investigative Training in the United States. Nate has become a valued friend and colleague and has invited me to be guest lecturer on some of his courses. Nate and his colleagues devised the Lafayette pre-employment screening questionnaire, in which they included a table comprising the following observable elements:

- Personal grooming
- Friendliness
- Physical appearance
- Poise stability
- Self-confidence
- Expression of ideas
- Mental alertness
- Motivation and ambition
- Experience and education
- Personality and maturity

They present these elements in table form and the observer allocates a score of one to five to each element. The scores for all elements are then added together. I have found that the higher a subject's score, the closer he is to Maslow's self-actualisation level.

In my experience these characteristics can also be useful in profiling a known subject. They can be observed either in an informal or a formal situation. An informal situation is just a discussion. A formal situation may be an interview with the subject.

Leadership

Some people are natural leaders and others are natural followers. Some are neither. By observing a subject's behaviour one will easily be able to establish whether he is a leader, a follower, or both, depending upon the circumstances. Once it has been established who is the leader, and what kind of leader he is, the profiler can offer several tactical options to the client in order to influence the subject's behaviour. One can influence a leader to follow a certain route and his group will follow. Or one can influence the second in charge to challenge the leader's convictions by promising him leadership. One can also incite the followers to uprising. These are called *divide and conquer* tactics. Most people do not like to admit that they are wrong, especially if they are in leadership positions. Therefore the client not only has to sway a leader to share his opinion; he also has to provide him with a plausible way of saving face. Usually one achieves this by making him believe it was his good idea in the first place.

Knowledge of and training in industrial psychology will be useful to the profiler. Useful sources I have found include Fiedler's leader-match theory on task- and people orientated leadership, Vroom's contingency theory regarding management decision styles, and Argyris' model theory on the psychological maturity of leaders and subordinates (to be found in Schein's *Organizational Psychology*, 1980). Once a subject's leadership style is determined, the profiler can predict his behaviour and devise a strategy to influence it.

Threats

Threats have been discussed in the chapter on stalking (page 339). The understanding of threats has a double purpose. The client needs to know when he should, or should not, make threats and, secondly, the client needs to understand the person who makes threats. Recall De Becker's advice: When a person has made a threat that person can only advance or retreat.

Predicting dangerous behaviour

Dangerousness is not a permanent state of being, nor is it a permanent characteristic of a person – dangerousness is situational.

De Becker identified two principles to consider when determining dangerousness, namely *value* and *vulnerability*. *Value* is an evaluation of the circumstances and intent of the perpetrator, and *vulnerability* is an assessment of the vulnerability of the target. When the threat is undervalued and vulnerability is ignored, the situation favours the perpetrator. When the perpetrator is evaluated by an expert and the target takes precautions to safeguard his vulnerabilities, dangerousness can be managed and avoided.

The principles of understanding danger are applicable within an intelligence situation when there is a threat of a company takeover, merger or rivalry among opposing leaders.

Content analysis

I was fortunate to have been personally trained by Avinoam Sapir, former expert on polygraphing in the Israeli Police and current director of the Laboratory for Scientific Interrogation in the United States. Sapir devised the Scientific Content Analysis (SCAN) system, by means of which a person's written or spoken words can be analysed. Both Avinoam Sapir and Nate Gordon provide training in SCAN from time to time in South Africa and I highly recommend students of profiling to attend their courses. They also offer training in the use of the VIEW questionnaire, which is especially useful for identifying perpetrators. I prefer this resource when profiling a known person, for it provides me with a tangible product of the subject and it is one of the most effective and reliable methods available.

Personality disorders

There are twelve personality disorders, each with observable characteristics. It is easy for anyone to read up
about these disorders in a textbook, but a layperson will
not have the insight to recognise or predict the behaviour
of the individual concerned. A competent profiler needs an
academic qualification in psychology and the experience
of having worked with patients suffering from personality
disorders. To achieve this level of diagnosis the profiler
must have attained at least a master's degree. As a group,
persons suffering from personality disorders are very
unpredictable and only an expert can make meaningful
deductions about their behaviour and how to manage
them.

For example, people who are over-perfectionistic, preoccupied with details and lists, always insist that others
follow their lead, have difficulty in making decisions
because they spend too much time on detail, or who are
overconscientious, lack generosity and have restricted
expression of affect, suffer from obsessive-compulsive
personality disorder. Rub them up the wrong way and they
will refuse to respond or deliberately sabotage a project.

Body language

There are many books on body language available to
the general public, but the profiler needs training and
experience in interpreting the finer nuances of body
language. He or she needs to understand the scientific
principles underlying body language: for example, a subject may wilfully try to repress a certain state of mind
(perhaps to conceal deception), but certain muscle groups
will involuntarily respond to this repression and reveal
the discomfort. The experienced profiler will be able to
detect these telltale signs.

Nate Gordon and William Fleisher in their book *Effective Interviewing and Interrogation Techniques* (2002) cite the following quotation from Freud: *He that has no eyes to see, no ears to hear, may convince himself that no mortal can keep a secret. If his lips are silent, he chatters with his fingertips; betrayal oozes out of him from every pore.*

Gordon and Fleisher list three categories of non-verbal behaviour:

- Emblems: These are non-verbal behaviours that in themselves express the total communication. An example is a person standing next to the road with his thumb in the air
- Illustrators: These are non-verbal communications that help the listener understand the verbal communication better; for example, a person banging his fist on the table while speaking angrily
- Adapters: These are primary subconscious non-verbal behaviours that can frequently detract from verbal behaviour. They are indicators of deception. For example, a person who insists that he is telling the truth, but covers his mouth with his hands.

An experienced profiler will also realise that the senses are aroused under stressful circumstances and will be alert to any behaviour indicating arousal of the senses.

The scientific application of body language therefore comprises much more than just making common deductions about a person crossing his arms and the profiler needs to be proficient in translating non-verbal behaviour, while at the same time analysing the verbal contents and context of the subject. Obviously this requires intense concentration, but it becomes easier with experience.

Neurolinguistic programming

Neurolinguistic programming (NLP) is a specialised field within psychology. It explains the link between the mind (neuro) and the speech (linguistic) of a subject. When a subject relates a story, the movement of the eyes will tell the profiler whether or not the subject is telling the truth.

Neurolinguistic programming also identifies the following three modalities, by which an individual predominantly operates:

- Visual: A subject will give clues in his speech, for example: 'I see what you mean'
- Auditory: A subject will give clues in his speech, for example: 'Now listen here ...'
- Kinaesthetic: A subject will give clues in his speech, for example: 'As I understand it ...'

Once the profiler has determined the preferred modality of the subject, he or she can advise the client to adopt that modality. The subject will subconsciously feel that the client understands him better and be more inclined to be influenced.

There are a number of agencies and psychologists who provide training in neurolinguistics.

Graphology

Handwriting analysis can be a very useful tool in profiling. As with body language there are many popular books available, but I recommend that profilers understand the underlying scientific principles of graphology. A person's handwriting is recognised as a projective technique, which can be psychologically analysed. I strongly advise that profilers do not attempt an amateur analysis of handwriting, but either be professionally trained or acquire the services of an expert. A colleague of mine, Dr Charmaine Elliott, is a qualified industrial psychologist and I have often sought her services. She has developed an eight graphology factors scale measuring the following polarities:

- Task orientation (considerate) – Task orientation (directive)
- Task orientation (less conscientious) – Task orientation (more conscientious)
- Emotional – Emotionally stable
- Introverted interpersonal orientation – Extroverted personal orientation
- Dependent – Independent
- Conceptualisation (concrete) – Conceptualisation (abstract)
- Conventional – Open to experience
- Lower need of power – Higher need of power

Dr Elliott can provide graphology reports for the purpose of pre-employment screening or a more comprehensive report on the personality of the writer.

Psychometrics

As a qualified registered psychologist the profiler can employ psychometrics as a tool in profiling, provided of course that the subject gives consent. The Health Professions Council of South Africa requires that psychologists and psychometrists adhere to strict ethical codes when administering psychological tests and I would advise any future profiler to keep up to date on these codes and adhere to them. A profiler should never allow the requirements of a client to influence his or her ethical code. All subjects that I have tested have signed written consent, as well as indemnity forms. It should also be remembered that any person being psychologically tested is legally entitled to feedback.

Psychoanalytical psychology

This entails a basic knowledge of Freudian psychology. Freud maintained that an individual's personality was determined within the first six years of his or her life.

(This is discussed in the chapter on serial killers, pages 124-36.) I firmly believe this. One should never underestimate the importance of trying to establish what kind of relationship the subject had with his parents. Adults often project feelings they had towards their parents on to other people. Old scripts are replayed every day. As I have said, people are creatures of habit, not just in what they do, but in how they think and react. When available, I find that the developmental history of a subject provides the most reliable information for me to be able to make predictions about future behaviour. For example, children who did not experience basic security during their youth will always compensate for this during adulthood. This can manifest either as being over-dependent on someone else, a need for approval, problems with authority or substituting security for money.

Erik Erikson corroborated Freud's theory on childhood developmental stages, but also explored adult developmental stages. He devised the following life cycle stages:

- Oral-sensory stage: trust versus mistrust. If a child's basic trust was gratified as an infant, he will remain optimistic about life
- Muscular-anal stage: autonomy versus shame and doubt. The child's self-confidence as opposed to self-consciousness will be established during this phase
- Locomotor-genital stage: initiative versus guilt. The child begins to mimic the adult world in this phase. Sibling rivalry is rife. Children who are encouraged to explore life despite their failures are successful, while those who are ridiculed in their attempts will suffer from guilt, often setting themselves up for failure as adults
- Stage of latency: industry versus inferiority. The child needs to develop his talents and acquire social skills.

Failure will result in feelings of inadequacy during adulthood
- Stage of puberty and adolescence: ego identity versus role confusion. Group identity, establishment of ego identity and incorporating the moral and ethical values of society are the important factors of this stage
- Stage of young adulthood: intimacy versus isolation. This stage incorporates establishing sexual identity and finding a life partner
- Stage of adulthood: generativity versus stagnation. Establishing a career, leadership or follower roles and authority confusion are issues to be resolved in this stage
- Stage of maturity: ego integrity versus despair. Ideological commitment versus confusion of values are relevant to this stage

Freud's and Erikson's theories have become a tool to identify certain characteristics in an adult personality and lead to a better understanding of the individual, especially when one recognises how these characteristics developed since childhood. If one wanted to change or influence the subject's behaviour on a long-term basis, one would have to correct the mistakes that were made during the childhood years. However, just by identifying the developmental stage a subject finds himself in, the profiler can devise a strategy that would incorporate the basic elements of that particular stage to influence short-term changes in behaviour.

PROFILING IDENTIFIED SUBJECTS

Once the profiler has established the subject's most likely motives, tapped all available resources and analysed the information, he or she is able to start compiling the profile.

The profile will usually include basic demographic information, an analysis of the subject's personality and predictions on the subject's most likely behaviours. Thereafter the profiler can devise a strategy on how to approach or influence the subject or his circumstances, should the client require this.

The profiler should take the following elements into consideration when profiling a known individual:

- The profiler should take cognisance of his or her own convictions and avoid being judgemental
- The profiler should try to place him- or herself squarely in the subject's shoes and circumstances when trying to figure out why he did something
- Always double check facts
- Enlist a partner to play 'devil's advocate' when you are compiling a profile
- People lie when they are afraid. They fear reprisal, they fear getting into trouble, they fear someone else will harm them if they tell the truth, they fear someone they love will get hurt if they tell the truth, they fear they will make a fool of themselves. Once the fear which motivates them to lie is identified, the lie can be transformed into a truth by appeasing that fear. Always try to make the truth sound more rewarding.

CASE STUDY: CORPORATE MERGER

Background information

In the following case, the client presented me with the curriculum vitae of the subject, a company alumni profile and several newspaper clippings containing direct quotes of the subject. The client envisaged a corporate merger with the subject and needed a strategy with which to approach the subject favourably during a presentation. I analysed the limited resources available and came up with the following profile:

Profile of the subject

Personality: Type A

Friedman and Rosenman define *Type A personality* as: *A hard-driving, aggressive, action-orientated person who will struggle to achieve poorly defined goals by means of competitive hostility and who is driven by time urgency.*

The subject recorded several achievements during his early adulthood. Before the age of twenty-five he had assumed a leadership position and represented his organisation at an international conference. It is possible that a sub-economic childhood motivated him to achieve a higher standard of living. He was exposed to a global environment at a young age, which would have boosted his self-confidence and honed his negotiation and self-assertion skills. He is opportunistic and seeks new stimulation on a daily basis. He is a man of vision and appreciates innovation. I determined this from his curriculum vitae.

Current life cycle

At the age of thirty-five the subject came into his own and now, ten years later, he has reached his peak. His current life challenge will be that he is approaching middle adulthood.

Erikson defines this phase as the generativity vs stagnation phase. Individuals at this stage of life are reviewing the past and deciding on the future. They compare their early aspirations with their current achievements and redefine their roles. Generativity points to guiding the upcoming generation and promoting self-actualisation.

The subject does not have a son. For someone in his position it is important to have a 'crown prince'. This position cannot be fulfilled by his own son and he will therefore subconsciously be searching for such a contender within his organisational ranks. An innovative up-and-coming contender, who has proved himself already and who will be willing to follow the subject's lead until he is ready to abdicate, will fill this position.

Current rivalry from management within his organisation will be threatening to him, since he is 'a king without a crown prince' and he might be ousted.

His fears at this stage will be disillusionment or frustration because he can no longer anticipate new work challenges, coupled with the threat that he might be overthrown by a new contender who is not his personal choice. The subject is not yet ready to abdicate, as is evident by his consideration of merging companies.

A Type A personality is also called a coronary personality and is predisposed to heart attacks. Since the subject is overweight this is a possibility. He may also be faced with a decline in physical vigour.

Motivational drives

Maslow's hierarchy presents five stages of consecutive needs to be gratified, which manifest as motivational drives. They are: physiological, security, affiliative, self-esteem and self-actualisation.

The subject has gratified the three lower need stages (physiological, security and affiliative) and at this stage of his life, in middle adulthood, is hovering between the self-esteem and self-actualisation stages of need fulfilment.

Self-esteem is represented by wealth, status and acknowledgement and is related to persuasibility. Self-actualisation is characterised by altruism and exceeding the self.

The subject has two main drives at this stage and they are *profit* and *benevolence*, each representing the top two need stages.

Profit: He is capitalistic and interested in the bottom line.

Benevolence: He is ideological, interested in upliftment, training and skills development, environmental impact and empowerment.

Whatever approach is taken with the subject, these two motivational drives should feature strongly.

Intelligence

The subject probably has a superior intelligence. The higher the IQ, the less a person will be moved by persuasive arguments. Unsubstantiated generalisations and irrelevant arguments will not impress him. An approach relying on impressive arguments with abundant factual support, will be more likely to persuade him. The subject is an independent thinker and will appreciate this characteristic in other people.

He is probably more concrete than abstract, given his financial background, therefore when he is faced with a presentation he will appreciate the analytical process having been completed, and the focus should be on the concrete facts. The presentation should be objective and rational.

Leadership

Fiedler's theory on leadership identifies two types of leaders namely: utilitarian and normative:

- Utilitarian: In this case, unless the leader meets the requirements, he may be voted out or fired. The basic form of involvement is calculative. The investors'/ subordinates' attitudes may be cautious, suspicious, independent, concerned with equity, self-protective and uninvolved
- Normative: This leader is charismatic and his basic form of involvement is moral.

The subject is a task-orientated leader, interested in the bottom line. He occupies a utilitarian position (profit making) within his company, but would also like to see himself as a normative leader (benevolent).

As a utilitarian leader, the subject has to appease the above-mentioned attitudes of the investors and shareholders as well as the state. This ties in with his first basic motivational drive, which is financial.

Since he also wants to be normative, he will attach value to upliftment and empowerment, which ties in with his second motivational need for benevolence.

He appreciates innovative high risk taking, coupled with accountability.

Value system

The subject is quoted as saying that he owes a great deal to his company. His value system is characterised by reciprocity. There is an element of reciprocal giving and taking. He used the word 'owe' not 'I am grateful to'. 'Owe' indicates reciprocal value, give and take, tit for tat.

Proposed strategy to approach the subject

Every person has a latitude for acceptance and a latitude for rejection. Ego involvement refers to the emotional investment a person makes in a business opportunity. The more highly ego-involved a person is in his projects, the greater his latitude for rejection of ideas that do not conform with his way of thinking. The subject is highly ego-involved in his work. Therefore proposals should fall securely within his latitude of acceptance. To accomplish this, anything presented to the subject should focus sharply on his two needs, namely, opportunity for profit-making and benevolence, in that order. If the focus falls only on profit-making, the subject will raise questions about the empowerment benefits of such a presentation, and vice versa. An ideal strategy would be to present both, and to emphasise the point that by accepting the proposal, he will be in a position to accomplish/bestow both.

This strategy will support his cognitive consistency, in other words, his ability to maintain balance regarding his beliefs, feelings and actions. This is important, especially since he is in his middle adulthood phase and needs reconfirmation.

The subject has reached the motivational need stage of self-esteem. The higher a person's self-esteem, the more difficult it is to persuade him. A person who has confidence in his personal opinion is not threatened when presented with conflicting arguments. Only if he considers another individual to have more authority than himself will he conform to that individual, otherwise he will not be persuaded by status in itself, but rather by the innovative substance of the message.

As pointed out previously, because the subject is intelligent and has reached a level of high self-esteem, he will not conform to authority simply for the sake of it. He will only conform to authority if he considers that the person wielding it has authority over him.

Arguments presented to the subject should therefore not be enforced purely on a power basis of authority. They should be logical, supportive, factual, concrete, support his two motivational needs and have a firm bottom line. Bohemian, fanciful and tangent arguments will only frustrate his sense of time urgency.

It is suggested that the subject only be approached by a person who has at least the same status as he does. He likes people who are like him, who share his interests and his way of thinking. Such a person should be in the same age group, the same executive status, Type A personality, stature, etc, but this person should be careful not to try to persuade the subject. The moment obvious persuasive tactics are implemented, the subject will view this as a lack of self-confidence. The benefits of a joint venture should support the subject's being placed a position to be seen as the one who addressed the profit-making and benevolent elements of the project. He should stand out as the hero.

Regarding the self-actualisation stage, the subject is at present still confusing benevolence with altruism. He will appreciate elements of training and developing skills, as well as a positive impact on the environment, being included in any proposal, but he will need recognition for it.

The information provided was not sufficient to determine the subject's decision-making style or problem-solving style, but enabled me to point out that he refused to comment on a certain issue. (This cannot be divulged as it might identify the subject.) This indicates that he will keep his cards to himself and will probably be more autocratic than democratic. Yet he has the persona/charisma to convince/influence others to follow him, probably provided by his exposure to international arenas at a young age. He should be regarded as a sophisticated manipulator.

Whoever presents the proposal should keep in mind that he is being evaluated by the subject. This resembles an interview situation. Points to focus on are the following:

- Attitude towards interviewee (the subject): Keep eye contact and be sensitive to his body language as well as your own. Mirror his hand and body movements unobtrusively, read his animated facial expressions, change direction immediately when boredom or irritation is detected. Establish whether the subject uses an auditive, visual or kinaesthetic modem of communication, eg: 'Listen here ...' / 'I see ...' / 'I feel that ...' and copy this in your own speech
- Mood and affect: Evaluate whether the interviewee

is irritable, relaxed, stable, fluctuating, reserved or forthcoming and change direction to support the positive affects

- Perception: Evaluate whether your message is clear or vague and rely on his questions or facial expressions to determine this
- Thought process: Keep your thought processes logical and coherent and avoid disjointed conjecture and loose associations
- Sensorium and cognition: Be aware of reality; that is, the time constraints of the presentation (lunch time, etc), the atmosphere of the environment where the presentation is made (luxurious and professional) and allow time for informal affiliation afterwards, if the subject is open to such a suggestion, but be sensitive to remain within corporate guidelines in this regard. He still values reciprocal tit-for-tat gestures, but he will be sensitive towards this, because of a previous negative experience.

It will be a crucial mistake to underestimate him, patronise him, bore him or to play one-upmanship.

Outcome

The merger was successful.

CASE STUDY: CORPORATE PROFILE

In this case the client was only able to provide me with the transcripts of three radio interviews, a condensed curriculum vitae and an article on the subject's home in a magazine. I used SCAN and neurolinguistic programming to compile the profile. The client needed a profile of the subject at short notice and a strategy to approach him.

Profile of the subject

An analysis of the transcripts reveals four main elements:
* Kinaesthetic modality
* Long-term perspective
* Calculated risk-taking
* Democratic management style

Kinaesthetic modality

The subject generally begins every sentence with the words: *I think* ... It would therefore be advisable to adopt this modality when speaking to him. Structures such as: *Our reasoning is ...; We are of the opinion that ...; Our rationale is ...; We believe that ...; What do you think/what is your view?* should litter the speech of the presenter of the proposal. Adopting the same modality is conducive to affiliation.

By preferring a kinaesthetic modality, the subject is indicating that he values careful, analytical, rational thought processes. He likes to give consideration to a subject before he gives his opinion on it. His use of phrases such as *not directly, about, maybe, possibly,* indicates that he is careful to commit himself to hard facts. This is probably to avoid future confrontation if promises are not lived up to.

Long-term perspective

The subject uses phrases such as at *this stage, over a period of time, progressively, long term, this will take time, steadily as market conditions will permit, from time to time, gradually,* etc when discussing his company's future plans, but he uses phrases such as *hope long before then, as soon as possible* when discussing another company's plans.

This indicates the subject will not react positively when he is pressured to perform, but expects speedy action from others. He should not be obliged to take an immediate decision on a matter.

Calculated risk-taking

The subject will not take impulsive risks. He will analyse and weigh all options before coming to an informed decision and he will not be rushed in this process. He needs to feel safe before venturing a risk.

Democratic management style

The subject frequently uses the words *we* and *our* when referring to his company's plans. Words such as *reasonable consensus, satisfactory outcome for all parties*, indicates that everything is negotiable.

He is probably a people-orientated leader, as he is more interested in motivating, encouraging, empowering and providing incentives to people than enforcing them. It seems he has more of a Type B personality.

The presenter of the proposal should be of the same status, stature, age group and personality type as the subject, so as not to make him feel uncomfortable.

Personal information

The following deductions are based upon the condensed curriculum vitae and an article on the home of the subject. The subject will place a high premium on family roots, tradition, 'old boys club', history and heritage. He also values environmental preservation. Any proposal which includes some of these values will appeal to him. If these values cannot be included in a formal proposal, they should be incorporated into an informal approach. Conducting social or business meetings within historical settings, complete with leather furniture, old books, formal gardens, etc will be advantageous. He is not a hi-tech, chrome and glass man. Old-fashioned values and good manners will make him feel at ease.

Outcome

Owing to the lack of further information, the profile could not be extended, but it provided the client with enough intelligence to approach the subject.

CASE STUDY: CUSTODY

In the following case study I was approached by an attorney on behalf of his client to (1) submit a profile on a subject's behaviour with specific reference to allegations of voyeurism, alcohol and drug abuse, inappropriate sexual behaviour towards children, and (2) the effect this might have upon his son. The attorney provided me with a file of statements and other documents, among them psychometric reports. Psychological reports are confidential, but with a subject's permission, they may be presented in court, which was the case in this instance. The subject rents a one-bedroom flat in an apartment building and has been identified as a peeping tom by female residents. He watches them through their bathroom windows. In one incident, he tried to climb though the window, but ran away when the woman screamed.

Profile of the subject

Narcissism

Psychometric reports of the subject reveal narcissistic traits in his personality. This raises the concern that he would place his own needs before those of his children.

The concept of narcissism needs to be explored.

Kaplan and Sadock in *The Synopsis of Psychiatry: Behavioral Sciences Clinical Psychiatry* (1991) define Narcissistic Personality Disorder as follows: *Persons with narcissistic personality disorder are characterized by a heightened sense of self-importance and grandiose feelings that they are unique in some way.*

Clinical features are described as follows:

> They handle criticism poorly and may become enraged that anyone would dare to criticize them, or they may appear to be completely indifferent to it. They want their own way and are frequently ambitious, desiring fame and fortune. Their sense of entitlement is striking. Their relationships are fragile, and they make others furious because they refuse to obey conventional rules of behavior. They are unable to show empathy, and they feign sympathy only to achieve their selfish ends. Interpersonal exploitiveness is commonplace. These patients have fragile self-esteem and are prone to depression. Interpersonal difficulties, rejection, loss and occupational problems are among the stresses that narcissists commonly produce by their behavior – stresses they are least able to handle.

The course and prognosis is described as follows: *The disorder is chronic and difficult to treat.*

According to Kaplan and Sadock, narcissistic personality disorder forms part of the Cluster B personality disorders, which demonstrate a generic predisposition for antisocial personality disorder (psychopath), and which is also associated with alcoholism.

Fantasy life and Voyeurism
The psychological report revealed that the subject has an undisciplined, immature imagination and fantasy life.

Since allegations of voyeurism – which is a sexual offence – have been levelled at the subject in various statements provided to me, the role of fantasy in sexual offences will be explored. MacCulloch, Snowden, Wood and Mills (1983) studied a group of sixteen sexual sadists. In thirteen of the cases, sadistic masturbatory fantasies were found to have inspired the sadistic acts. MacCulloch et al found that thirteen of the sadists had behavioural 'try-outs' where their fantasies corresponded with their sadistic behaviour. In some cases they found a progression in the contents of their sadistic fantasies.

Prentky, Wolbert-Burgess, Rokous, Lee, Harman, Ressler and Douglas (1989) examined the role of fantasy by comparing twenty-five serial killers with seventeen murderers who committed only a single murder. The authors hypothesised that the drive mechanism for serial killers is an intrusive fantasy life manifesting in higher prevalences of paraphilias (voyeurism is diagnosed as a paraphilia), documented or self-reported violent fantasies and organised crime scenes in serial homicides. All three of their hypotheses were supported.

Prentky et al (1989) report that Burgess, in a study she conducted in 1986, had found evidence of daydreaming and compulsive masturbation in over 80 per cent of a sample of thirty-six serial murderers in childhood as well as adulthood.

Prentky et al summarise the research of MacCulloch et al as follows:

While the precise function of consummated fantasy is speculative, we concur with MacCulloch et al that once the restraints of inhibiting the acting out of the fantasy are no longer present, the individual is likely to engage in a series of progressively more accurate 'trial runs' in an attempt to enact the fantasy as it is imagined. Since the trial runs can never precisely match the fantasy, the need to restage the fantasy with a new victim is established.

By no means is there any suggestion in my report that the subject is a serial killer or a sadist. What is important in the above quotations is that research has found a relationship between fantasy life and repetitive sexual offences.

It is common that perversions or paraphilias – such as voyeurism (a sexual offence) – are fuelled by fantasy. The fact that the ex-wife referred in her statements to the subject's habit of watching pornography is relevant. (The sense of sight is used in voyeurism to cause sexual arousal and the sense of sight is also used with pornography to cause sexual arousal.)

Freud described voyeurism as a violation of others' sexual activity, which would replace indulging in normal sex. Voyeurism does not only pertain to the sexual activity of others, but also to undressing, bathing and being naked. The element of risk involved – peeping tom activities – provides sexual pleasure to the voyeur as well. Acting out the fantasy will commence by dressing up to go out, taking binoculars, planning the route, identifying the victim beforehand, etc.

The authors of the research discussed above point out that when there are no internal inhibitors present, individuals will act out sexual fantasies. This implies that since the subject has an immature and undisciplined fantasy life, when he has a sexual urge he is likely to act upon it, notwithstanding social or moral disapproval. Evidence of his violent verbal and physical abuse – as reported by several witnesses – is also indicative of the fact that he cannot control his basic impulses. Adequate impulse control will be an inhibitor to acting out sexual fantasies.

The FBI's *Crime Classification Manual* (1993) classifies voyeurism as a nuisance offence. However it warns investigators that if an individual has escalated his behaviour from peeping tom (outside) to burglarising (indoor) and thus progressing to more serious invasive activity, this is a sign of danger.

Witnesses report that the subject has progressed from peeping tom activities to engaging in contact. One cannot at this stage confirm that the subject is a rapist in the making, but one can speculate as to what his next action would have been if he had managed to enter the premises. The first step was to watch – which might be harmless to the individual being observed – the next progression was to approach – which might frighten and be potentially harmful to the victim – the next logical step would be to touch, which would constitute rape or sexual assault. Clearly he is escalating to more aggressive sexual behaviour, which is dangerous.

The allegations of continuous watching of pornography, alleged voyeurism as well as the breaking-in indicates that the subject is exhibiting the profile of a sexual predator, with escalating uninhibited fantasies. This, given his narcissistic tendencies (an individual who places his own needs above those of others) and his low impulse control, makes the subject a potentially dangerous individual. His sexual fantasy life is beginning to overtake his concept of reality. He is running the risk of being charged with breaking and entering, but discards this risk because of his growing overwhelming need to act upon his sexual fantasies. The risk itself is arousing to the voyeur. Discarding the risk of being apprehended for the sake of acting out the fantasy is an indication that the fantasy life is becoming more important than reality.

Paedophilia and child molestation

The ex-wife reported that the subject would sleep naked with his son and that he would bath naked with the son for longer than an hour, more than once a day, and would regularly videotape the son and his friends naked. It is not necessary to bath children for an hour, nor twice a day. Clearly the purpose of the escapades was not for bathing but for something else, especially since he entered the bath naked as well. The question has to be asked: might this be for the pleasure of spending time with the son naked under the guise of innocent bathing? It is not uncommon for parents to videotape or take pictures of their children naked. Most family albums will have one or two photos of naked toddlers in a bath. However the differentiating factor will be the number of naked photos compared with clothed photos. The subject will probably contest that he loves his child and would never harm him. It is worth noting that the majority of child molesters, when confronted, say that they love children and had no intention of harming them.

However, in the light of the subject's alleged preference for pornography, his alleged voyeurism and immature fantasy life, his videotaping, sleeping and bathing naked with the child is inappropriate, especially given his low impulse control. The ex-wife also reported marijuana abuse which, coupled with alcohol abuse would lower his impulse control even further.

Child-rearing

The ex-wife has a valid concern that the subject was not aware of his son's age-related needs, the fact that he ignored his illnesses and that he acted as a playmate and not a responsible adult and furthermore allowed his son to play with a firearm.

The fact that the child does not have his own bed in his father's flat is also worth noting. The subject appears to treat his son as an extension of himself (narcissistic trait) and not as an individual who needs his own space.

Effect on the child

The theories of renowned historical child psychologists will be explored.

The son is currently in what Freud (European child expert) described as the Oedipus/phallic phase. Subconsciously he is in love with his mother and resents his father as the competition. This is normal and might explain why he has made derogatory remarks about his father. At the end of this phase (5-6 years) he will begin identifying with his father as a role model. The subconscious reasoning is: 'If I am like my father I will get a woman like my mother.' His father is now becoming a very important role model for him. Also at the end of this phase the father figure role model will influence the boy's developing of a conscience – internal differentiation between right and wrong. According to Freud, before the age of six, children avoid doing wrong for fear of punishment, but after identifying with the father figure, they internalise this aspect of the conscience.

Eric Erickson (American child expert) identifies 3-5 years as the Initiative vs Guilt phase. Children in this phase want to mimic the adult world and their social role identification is important. Whatever example the boy's father sets him in this phase will influence his own concept of his social role as a man.

Jean Piaget (French child expert) is of the opinion that the child's ability for logical cause-and-effect thinking and his ability to appreciate others' points of view will commence at seven years. This pertains to developing a conscience. (Lack of a conscience is what mostly differentiates psychopaths from other individuals.)

Bathing and sleeping naked with a child in this age group is inappropriate to his developmental needs. Frequent videotaping of him naked may be humiliating, especially when he grows older. If discipline and routines are ignored, the child will feel insecure. If the allegations levelled at the subject are true, his current behaviour will have a devastating negative effect on his child for the rest of his life, especially with regard to sexuality and conscience.

Conclusion

If the allegations levelled at the subject are proved to be true, he is a potentially dangerous sexual predator. I would be negligent in my duty as a forensic and investigative psychologist if I did not issue a warning that a child in his custody could be in danger of being exposed to sexual molestation/exploitation and moral corruption.

Outcome

The allegations of voyeurism were proved when the subject was caught red-handed. An investigation was conducted into his illegal possession of child pornography. He was granted limited custody under supervision and made several attempts to outmanoeuvre the supervision. At the time of writing another court case is forthcoming, pending the outcome of the child pornography investigation.

These case studies indicate how much can be deduced and transformed into intelligence from very limited resources. Education, training and experience provided the building blocks for these profiles.

References

Brussel, J A (1968). *Casebook of a Crime Psychiatrist*. London: Mayflower.

Cameron, D & Fraser, E (1987). *The Lust to Kill*. Cambridge: Polity Press.

Canter, D (1991). *A facet approach to offender profiling*. Surrey University.

Canter, D (1995). *Criminal Shadows: Inside the mind of a serial killer*. London: Harper Collins Publishers.

Davies, A (1992). 'Rapists' behaviour: A three aspect model as a basis for analysis and the identification of a serial crime'. *Forensic Science International*, 55: 173-194.

De Becker, G (1997). *The Gift of Fear*. Little Brown & Company.

Dietz, P E; Matthews, D; Van Duyne, C; Martell, D A; Perry, C D H; Stewart, T; Warren, J & Crowder, J D (1981). 'Threatening and otherwise inappropriate letters to Hollywood celebrities'. *Journal of Forensic Sciences*, No 1: 185-209.

Dietz, P E; Matthews, D B; Martell, D A; Stewart, T M; Hrounda, D R; & Warren J. 'Threatening and otherwise inappropriate letters to members of US Congress'. *Journal of Forensic Sciences*, March 1991.

Douglas, J (1986). 'Criminal Profiling from Crime Scene Analysis'. *Behavioral Sciences and the Law*, 4 (4).

Douglas, J & Olshaker, M (1996). *Practical Homicide investigation tactics, procedures and forensic techniques*. Boca Raton: CRC Press.

FBI (1986). *Criminal Profiling: A viable investigative tool against violent crime*. US Department of Justice.

FBI. *The Firesetter: A Psychological Profile*. US Department of Justice.

Gerberth, V J (1996). *Practical Homicide Investigation: tactics procedures and forensic techniques*. New York: Elsevier.

Gordon, N J & Fleisher, W L (2002). *Effective Interviewing and Interrogation Techniques*. Academic Press.

Hare, R (1993). *Without conscience*. London: Warner Books.

Hazelwood, R R & Burgess, A (1987). 'Introduction to the serial rapist: research by the FBI'. *FBI Law Enforcement Bulletin*, 58: 16-24.

Hazelwood, R R & Warren, J I (1995). *The Serial Rapist: Criminal Personality Profiling and Crime Scene Assessment*. Dundee.

Hickey, E W (2002). *Serial murderers and their victims*. USA: Wadsworth Group.

Hollin, C R (1989). *Psychology and Crime*. London: Routledge.

Holmes, R M (1989). *Profiling Violent Crimes*. Sage Publications.

Holmes, R M & De Burger, J (1988). *Serial Murder*. Newbury Park: Sage Publications.

Ivey, G (1993). Psychodymamic aspects of demonic possession and Satanic worship. *Suid-Afrikaanse Tydskrif vir Sielkunde*, 23 (4): 186-194.

Jeffers, H P (1993). *Profiles in Evil*. London: Warner Books.

Kaplan, H I & Sadock, B J (1991). *Synopsis of Psychiatry*. Baltimore: Williams & Wilkins.

Keeny, B & Heide, K (1994). 'Gender differences in serial murderers: a preliminary analysis'. *Journal of Interpersonal Violence*, 9 (3): 383-398.

Kelleher, M & Kelleher, C (1998). *Murder most Rare: the female serial killer*. New York: Dell.

Kirby, P. 'A typical child molester'. *Police Review*, May 1994.

Knight, R & Prentky, R (1987). 'The developmental antecedents and adult adaptations of rapist subtypes'. *Criminal Justice & Behavior*, 14: 403-426.

Labuschagne, G N (1997) *Serial Murder: An Interactional Analysis*. University of Pretoria Master's thesis.

Lane, B & Gregg, W (1992). *The Encyclopedia of Serial Killers*. Headline Book Publishing.

Lanning, K (1987). *Child Molesters: A behavioral analysis*. National Center for Missing and Exploited Children in USA.

Lanning, K (1989). *Child Sex Rings*. National Center for Missing and Exploited Children in USA.

Leibman, F H (1989). Serial Murders: four case histories. *Federal Probation*, 53 (4): 41-45.

Levin, J & Fox, A J (1991). *America's growing menace – Mass Murder*. New York: Berkley Books.

Leyton, E (1986). *Compulsive Killers: The story of modern multiple murder*. New York: Washington Mews Books.

MacCulloch, M J; Snowden, P R; Wood, P J W & Mills, H E (1983). 'Sadistic Fantasy, Sadistic Behaviour and Offending'. *British Journal of Psychiatry*, 143: 20-29.

Maslow, A H (1970). *Motivation and Personality*. New York: Harper & Row Publishers.

McIvor, D L & Duthie, B. 'MMPI profiles of incest offenders'. *Criminal Justice and Behavior*, December 1986.

Money, J (1990). 'Forensic Sexology: Paraphiliac Serial Rape (Biastophilia) and Lust Murder (Erotophonophilia)'. *American Journal of Psychotherapy*, XLIV (1): 26-36.

Netto, L (2000). *The development of a pro-forma document for use in police rape investigations*. Rhodes University, Master's thesis.

Pienaar, A & Schurink, E (1996). *Analysis of the patterns of crimes against children*. South Africa: Human Sciences Research Council.

Pistorius, M (1996). *A Psychoanalytical Approach to Serial Killers*. University of Pretoria, Doctoral thesis.

Pistorius, M (2004). *Fatal Females: Women who kill*. Johannesburg: Penguin.

Prentky, R A; Wolbert-Burgess, A; Rokous, F; Lee, A; Hartman, C; Ressler, R K & Douglas, J (1989). 'The Presumptive Role of Fantasy in Serial Homicide'. *American Journal of Psychiatry*, 147 (7): 887-891.

Ressler, R K; Douglas, J; Burgess, A W & Burgess, A G (1992). *Crime Classification Manual*. USA: Simon & Schuster.

Ressler, R K & Shachtman, T (1993). *Whoever fights Monsters*. London: Simon and Schuster.

Rumbelow, D (1988). *The Complete Jack the Ripper*. London: Penguin Books.

Schein, E (1980). *Organizational Psychology*. Englewood Cliff : Prentice Hall Inc.

Schwartz, A E (1992). *The man who could not kill enough – the secret murders of Jeffrey Dahmer*. New York: Carol Publishing Group.

Turvey, B (1999). Criminal Profiling: an introduction to behavioral science. London: Academic Press.

Vogelman, K (1990). *The sexual face of violence: rapists on rape*. Johannesburg: Ravan Press.

Williams, W L; Lane, J & Zona, M A. 'Stalking: successful intervention strategies'. *The Police Chief*, LXIII (2): 24-28. February 1996.

Zona, M A; Kaushal, K S & Lane, J (1993). 'A comparative study of erotomanic and obsessional subjects in a forensic sample'. *Journal of Forensic Sciences*. July 1993.